CLEP

College Level Examination Program

Composition & Literature Series

Copyright © 2016

All rights reserved. No part of the material protected by this copyright notice may be reproduced or utilized in any form or by any means, electronic or mechanical, including photocopying or recording or by any information storage and retrievable system, without written permission from the copyright holder.

To obtain permission(s) to use the material from this work for any purpose including workshops or seminars, please submit a written request to:

XAMonline, Inc.
21 Orient Avenue
Melrose, MA 02176
Toll Free: 1-800-301-4647
Email: info@xamonline.com
Web: www.xamonline.com
Fax: 1-617-583-5552

Library of Congress Cataloging-in-Publication Data
Wynne, Sharon

CLEP Composition and Literature Series/ Sharon Wynne
   ISBN: 978-1-60787-583-3

1. CLEP   2. Study Guides   3. Literature

Disclaimer:

The opinions expressed in this publication are the sole works of XAMonline and were created independently from the College Board, or other testing affiliates. Between the time of publication and printing, specific test standards as well as testing formats and website information may change that are not included in part or in whole within this product. XAMonline develops sample test questions, and they reflect similar content as on real tests; however, they are not former tests. XAMonline assembles content that aligns with test standards but makes no claims nor guarantees candidates a passing score.

Cover photo provided by © Can Stock Photo Inc./Kurhan/4831346; © iStockphoto.com/Jordan Chesbrough/712377; © iStockphoto.com/Alex Stukkey/9957164; © iStockphoto.com/Ken Brown/18568050; © iStockphoto.com/ClaudeLux/43649652

Printed in the United States of America
CLEP Composition and Literature Series
ISBN: 978-1-60787-583-3

TABLE OF CONTENTS

Analyzing and Interpreting Literature 1

Practice Test 2

Answer Key 28

Explanations 29

American Literature 78

Practice Test 80

Answer Key 100

Explanations 101

College Composition 151

Practice Test 152

Practice Test Essay 1 167

Practice Test Essay 2 168

Answer Key 169

Explanations 170

College Composition Modular 197

Practice Test 199

Practice Test Essay 1 223

Practice Test 2 224

Answer Key 225

Explanations 226

English Literature 272

Practice Test 273

Answer Key 295

Explanations 296

ANALYZING AND INTERPRETING LITERATURE

CLEP Practice Exam: Analyzing and Interpreting Literature

INSTRUCTIONS

This exam gives passages from known writings (fiction, poems, non-fiction/history, biographies, drama and more) over the past five hundred years. While the student taking the exam is not expected to have read the material or have familiarity with the passage prior to the exam, the test taker is expected to have the knowledge of an undergraduate English and writing class.

TIP: As the writing changes and the time periods change, it's important for a student to note the author and time period as that may assist in answering questions by either eliminating unlikely answers or allow the student to recall items about the author.

At the end of the test passages and answers, there is an answer key and a "rationale" key for each question. Take the test without referencing these guides. For questions that you guess The correct answers or get wrong, the rationale is provided to help you see how test makers frame answers to questions or explain pieces of information with which you are unfamiliar.

There are 80 questions on this particular practice test, and the CLEP also uses around 80 for the credit exam. As with the CLEP exam, the passages are taken primarily from American and British Literature - though at least once question, just as in the actual exam, is taken from another area of literature. Within the questions of the CLEP, the mixture of genre types falls typically almost 80-90% between poetry and prose (both fiction and non-fiction within the prose selections) and the remaining on drama. The entire test is balanced between three main eras - Renaissance/17th Century, 18th/19th Century, as well as 10th/21st Century; in the past, there is a slightly heavier emphasis on 18th/19th work, and usually there is one passage from the Classical/pre-Renaissance period.

The CLEP allows 98 minutes to take the exam of approximately 80 questions. Time yourself during the exam, but as you practice, focus more attention on accurately answering questions as the total number of correct answers impacts your score, not how many you skip or get wrong. If you skip any questions, make sure that you also skip that line on The correct answer sheet - or you may spend a lot of time erasing and redoing your answer key.

These passages do not actually appear on the CLEP exam, but are meant to show how the exam is written and the various range of questions, answers, and key knowledge points required in order to pass the CLEP exam. Read each question carefully and provide the best answer choice. Good luck.

ANALYZING AND INTERPRETING LITERATURE

PASSAGE 1
(Prose fiction, American, 21st century)

Mornings, he likes to sit in his new leather chair by his new living room window, looking out across the rooftops and chimney pots, the clotheslines and telegraph lines and office towers. It's the first time Manhattan, from high above, hasn't crushed him with desire. On the contrary the view makes him feel smug. All those people down there, striving, hustling, pushing, shoving, busting to get what Willie's already got. In spades. He lights a cigarette, blows a jet of smoke against the window. Suckers.
~J.R. Moehriger, 2012 p120

1. The subject in this passage is:

   [A] a character, and seems to be the lead of the story

   [B] a supporting character

   [C] someone with an attitude of a criminal

   [D] female

   [E] has been poor his whole life

2. What kind of description is the author providing of this scene?

   [A] Backstory of the character

   [B] A characterization of what the character is like

   [C] A narrative, with the end of the selection giving thoughts in the first person

   [D] The unreliable narrative about a character

   [E] The author is using a persuasive argument

3. What types of words are "striving, hustling, pushing, shoving, bustling"?

   [A] Adjectives

   [B] Adverbs

   [C] Nouns

   [D] Gerunds

   [E] Verbs

ANALYZING AND INTERPRETING LITERATURE

4. **If you had to explain the phrase "crushed him" in the paragraph above and context of the paragraph, what would be the best appropriate explanation?**

   [A] The city sustained him with all the opportunity available.

   [B] The city called to him to be part of its life.

   [C] The city complimented him for everything he has achieved.

   [D] The city had energized him to get what he felt he deserved.

   [E] The city smothered him with all its offerings.

5. **The author portrays the attitude of the character toward the people on the street below as:**

   [A] condescending

   [B] sarcastic

   [C] affectionate

   [D] tolerant

   [E] encouraged

PASSAGE 2
(Poetry, American, 19th century)

> There is no frigate like a book
> To take us lands away,
> Nor any coursers like a page
> Of prancing poetry;
> This traverse may the poorest take
> Without oppress of toll;
> How frugal is the chariot
> That bears the human soul!
> ~Emily Dickinson (1830-1886)

6. **Authors use particular literary structures for descriptions. What best explains the one that Emily Dickinson employs in this poem?**

   [A] A literary allegory

   [B] Personification

   [C] Idioms

   [D] Similes

   [E] Flashbacks

7. **How many types of transport types does the author incorporate?**

   [A] Two

   [B] Three

   [C] Four

   [D] Five

   [E] None

ANALYZING AND INTERPRETING LITERATURE

8. **If the words 'frigate, coursers, and chariot' were replaced with synonyms, what would the best choice of the following options include?**

   [A] Train, car, carriage

   [B] Train, horse, carriage

   [C] Ship, car, carriage

   [D] Ship, car, train

   [E] Ship, horse, carriage

9. **Which of the following descriptions more closely describes the author's intended meaning of poem?**

   [A] Difficulties at work

   [B] The importance of books

   [C] Confessions for the soul

   [D] Poverty makes things difficult

   [E] Describing modes of transportation

10. **There are very descriptive and strong feelings conveyed by the poet. Which of the following is not a feeling that this poem expresses?**

    [A] Enjoyment of reading

    [B] Excitement of where reading can take you

    [C] Encouragement to get others to read

    [D] Fascination with topics in books

    [E] Discouragement for new readers

11. **What is a good paraphrase of "To take us lands away" that Ms. Dickinson writes in this poem?**

    [A] War makes it unsafe to travel, so we can just read about places.

    [B] Poems will drive us to save our souls.

    [C] Books can engage us to see new things.

    [D] Authors can show us how to go on vacation.

    [E] It shows poems are short and fun.

ANALYZING AND INTERPRETING LITERATURE

PASSAGE 3
(Poetry, British, 17th century)

Since brass, nor stone, nor earth, nor boundless sea,
But sad mortality o'ersways their power,
How with this rage shall beauty hold a plea,
Whose action is no stronger than a flower? (line 4)
O how shall summer's honey breath hold out
Against the wrackful siege of batt'ring days,
When rocks impregnable are not so stout,
Nor gates of steel so strong, but Time decays? (line 8)
O fearful meditation! where, alack,
Shall Time's best jewel from Time's chest lie hid?
Or what strong hand can hold his swift foot back?
Or who his spoil of beauty can forbid? (line 12)
O none, unless this miracle have might,
That in black ink my love may still shine bright.
~William Shakespeare, 1609

12. In line four, what is the strength of a flower describing?

   [A] Beauty (beauty line above)
   [B] Time
   [C] Summer's honey breath
   [D] Strong hand
   [E] Meditation

13. The first line of the poem tries to explain _____.

   [A] that there are a lot of things discussed in the poem.
   [B] that the strongest natural things are no match for beauty.
   [C] where you can find love.
   [D] what the author went through to write this poem.
   [E] that prayer can solve any problems.

14. "Black ink" references what in the last line?

   [A] Written poems
   [B] Street signs
   [C] Black diamonds
   [D] Summer flowers dying
   [E] Graffiti

15. The main idea of this poem is describing all of the following except:

   [A] hope
   [B] time, aging and death overthrow beauty
   [C] marriage
   [D] things that time cannot destroy
   [E] the author's victory

16. Shakespeare creates emotions in this poem, and expresses all of the following except:

    [A] rage

    [B] defeat

    [C] love

    [D] devotion

    [E] mortality

PASSAGE 4
(Prose non-fiction, American, 20th century)

When rays of light pass through a prism, they undergo a change of direction: they are always deflected away from the refractive edge. It is possible to conceive an assembly of prisms whose refractive surfaces progressively become more nearly parallel to each other towards the middle: light rays passing through the outer prisms will undergo the greatest amount of refraction, with consequent deflection of their path towards the center, whereas the middle prism with its two parallel surfaces causes no deflection at all. When a beam of parallel rays passes through these prisms, the rays are all deflected towards the axis and converge at one point. Rays emerging from a point are also deflected by the prisms that they converge. A lens can be conceived as consisting of a large number of such prisms placed close up against one another, so that their surfaces merge into a continuous spherical surface. A lens of this kind, which collects the rays and concentrates them at one point, is called a convergent lens. Since it is thicker in the middle than at the edge, it is known as a convex lens. In the case of a concave lens, which is thinner in the middle than at the edge, similar considerations show that all rays diverge from the center. Hence such a lens is called a divergent lens. After undergoing refraction, parallel rays appear to come from one point, while rays remerging from a point will, after passing through the lens, appear to emerge from another point. Lenses have surfaces in the same direction but having a different radii of curvature, these are known as meniscus lenses and are used more particularly in spectacles.
~The Way Things Work, ©1963

17. According to the passage above, light rays hit convex mirror and:

    [A] the rays pass straight through

    [B] the rays bounce only straight back to the light source

    [C] bend together to cross at a single point on the other side

    [D] are refracted to open outward on the other side

    [E] are reflected outward at angles back toward the light source

18. Light rays hit a concave surface. As the passage explains, light:

   [A] travels through the prism's surface, angling together to a point

   [B] moves in the same direction but has a different radii of curvature

   [C] the light merges to a point on the continuous spherical surface

   [D] is always reflected away from the refractive edge

   [E] experiences no deflection

19. Spectacles use meniscus lenses, which are explained by the author that these lenses are:

   [A] flat

   [B] concave lenses

   [C] convex lenses

   [D] round on both sides of the lens, meaning they have double refraction

   [E] always convergent lenses

PASSAGE 5
(Prose fiction, British, 18th century)

   There is likewise another diversion, which is only shown before the Emperor and Empress, and first minister, upon particular occasions. The Emperor lays on a table three fine silken threads of six inches long. One is blue, the other red, and the third green. These threads are proposed as prizes for those persons whom the Emperor hath a mind to distinguish by a peculiar mark of his favor. The ceremony is performed in his Majesty's great chamber of state; where the candidates are to undergo a trial of dexterity very different from the former, and such as I have not observed the least resemblance of in any other country of the old or the new world. The Emperor holds a stick in his hands, both ends parallel to the horizon, while the candidates, advancing one by one, sometimes leap over the stick, sometimes creep under it backwards and forwards several times, according as the stick is advanced or depressed. Sometimes the Emperor holds one end of the stick, and his first minister holds the other; sometimes the minister has it entirely to himself. Whoever performs his part with most agility, and holds out the longest in *leaping* and *creeping,* is rewarded with the blue-colored silk; the red is given to the next, and the green is given to the third, which they all wear girt twice round the middle; and you see few great persons about this court who are not adorned with one of these girdles.
   ~Jonathan Swift, 1704

ANALYZING AND INTERPRETING LITERATURE

20. The stick game described by the author in this passage is an allusion to what?

    [A] Jumping to the tune of the Emperor's (his boss') direction

    [B] Baseball

    [C] War games

    [D] A circus

    [E] Tennis

21. Why are the silk threads highly valued?

    [A] Silk is a common material.

    [B] Green is the Empress' favorite color.

    [C] People don't give gifts very often.

    [D] Silk was very expensive in the 1700s, when the story was written.

    [E] All great persons wear silk.

22. Using the information only in the passage, are the colors of the silk threads significant?

    [A] Yes, because they are royal colors.

    [B] Yes, because they represent places of winners.

    [C] No, because everyone has them.

    [D] No, because hardly everyone has them.

    [E] You cannot determine from the passage if the colors are important.

PASSAGE 6
(Prose non-fiction, 20th century)

On the other hand, however, we have no intention whatever of maintaining such a foolish and doctrinaire thesis as that the spirit of capitalism could only have arisen as the result of certain effects of Reformation, or even that of capitalism as an economic system is a creation of the Reformation. In itself, the fact that certain important forms of capitalistic business organizations are known to be considerably older than the Reformation is a sufficient refutation of such a claim. On the contrary, we only wish to ascertain whether and to what extent religious forces have taken part in the qualitative formation and the quantitative expansion of that spirit over the world. Furthermore, what concrete aspects of our capitalistic culture can be traced to them. In the view of the tremendous confusion of interdependent influences between the material basis, the forms of social and political organization, and the ideas current in the time of Reformation, we can only proceed by investigating whether and at what points certain correlations between forms of religious belief and practical ethics can be worked out. At the same time, we shall as far as possible clarify the manner and the general direction which, by virtue of those relationships, the religious movements have influenced development of material culture. Only when this has been determined with reasonable accuracy can the attempt be made to

estimate to what extent the historical development of modern culture can be attributed to those religious forces and to what extent others.
~Max Weber, 1904

23. Capitalism is what type of system according to this passage?

   [A] Democratic

   [B] Economic

   [C] Religious

   [D] Cultural

   [E] Expansionist

24. When the author compares capitalism to the Reformation, what were the main ideas of the Reformation?

   [A] Democratic

   [B] Economic

   [C] Religious

   [D] Cultural

   [E] Expansionist

25. What word or phrase originating at least in part in the above passage best describes the goal or target of capitalism?

   [A] Ethics based

   [B] Culture driven

   [C] Historical application

   [D] Material accumulation

   [E] Force of nature

26. From the passage above, which of the following phrases best describes the author's attitude toward capitalism?

   [A] The author approves of capitalism if it involves religion.

   [B] The author approves of capitalism when it is driven by "qualification expansion of spirit".

   [C] The author disapproves of capitalism when it involves modern culture.

   [D] The author disapproves of capitalism when Reformation is involved.

   [E] The author disapproves of capitalism but wants to investigate why it is wrong.

ANALYZING AND INTERPRETING LITERATURE

PASSAGE 7
(Prose non-fiction, 20th century)

I'd like to say here, that I wasn't the only important one. I was part of a family, just like all of my brothers and sisters. The whole community was important. We used to discuss many of the community's problems together, especially when someone was ill and we couldn't buy medicine, because we were getting poorer and poorer. We'd start discussing and heaping insults on the rich who'd made us suffer for so long. It was about then I began learning about politics. I tried to talk to people who could help me sort my ideas out. I wanted to know what the world was like on the other side. I knew the *finca*, I knew the *Altiplano*. But what I didn't know was about the other problems of the Indians in Guatemala. I didn't know the problems the other groups had to holding onto their land. I knew there were lots of other Indians in other parts of the country, because I'd been meeting them in the *finca* since I was a child, but though we all worked together, we didn't know any of the names of the towns they came from, or how they lived, or what they ate. We just imagined that they were like us.
~Rigoberta Menchu,
Nobel Peace Prize Winner 1992

27. From the context of the passage, what is a *finca*?

[A] A farm

[B] A village or town

[C] A mountain range

[D] A house

[E] It cannot be determined

28. The author is telling a story about her own life. What is this kind of document called?

[A] Autobiography

[B] Mystery

[C] Biography

[D] Narrative

[E] Romance

ANALYZING AND INTERPRETING LITERATURE

29. Given the information in the passage, the author most likely worked as:

    [A] a washer woman

    [B] a seamstress

    [C] a farmer

    [D] a teacher

    [E] it cannot be determined from the passage

30. The author describes who is the most important. She defines it as:

    [A] herself

    [B] her family

    [C] her community

    [D] the rich people that employed them

    [E] the *finca*

PASSAGE 8
(Poetry, British, 18th century)

Tyger! Tyger! burning bright
In the forests of the night,
What immortal hand or eye
Could frame thy fearful symmetry?

In what distant deeps or skies
Burnt the fire of thine eyes?
On what wings dare he aspire?
What the hand dare seize the flame?

And what shoulder, & what art,
Could twist the sinews of they heart?
And when thy heart began to beat,
What dread hand? & what dread feet?
    ~Excerpt, William Blake, 1794

31. Which of the topics below is this best description of the poem's main idea?

    [A] Strength, as sinews of the heart are strong.

    [B] Creationism, and the author asks what immortal being created the tiger.

    [C] Flying, because it talks about wings.

    [D] Fire, with references to flames and burning forests.

    [E] Love, describing the heart and how it beats.

32. Sinews, in the third stanza, can be best compared to:

    [A] thread

    [B] a cage

    [C] rope

    [D] heart strings or emotions

    [E] burnt fire, from the second stanza

ANALYZING AND INTERPRETING LITERATURE

33. Another phrase for "deeps or skies" that would fit in this poem could be:

    [A] caves or planes

    [B] trees or forests

    [C] seas or air

    [D] waves or wind

    [E] oceans or lakes

34. What is personified in the poem?

    [A] A lion

    [B] Birds

    [C] Candle

    [D] A tiger

    [E] The sky

35. In line 7 of this poem, what word below most nearly means "aspire"?

    [A] Soar

    [B] Plunge

    [C] Scheme

    [D] Travel

    [E] Admire

36. The poet, William Blake, uses all of the following literary tools to convey his message, except:

    [A] metaphors

    [B] rhymed couplets

    [C] personification

    [D] symbols

    [E] lyrics

PASSAGE 9
(Prose fiction, British, 19th century)

"Without their visits you cannot hope to shun the path I tread. Expect the first tomorrow night, when the bell tolls One. Expect the second on the next night at the same hour. The third, upon the next night, when the last stroke of Twelve has ceased to vibrate Look to see me no more; and look that, for your own sake, you remember what has passed between us!"

It walked backward from him; and at every step it took, the window raised itself a little, so that, when the apparition reached it, it was wide open.

Scrooge closed the window, and examined the door by which the Ghost had entered. It was double-locked, as he had locked it with his own hands, and the bolts were undisturbed. Scrooge tried to say "Humbug!" but stopped at the first syllable. And being, from the emotion he had undergone, or the fatigues of the day, or his glimpse of

the invisible world, or the dull conversation of the Ghost, or the lateness of the hour, much in need of repose, he went straight to bed, without undressing, and fell asleep on the instant.
            ~Charles Dickens, 1843

37. What quality of the Ghost is the most likely trait that Scrooge dislikes the most?

   [A] The Ghost's old fashioned speech bothers Scrooge the most.

   [B] The authoritative nature the Ghost takes with Scrooge is the quality disliked the most.

   [C] The fact that the Ghost could break into his house is the trait that Scrooge dislikes.

   [D] The Ghost is taller than Scrooge, and that bothers him.

   [E] Scrooge dislikes that his bedtime was later than usual.

38. The way Scrooge's reaction to the Ghost is portrayed could mean that according to this passage that Scrooge is:

   [A] tired

   [B] angry

   [C] looking for excuses

   [D] forgetful

   [E] planning to ignore the Ghost

39. The Ghost's remarks listed in the passage can most likely be inferred as:

   [A] a warning to Scrooge

   [B] the Ghost is talking to the wrong person

   [C] Scrooge is hallucinating

   [D] a friend was playing a joke on Scrooge

   [E] no inference can be made

40. Scrooge's reaction to the Ghost in this passage leads a reader to conclude:

   [A] that Scrooge was just conducting a normal nighttime house-check

   [B] when the Ghost comes back for him, Scrooge will go along willingly

   [C] even wealthy people like Scrooge lock their houses

   [D] that Scrooge does not believe in the supernatural

   [E] Scrooge is likely overcome with exhaustion

41. The tone of the passage is intended to:

[A] serve as a warning to Scrooge about things he will be shown

[B] serve as a reminder that Scrooge has forgotten appointments

[C] describe how disconcerted Scrooge felt after the warning was given by the Ghost

[D] provide backstory

[E] explain why Scrooge is so stingy

PASSAGE 10
(Prose, non-fiction, American, 20th century)

Using the Constitution to protect the minorities, James Madison's system of government is largely an attempt to divide and frustrate the majority. Madison envisioned a political system with the broadest possible power base. For example, he rejected the common belief that a democracy could work only in a very small area, arguing that it could succeed in a large country like the United States. A large population spread over a huge area would make it very difficult to force a permanent majority. Such a society would probably divide into varied and fluctuating minorities, making a long lasting majority unlikely. Instead, majorities would be created out of combinations of competing minorities. Thus, any majority would be temporary, and new ones would be elusive. This system, political scientists now term *pluralism.*

~Leon Baradat, 1973

42. According to the passage, what is pluralism?

[A] Majorities created out of combinations of competing minorities

[B] A new division of political science

[C] A political system with the smallest possible power base

[D] A new name for a permanent majority

[E] The system for democracy to work in a very small area

43. The Constitution mentioned in the first line, in context to this passage, is:

[A] James Madison's document to create a permanent majority

[B] the document creating the United States

[C] the personality of James Madison

[D] the health of the majority

[E] instructions on how to create combinations of competing minorities

ANALYZING AND INTERPRETING LITERATURE

44. The passage talks about democracy. Another phrase for a democracy is:

   [A] the rule of a few over the many

   [B] the welfare state

   [C] a laissez-faire economy

   [D] an elected government system

   [E] an appointed government by a monarch

PASSAGE 11

American black music was going along like an express train. But white cats, after Buddy Holly died and Eddie Cochran died, and Elvis was in the army gone wonky, white American music when I arrived was the Beach Boys and Bobby Vee. They were still stuck in the past. The past was six months ago; it wasn't a long time. But things changed. The Beatles were the milestone. And then they got stuck inside their own cage. "The Fab Four." Hence, eventually, you got the Monkees, all this ersatz stuff. But I think there was a vacuum somewhere in white American music at the time.

When we first got to America and to LA, there was a lot of Beach Boys on the radio, which was pretty funny to us - it was before *Pet Sounds* - it was hot rod songs and surfing songs, pretty lousily played, familiar Chuck Berry licks going on. "Round, round get around / I get around," I though that was brilliant. It was later on, but Brian Wilson had something. "In My Room," "Don't Worry Baby." I was more interested in their B-sides, the ones he slipped in. There was no particular correlation with what we were doing so I could just listen to it on another level. I thought these are very well-constructed songs. I took easily to the pop song idiom. I'd always listened to everything, and America opened it all out - we were hearing records there that were regional hits. We'd get to know local labels and local acts, which is how we came across "Time Is on My Side," in LA, sung by Irma Thomas. It was a B-side of a record on Imperial Records, a label we'd have been aware of because it was independent and successful and based on Sunset Strip.
   ~Keith Richards, 2010

45. How many unique singers versus unique bands, respectively, are named in the passage above?

   [A] Seven and Four

   [B] Six and Three

   [C] Eight and Three

   [D] Seven and Three

   [E] Six and Four

ANALYZING AND INTERPRETING LITERATURE

46. **How many songs are referenced in the passage above?**

    [A] Two

    [B] Three

    [C] Four

    [D] Five

    [E] Six

47. **In the context of the selection's first paragraph, how many white singers or groups are named by the author?**

    [A] Four

    [B] Five

    [C] Three

    [D] Seven

    [E] One

48. **Given what the author says about the B-side of a record, which of the following sentences is closest to the author's opinion?**

    [A] The B-side had more creativity and outlets for artists, making it unique.

    [B] It was called the B-side because the songs were generally not as good.

    [C] Only regional labels took the time to press B-sides.

    [D] The B-side was where all the surfing songs were recorded.

    [E] Labels were strict about the contents of the B-sides.

49. **When the author talks about the Beatles and says "they got stuck inside their own cage," the author most likely means:**

    [A] that the Beatles always had to hide in hotels because they were so famous

    [B] that successful musical groups could never enjoy the publicity

    [C] that the Beatles were trapped on planes all the time

    [D] that the Beatles couldn't perform with anyone outside of their four members

    [E] the Beatles outgrew the standard previously set for successful musicians, and were trapped in their own famous sensation

50. Given the descriptions in the passage, the author's profession is likely:

[A] a roadie

[B] a writer

[C] a singer

[D] a photographer

[E] a teacher

PASSAGE 12
(Prose fiction, British, pre-Ren/Classic)

A marvelous case is it to hear, either the warnings of that he should have voided, or the tokens of that he could not void. For the self night next before his death, the lord Stanley sent a trusty secret messenger unto him at midnight in all the haste, requiring him to rise and ride away with him, for he was disposed utterly no longer to bide; he had so fearful a dream, in which him thought that a boar with his tusks so raced them both by the heads, that the blood ran about both their shoulders. And forasmuch as the protector gave the boar for his cognizance, this dream made so fearful an impression in his heart, that he was thoroughly determined no longer to tarry, but had his horse ready, if the lord Hastings would go with him to ride so far yet the same night, that they should be out of danger ere day. Ay, good lord, quoth the lord Hastings to this messenger, leaneth my lord thy master so much to such trifles, and hath such faith in dreams, which either his own fear fantasieth or do rise in the night's rest by reason of his day thoughts? Tell him it is plain witchcraft to believe in such dreams; which if they were tokens of things to come, why thinketh he not that we might be as likely to make them true by our going if we were caught and brought back (as friends fail fleers), for then had the boar a cause likely to race us with his tusks, as folk that fled for some falsehood, wherefore either is there no peril (nor none there is indeed), or if any be, it is rather in going than biding. And if we should, needs cost, fall in peril one way or other, yet had I livelier that men should see it were by other men's falsehood, than think it were either our own fault or faint heart. And therefore go to thy master, man, and commend me to him, and pray him be merry and have no fear: for I ensure him I am as sure of the man that he wotteth of, as I am of my own hand. God send grace, sir, quoth the messenger, and went his way.

~Sir Thomas More, 1513

51. The beginning of the passage is describing what?

[A] An injury sustained by the main character

[B] A rider that is trying to escape injury

[C] The main character's dream

[D] A witch's story

[E] The boar that the character will grill for dinner

ANALYZING AND INTERPRETING LITERATURE

52. **What is the cautionary message that the rider gets when he reaches his destination?**

    [A] Dreams are witchcraft if you believe in them.

    [B] Dreams can come true if you believe in them.

    [C] God sends His grace.

    [D] Those faint of heart do not have dreams.

    [E] Men cannot fall for other men's falsehoods.

53. **Did the main character in this passage believe he could out run bad visions?**

    [A] No, the passage makes it clear you always get what's coming in a dream.

    [B] No, dreams mean nothing, so the main character didn't pay any attention to it.

    [C] Yes, it was possible to escape bad visions on horseback.

    [D] Yes, the main character thought dancing would rid himself of bad dreams.

    [E] There is nothing in the passage that assists in answering this question.

PASSAGE 13
(Prose fiction, British, 19th century)

To go into solitude, a man needs to retire as much from his chamber as from society. I am not solitary whilst I read and write, though nobody is with me. But if a man would be alone, let him look at the stars. The rays that come from those heavenly worlds, will separate between him and what he touches. One might think the atmosphere was made transparent with this design, to give man, in the heavenly bodies, the perpetual presence of the sublime. Seen in the streets of cities, how great they are! If the stars should appear one night in a thousand years, how would men believe and adore; and preserve for many generations the remembrance of the city of God which had been shown! But every night come out these envoys of beauty, and light the universe with their admonishing smile.
   ~Ralph Waldo Emerson, 1836

54. **The first two lines of this passage imply what?**

    [A] A man is never alone.

    [B] A man is always alone.

    [C] A man can be alone if he turns his back on people.

    [D] A man can be alone if he makes his mind focus.

    [E] A man who is lonely is considered alone.

ANALYZING AND INTERPRETING LITERATURE

55. Given the whole passage, which of the following is the best match for the author's opinion about nature?

[A] The author prefers to seek to retire in his chamber.

[B] The author sees wonder in the sky and beauty at night.

[C] The author does not like trees.

[D] The author can only see stars one night in a thousand years.

[E] You cannot tell the author's opinion from this passage.

56. The phrase "light the universe with their admonishing smile" is an example of:

[A] personification

[B] a simile

[C] a metaphor

[D] irony

[E] satire

PASSAGE 14

Two roads diverged in a yellow wood,
And sorry I could not travel both
And be one traveler, long I stood
And looked down one as far as I could
To where it bent in the undergrowth;

Then took the other, as just as fair,
And having perhaps the better claim,
Because it was grassy and wanted wear;
Though as for that the passing there
Had worn them really about the same,
 And both that morning equally lay
In leaves no step had trodden black.
Oh, I kept the first for another day!
Yet knowing how way leads on to way,
I doubted if I should ever come back.

I shall be telling this with a sigh
Somewhere ages and ages hence:
Two roads diverged in a wood, and I—
I took the one less traveled by,
And that has made all the difference.
~Robert Frost, 1920

57. **When the author uses the phrase "wanted wear" in the third stanza, what does that mean?**

    [A] It looked just as fair as the other path.

    [B] It was not as inviting.

    [C] The path didn't go the same way as the other one.

    [D] The path was less traveled than the other one.

    [E] You cannot determine what the author means.

58. **The author says that he "took the one less traveled by"; what does that mean?**

    [A] The other path looked like it was used more.

    [B] He did the right thing when others chose the wrong one.

    [C] He took the one on the left.

    [D] He took the one on the right.

    [E] It cannot be determined what the author meant by this short selection.

59. **What is another way the author states his path was the "one less traveled by"?**

    [A] "both that morning equally lay"

    [B] "no step had trodden black"

    [C] "Somewhere ages and ages hence"

    [D] "bent in the undergrowth"

    [E] "having perhaps the better claim"

60. **What does the author imply since he took the path less traveled?**

    [A] He has run into fewer people that try to bully him into doing what they want.

    [B] Life is tougher getting to see the light.

    [C] He was sorry he didn't chose to go the more well-trod path.

    [D] He didn't make as much money as the people that took the other path.

    [E] His life is better for choosing to go his own path.

PASSAGE 15
(Prose fiction, American, 20th century)

His memories of the Boston Society Contralto were nebulous and musical. She was a lady who sang, sang, sang in the music room on their house on Washington Square - sometimes with guests all about her, the men with their arms folded, balanced breathlessly on the edges of sofas, the women with their hands in their laps, occasionally making little whispers to the men and always clapping very briskly and uttering cooing cries after each song - and she often sang to Anthony alone, in Italian or French or in a strange and terrible dialect...

Oblivious to the social system, he lived for a while alone and unsought in a high room in Beck Hall - a slim dark boy of medium height with a shy sensitive mouth. His allowance was more than liberal. He laid the foundations for a library by purchasing from a wandering bibliophile first editions of Swinburne, Meredith, and Hardy, and a yellowed illegible autograph letter of Keats', finding later he had been amazingly overcharged. He became an exquisite dandy, amassed a rather pathetic collection of silk pajamas, brocaded dressing-gowns, and neckties too flamboyant to wear; in this secret finery he would parade before a mirror in his room or lie stretched in satin along the window-seat looking down on the yard and realizing this clamor, breathless and immediate, in which it seemed he was to never have a part.
~F. Scott Fitzgerald, 1922

61. Based on the information in the passage, what is a "contralto"?

[A] A Boston slang term for a high class man

[B] A female singer

[C] A female dancer

[D] A writer

[E] A bibliophile

62. Based on the information in the passage, an "exquisite dandy" refers to:

[A] the first editions of the books listed in the passage

[B] anyone who wears silk pajamas

[C] a gentleman who has money to spend extravagantly on fancy things

[D] someone who likes to parade before a mirror

[E] someone who likes candy

63. Why would the social system be important in this reading selection?

   [A] Richer classes don't have dandies, so the main character can't be dandy.

   [B] A rich man with no female friends is called a dandy, and it helps explain the story.

   [C] The character seems ostracized and that can't happen in certain social classes.

   [D] If the main character was of a lower class, he could not live the life described.

   [E] No one lives the luxurious life described in the passage.

PASSAGE 16
(Prose fiction, American, 20th century)

These are morning matters, pictures you dream as the final wave heaves you up on the sand in the bright light and drying air. You remember pressure, and a curved sleep you rested against, soft, like a scallop in its shell. But the air hardens your skin; you stand; you leave the lighted shore to explore some dim headland, and soon you're lost in the leafy interior, intent, remembering nothing.

I still think of that old tomcat, mornings, when I wake. Things are tamer now; I sleep with the window shut. The cats and our rites are gone and my life is changed, but the memory remains of something powerful playing over me. I wake expectant, hoping to see a new thing. If I'm lucky I might be jogged awake by a strange bird call. I dress in a hurry, imagining the yard flapping with auks, or flamingos. This morning it was a wood duck, down at the creek. It flew away.
   ~Annie Dillard, 1975 Pulitzer Prize

64. The tone of the selection is:

   [A] reflective

   [B] indulgent

   [C] indifferent

   [D] dishonest

   [E] ironic

65. The author uses _____ to describe the setting.

   [A] personification

   [B] ambivalence

   [C] satire

   [D] allusion

   [E] clichés

66. The phrase, "like a scallop in its shell" is an example of:

   [A] irony

   [B] a simile

   [C] a metaphor

   [D] personification

   [E] euphemism

67. **The author describes many of her feelings and situations by focusing the conversation on animals. Based on the information in the passage, one reason could be:**

   [A] animals are comforting and relax the reader

   [B] birds are flighty and the center of her story

   [C] the setting of this story is a farm

   [D] the lead character doesn't have many human friends

   [E] it is the backstory of how animals and nature are always present in the character's life

68. **The phrase "the air hardens your skin" within the context of the passage most likely refers to what?**

   [A] The morning air woke the character up from dreaming.

   [B] The scallop shell bed the character sleeps in has opened.

   [C] The air dries out the character's skin.

   [D] The coldness of the room turns off the brain of the character.

   [E] The air turns the character's skin cold when the cat leaves the bed.

PASSAGE 17
(Drama, British, 16th century/classical)

Bernardo : Welcome, Horatio: welcome, good Marcellus.
Marcellus : What, has this thing appear'd again to-night?
Bernardo : I have seen nothing.
Marcellus : Horatio says 'tis but our fantasy,
And will not let belief take hold of him
Touching this dreaded sight, twice seen of us:
Therefore I have entreated him along
With us to watch the minutes of this night;
That if again this apparition come,
He may approve our eyes and speak to it.
Horatio : Tush, tush, 'twill not appear.
Bernardo : Sit down awhile;
And let us once again assail your ears,
That are so fortified against our story
What we have two nights seen.
~William Shakespeare, 1599-1602

69. **The three men in the play can be said, in this passage:**

   [A] to disagree about a ghost that was seen

   [B] to disagree that two days ago they saw people meeting "twice seen of us"

   [C] that Horatio and Bernardo are trying to persuade Marcellus they saw something

   [D] that Horatio and Marcellus are trying to persuade Bernardo they saw something

   [E] to meet for a drink for "fortification"

ANALYZING AND INTERPRETING LITERATURE

70. When Marcellus speaks of "approving our eyes", what is he saying?

    [A] Marcellus and Bernardo need glasses.

    [B] Bernardo didn't believe what Marcellus saw.

    [C] Horatio believes what Marcellus saw.

    [D] Horatio should see what Bernardo and Marcellus saw.

    [E] Marcellus should believe what Bernardo saw.

71. When Bernardo says "once again assail your ears", what does he mean?

    [A] He wants to repeat himself to Marcellus to make him believe him.

    [B] He wants to repeat himself to Horatio to make him believe him.

    [C] He wants to repeat himself to help all three of them believe the story.

    [D] He wants Marcellus and Horatio to poke holes in the story.

    [E] None of these are the meaning of that phrase in the passage.

72. In the context of the passage, entreated means:

    [A] invited

    [B] engaged

    [C] demanded

    [D] refused

    [E] ignored

PASSAGE 18
(Drama, American, 20th century)

Edmund : That's foolishness. You know it's only a bad cold.
Mary : Yes, of course, I know that!
Edmund : But listen, Mama. I want you to promise me that even if it turns out to be something worse, you'll know I'll soon be alright again, anyway, and don't worry yourself sick, and you'll keep on taking care of yourself -
Mary : I won't listen when you talk so silly! There's absolutely no reason to talk as if you expect something dreadful! Of course, I promise you I give you my sacred word of honor! But I suppose you're remembering I've promised before on my word of honor.
Edmund : No!
Mary : I'm not blaming you, dear. How can you help it? How can any one of us forget? That's what makes it so hard - for all of us. We can't forget.
Edmund : Mama! Stop it!
Mary : All right, dear. I didn't beam to be so gloomy. Don't mind me. Here. Let me feel your head. Why,

24

it's nice and cool. You certainly don't have any fever now.
~Eugene O'Neill, 1955

73. It can be said that this passage of the drama:

[A] puts American dream against American nightmare

[B] describes the normal American family

[C] portrays Americans in a very resilient fashion

[D] was likely written during a war so obviously has negative overtones

[E] has the mother remembering the death of another child

74. Mary changes the direction of the conversation by:

[A] stopping Edmund from talking by taking his temperature

[B] making Edmund feel badly about the death of his brother

[C] walking out of the room

[D] tucking the covers up to his chin

[E] ignoring him

75. This portion of the play is a:

[A] monologue

[B] dialogue

[C] soliloquy

[D] entendre

[E] stichomythia

76. Mary talks about Edmund expecting something dreadful. What's a literary term for that action?

[A] Oxymoron

[B] Dissonance

[C] Foreshadowing

[D] Stream of consciousness

[E] Understatement

PASSAGE 19
(Prose fiction, British, 18th century)

But though thus largely indebted to fortune, to nature she had yet greater obligation: her form was elegant, her heart was liberal. Her countenance announced the intelligence of her mind, her complexion varied with every emotion of her foul, and her eyes, the heralds of her speech, now beamed with understanding and now glistened with sensibility.

For the short period of her minority, the management of her fortune and the care of her person, had by the Dean been entrusted to three guardians, among whom her own choice was to settle to her residence: but her mind, saddened by the lots of all her natural friends, coveted to regain its serenity in the quietness of the country, and in the bosom of an aged and maternal counsellor, whom she loved as her mother, and to whom she had been known from her childhood.

-Fanny Burney, 1782

77. From the context of this passage, which of the following statements is the most likely to be true?

   [A] The main character is poor.

   [B] The main character is an orphan.

   [C] The setting of the story is in England.

   [D] The main character is going to live with her aunt.

   [E] The main character doesn't like to live in town.

78. In the quote, "her heart was liberal", what is the author trying to express?

   [A] The author implies that the main character is of loose morals.

   [B] The author implies that while ladylike, she has a wild streak.

   [C] The author alludes that the woman is more open than her demeanor.

   [D] The author makes it clear that she is alone.

   [E] The author shows how she was older than her natural friends.

79. What does the word "minority" mean in the context of the passage?

   [A] The woman in the passage is a Native American.

   [B] The character is not yet an adult.

   [C] The group of people in the story are members of the minority political party.

   [D] The character has less money than her friends.

   [E] None of the given options explain "minority" in this passage.

ANALYZING AND INTERPRETING LITERATURE

80. **What is another word for serenity in this passage?**

    [A] Peacefulness

    [B] Counsellor

    [C] Bosom

    [D] Rambunctiousness

    [E] Prayerful

ANALYZING AND INTERPRETING LITERATURE

ANSWER KEY

Question Number	Correct Answer	Your Answer	Question Number	Correct Answer	Your Answer	Question Number	Correct Answer	Your Answer
1	A		28	A		55	B	
2	C		29	C		56	A	
3	E		30	C		57	D	
4	D		31	B		58	A	
5	A		32	D		59	B	
6	A		33	C		60	E	
7	B		34	D		61	B	
8	E		35	A		62	C	
9	B		36	C		63	D	
10	E		37	B		64	A	
11	C		38	C		65	D	
12	A		39	A		66	C	
13	B		40	D		67	E	
14	A		41	C		68	A	
15	C		42	A		69	A	
16	B		43	B		70	D	
17	E		44	D		71	B	
18	A		45	D		72	A	
19	B		46	C		73	E	
20	A		47	D		74	A	
21	D		48	A		75	B	
22	B		49	E		76	C	
23	B		50	C		77	B	
24	C		51	C		78	C	
25	D		52	A		79	B	
26	E		53	C		80	A	
27	B		54	D				

ANALYZING AND INTERPRETING LITERATURE

EXPLANATIONS

If there are words that are options for answers that you do not know, now is the time to look them up and prepare yourself for the CLEP exam! Many answer options includes words or phrases used in literary discussions, and some may not be familiar. It is possible they will be on the actual exam, so you should familiarize yourself with them now.

PASSAGE 1
(Prose fiction, American, 21st century)

> **Mornings, he likes to sit in his new leather chair by his new living room window, looking out across the rooftops and chimney pots, the clotheslines and telegraph lines and office towers. It's the first time Manhattan, from high above, hasn't crushed him with desire. On the contrary the view makes him feel smug. All those people down there, striving, hustling, pushing, shoving, busting to get what Willie's already got. In spades. He lights a cigarette, blows a jet of smoke against the window. Suckers.**

J.R. Moehriger, 2012 p120

1. The subject in this passage is:

   [A] a character, and seems to be the lead of the story

   [B] a supporting character

   [C] someone with an attitude of a criminal

   [D] female

   [E] has been poor his whole life

The correct answer is A.
The story being explained is about the main character. B is wrong because there are no other characters explained by the author, to have a main and a supporting character. You cannot tell if the person is a criminal or poor from this excerpt, so it is presumptuous to guess C or E could be The correct answers. D is also incorrect because the pronoun "he" is used so it is clearly wrong.

ANALYZING AND INTERPRETING LITERATURE

2. **What kind of description is the author providing of this scene?**

   [A] Backstory of the character

   [B] A characterization of what the character is like

   [C] A narrative, with the end of the selection giving thoughts in the first person

   [D] The unreliable narrative about a character

   [E] The author is using a persuasive argument

The correct answer is C.
The backstory of a character tells about some time in the past, and since this scene is of the present, that choice A is wrong. B is also incorrect as there is no descriptions about the main character, only the current scene he is observing. There is no basis to assume D is correct and in the option E, there is no argument for or against a topic. Therefore, the correct answer is C.

3. **What types of words are "striving, hustling, pushing, shoving, bustling"?**

   [A] Adjectives

   [B] Adverbs

   [C] Nouns

   [D] Gerunds

   [E] Verbs

The correct answer is E.
This is a simple definition of words. Verbs are listed for choice E.

ANALYZING AND INTERPRETING LITERATURE

4. **If you had to explain the phrase "crushed him" in the paragraph above and context of the paragraph, what would be the best appropriate explanation?**

   [A] The city sustained him with all the opportunity available.

   [B] The city called to him to be part of its life.

   [C] The city complimented him for everything he has achieved.

   [D] The city had energized him to get what he felt he deserved.

   [E] The city smothered him with all its offerings.

The correct answer is D.
When looking at the context of the paragraph, there are no leading clues that the city has sustained the character, complimented him or smothered him. Of the options B and D, the better answer is D, as the city didn't call the character to join in the opportunity directly. D offers a description back to the excerpt - that he "deserved" what he has achieved.

5. **The author portrays the attitude of the character toward the people on the street below as:**

   [A] condescending

   [B] sarcastic

   [C] affectionate

   [D] tolerant

   [E] encouraged

The correct answer is A.
Knowing what these words mean, the only choice that is close is A.

ANALYZING AND INTERPRETING LITERATURE

PASSAGE 2
(Poetry, American, 19th century)

> There is no frigate like a book
> To take us lands away,
> Nor any coursers like a page
> Of prancing poetry;
> This traverse may the poorest take
> Without oppress of toll;
> How frugal is the chariot
> That bears the human soul!
>   ~Emily Dickinson (1830-1886)

6. Authors use particular literary structures for descriptions. What best explains the one that Emily Dickinson employs in this poem?

    [A] A literary allegory

    [B] Personification

    [C] Idioms

    [D] Similes

    [E] Flashbacks

The correct answer is A.
This is another definition type of question, and the correct choice is A.

7. How many types of transport types does the author incorporate?

    [A] Two

    [B] Three

    [C] Four

    [D] Five

    [E] None

The correct answer is B.
This is a counting exercise - B, for three, as listed in the next question.

ANALYZING AND INTERPRETING LITERATURE

8. **If the words 'frigate, coursers, and chariot' were replaced with synonyms, what would the best choice of the following options include?**

   [A] Train, car, carriage

   [B] Train, horse, carriage

   [C] Ship, car, carriage

   [D] Ship, car, train

   [E] Ship, horse, carriage

The correct answer is E.
Defining frigate (ship), coursers (horses) and chariots (similar to a carriage drawn by a horse), the best choice is E.

9. **Which of the following descriptions more closely describes the author's intended meaning of poem?**

   [A] Difficulties at work

   [B] The importance of books

   [C] Confessions for the soul

   [D] Poverty makes things difficult

   [E] Describing modes of transportation

The correct answer is B.
This poem is about the journeys available through stories and books. From the first sentence, the author lays forth the meaning of the poem is B.

ANALYZING AND INTERPRETING LITERATURE

10. **There are very descriptive and strong feelings conveyed by the poet. Which of the following is not a feeling that this poem expresses?**

    [A] Enjoyment of reading

    [B] Excitement of where reading can take you

    [C] Encouragement to get others to read

    [D] Fascination with topics in books

    [E] Discouragement for new readers

The correct answer is E.
It is important to read the questions carefully. This is a reverse question, it is asking which is not something that is mentioned or implied in the poem. Therefore, the correct answer is E. If you don't know the correct answer, you can try to look at all five options to select the one that doesn't fit with the others.

11. **What is a good paraphrase of "To take us lands away" that Ms. Dickinson writes in this poem?**

    [A] War makes it unsafe to travel, so we can just read about places.

    [B] Poems will drive us to save our souls.

    [C] Books can engage us to see new things.

    [D] Authors can show us how to go on vacation.

    [E] It shows poems are short and fun.

The correct answer is C.
Option A is very abrupt and makes too many assumptions; Option E is not relevant to the subject of the poem - both of these are obviously out. Of the choices remaining, using the references with the different ways people traveled in her earlier lines, the best answer is C.

ANALYZING AND INTERPRETING LITERATURE

PASSAGE 3
(Poetry, British, 17th century)

    Since brass, nor stone, nor earth, nor boundless sea,
    But sad mortality o'ersways their power,
    How with this rage shall beauty hold a plea,
    Whose action is no stronger than a flower? (line 4)
    O how shall summer's honey breath hold out
    Against the wrackful siege of batt'ring days,
    When rocks impregnable are not so stout,
    Nor gates of steel so strong, but Time decays? (line 8)
    O fearful meditation! where, alack,
    Shall Time's best jewel from Time's chest lie hid?
    Or what strong hand can hold his swift foot back?
    Or who his spoil of beauty can forbid? (line 12)
    O none, unless this miracle have might,
    That in black ink my love may still shine bright.
        ~William Shakespeare, 1609

12. In line four, what is the strength of a flower describing?

   [A] Beauty (beauty line above)

   [B] Time

   [C] Summer's honey breath

   [D] Strong hand

   [E] Meditation

The correct answer is A.
This is a direct answer from line three - A.

ANALYZING AND INTERPRETING LITERATURE

13. **The first line of the poem tries to explain _____.**

    [A] that there are a lot of things discussed in the poem.

    [B] that the strongest natural things are no match for beauty.

    [C] where you can find love.

    [D] what the author went through to write this poem.

    [E] that prayer can solve any problems.

The correct answer is B.
The author does not mention love, personal struggles, or prayer in this poem. Of the remaining answers, A is too general and B is the correct answer (using many of the lines about strength that cannot compare to beauty).

14. **"Black ink" references what in the last line?**

    [A] Written poems

    [B] Street signs

    [C] Black diamonds

    [D] Summer flowers dying

    [E] Graffiti

The correct answer is A.
A is the best answer, as all others are not pertaining to the time period or not mentioned even indirectly with the poem.

ANALYZING AND INTERPRETING LITERATURE

15. **The main idea of this poem is describing all of the following except:**

    [A] hope

    [B] time, aging and death overthrow beauty

    [C] marriage

    [D] things that time cannot destroy

    [E] the author's victory

The correct answer is C.
This is another question where you must read carefully. All of the items are mentioned or alluded to with the exception of C; therefore, that is The correct answer that is NOT in the poem.

16. **Shakespeare creates emotions in this poem, and expresses all of the following except:**

    [A] rage

    [B] defeat

    [C] love

    [D] devotion

    [E] mortality

The correct answer is B.
Again, another question to make sure you are reading and not just going with the first answer that matches a word in the passage, making B the correct answer.

ANALYZING AND INTERPRETING LITERATURE

PASSAGE 4
(Prose non-fiction, American, 20th century)

When rays of light pass through a prism, they undergo a change of direction: they are always deflected away from the refractive edge. It is possible to conceive an assembly of prisms whose refractive surfaces progressively become more nearly parallel to each other towards the middle: light rays passing through the outer prisms will undergo the greatest amount of refraction, with consequent deflection of their path towards the center, whereas the middle prism with its two parallel surfaces causes no deflection at all. When a beam of parallel rays passes through these prisms, the rays are all deflected towards the axis and converge at one point. Rays emerging from a point are also deflected by the prisms that they converge. A lens can be conceived as consisting of a large number of such prisms placed close up against one another, so that their surfaces merge into a continuous spherical surface. A lens of this kind, which collects the rays and concentrates them at one point, is called a convergent lens. Since it is thicker in the middle than at the edge, it is known as a convex lens.

In the case of a concave lens, which is thinner in the middle than at the edge, similar considerations show that all rays diverge from the center. Hence such a lens is called a divergent lens. After undergoing refraction, parallel rays appear to come from one point, while rays remerging from a point will, after passing through the lens, appear to emerge from another point. Lenses have surfaces in the same direction but having a different radii of curvature, these are known as meniscus lenses and are used more particularly in spectacles.

~ *The Way Things Work*, ©1963

17. According to the passage above, light rays hit convex mirror and:

   [A] the rays pass straight through

   [B] the rays bounce only straight back to the light source

   [C] bend together to cross at a single point on the other side

   [D] are refracted to open outward on the other side

   [E] are reflected outward at angles back toward the light source

The correct answer is E.
The passage explains that a convex mirror "is thicker in the middle than at the edge" in the last line of the first paragraph. Thus, both A and B are wrong as the surface isn't flat (without curve). C describes a concave lens and D describes a lens not explained in the passage. Therefore, the correct answer is E.

ANALYZING AND INTERPRETING LITERATURE

18. **Light rays hit a concave surface. As the passage explains, light:**

    [A] travels through the prism's surface, angling together to a point

    [B] moves in the same direction but has a different radii of curvature

    [C] the light merges to a point on the continuous spherical surface

    [D] is always reflected away from the refractive edge

    [E] experiences no deflection

The correct answer is A.
Similar to 4.1, the definition is in the passage that matches A. The other four options are wrong or nonsensical as explained in the paragraphs.

19. **Spectacles use meniscus lenses, which are explained by the author that these lenses are:**

    [A] flat

    [B] concave lenses

    [C] convex lenses

    [D] round on both sides of the lens, meaning they have double refraction

    [E] always convergent lenses

The correct answer is B.
Think about a pair of glasses. They aren't flat, so A is wrong. If they were D, round on both sides, then they wouldn't work. Within E, an extreme modifier is used - always - and when words are extreme - such as always, never, every - that is usually an indicator of a wrong answer (unless it's a quote). Thus, the correct choice is B.

ANALYZING AND INTERPRETING LITERATURE

PASSAGE 5
(Prose fiction, British, 18th century)

There is likewise another diversion, which is only shown before the Emperor and Empress, and first minister, upon particular occasions. The Emperor lays on a table three fine silken threads of six inches long. One is blue, the other red, and the third green. These threads are proposed as prizes for those persons whom the Emperor hath a mind to distinguish by a peculiar mark of his favor. The ceremony is performed in his Majesty's great chamber of state; where the candidates are to undergo a trial of dexterity very different from the former, and such as I have not observed the least resemblance of in any other country of the old or the new world. The Emperor holds a stick in his hands, both ends parallel to the horizon, while the candidates, advancing one by one, sometimes leap over the stick, sometimes creep under it backwards and forwards several times, according as the stick is advanced or depressed. Sometimes the Emperor holds one end of the stick, and his first minister holds the other; sometimes the minister has it entirely to himself. Whoever performs his part with most agility, and holds out the longest in *leaping* and *creeping,* is rewarded with the blue-colored silk; the red is given to the next, and the green is given to the third, which they all wear girt twice round the middle; and you see few great persons about this court who are not adorned with one of these girdles.

~ Jonathan Swift, 1704

20. The stick game described by the author in this passage is an allusion to what?

    [A] Jumping to the tune of the Emperor's (his boss') direction

    [B] Baseball

    [C] War games

    [D] A circus

    [E] Tennis

The correct answer is A.
This is another passage where it makes sense to check the year the item was written. Baseball was not yet invented, and tennis as we know it today was not yet played - so both B and E are wrong. A circus doesn't have anything to do with a straight line, so D is also wrong. While A and C are both possible, only A is probable and directly connects to the passage.

ANALYZING AND INTERPRETING LITERATURE

21. Why are the silk threads highly valued?

[A] Silk is a common material.

[B] Green is the Empress' favorite color.

[C] People don't give gifts very often.

[D] Silk was very expensive in the 1700s, when the story was written.

[E] All great persons wear silk.

The correct answer is D.
A is not true, so it can be eliminated. B has no basis of support in the passage, so it is not true. E has some reference in the passage, but it uses one of those extreme words, so it can be eliminated. Between C and D, C has no mention in the passage whereas D references the time period of the story and is the best answer.

22. Using the information only in the passage, are the colors of the silk threads significant?

[A] Yes, because they are royal colors.

[B] Yes, because they represent places of winners.

[C] No, because everyone has them.

[D] No, because hardly everyone has them.

[E] You cannot determine from the passage if the colors are important.

The correct answer is B.
This question is straight from the passage and is explained in the third sentence. The correct answer is B.

ANALYZING AND INTERPRETING LITERATURE

PASSAGE 6
(Prose non-fiction, 20th century)

On the other hand, however, we have no intention whatever of maintaining such a foolish and doctrinaire thesis as that the spirit of capitalism could only have arisen as the result of certain effects of Reformation, or even that of capitalism as an economic system is a creation of the Reformation. In itself, the fact that certain important forms of capitalistic business organizations are known to be considerably older than the Reformation is a sufficient refutation of such a claim. On the contrary, we only wish to ascertain whether and to what extent religious forces have taken part in the qualitative formation and the quantitative expansion of that spirit over the world. Furthermore, what concrete aspects of our capitalistic culture can be traced to them. In the view of the tremendous confusion of interdependent influences between the material basis, the forms of social and political organization, and the ideas current in the time of Reformation, we can only proceed by investigating whether and at what points certain correlations between forms of religious belief and practical ethics can be worked out. At the same time, we shall as far as possible clarify the manner and the general direction which, by virtue of those relationships, the religious movements have influenced development of material culture. Only when this has been determined with reasonable accuracy can the attempt be made to estimate to what extent the historical development of modern culture can be attributed to those religious forces and to what extent others.

~ Max Weber, 1904

23. Capitalism is what type of system according to this passage?

   [A] Democratic

   [B] Economic

   [C] Religious

   [D] Cultural

   [E] Expansionist

The correct answer is B.
This is a question where you have to understand that the passage discusses business organizations and actually refutes the religious forces interference. C is wrong, as per the passage. D is mentioned in capitalistic culture, but as you should not answer a question with a the same word as is being asked, the choice C is wrong. Democracy is a governmental system, so it does not define the capitalism. Expansionist is not relevant to the passage, therefore B is the correct answer.

ANALYZING AND INTERPRETING LITERATURE

24. When the author compares capitalism to the Reformation, what were the main ideas of the Reformation?

   [A] Democratic

   [B] Economic

   [C] Religious

   [D] Cultural

   [E] Expansionist

The correct answer is C.
The passage describes the reformation as a religious movement; C is the correct answer.

25. What word or phrase originating at least in part in the above passage best describes the goal or target of capitalism?

   [A] Ethics based

   [B] Culture driven

   [C] Historical application

   [D] Material accumulation

   [E] Force of nature

The correct answer is D.
Items A, B and C are talked about differently in the passage, and not about the goal of capitalism. D and E are the only possible remaining choices. There is nothing about nature in the paragraph, so D is the correct answer.

ANALYZING AND INTERPRETING LITERATURE

26. From the passage above, which of the following phrases best describes the author's attitude toward capitalism?

[A] The author approves of capitalism if it involves religion.

[B] The author approves of capitalism when it is driven by "qualification expansion of spirit".

[C] The author disapproves of capitalism when it involves modern culture.

[D] The author disapproves of capitalism when Reformation is involved.

[E] The author disapproves of capitalism but wants to investigate why it is wrong.

The correct answer is E.
The tone of the passage is disapproval, so A and B are automatically incorrect. D is also incorrect as the author does not describe the interaction with religion so this applies. Between C and E, culture is used to describe different components within the passage but not in this manner; therefore, E is the best answer.

PASSAGE 7
(Prose non-fiction, 20th century)

> I'd like to say here, that I wasn't the only important one. I was part of a family, just like all of my brothers and sisters. The whole community was important. We used to discuss many of the community's problems together, especially when someone was ill and we couldn't buy medicine, because we were getting poorer and poorer. We'd start discussing and heaping insults on the rich who'd made us suffer for so long. It was about then I began learning about politics. I tried to talk to people who could help me sort my ideas out. I wanted to know what the world was like on the other side. I knew the *finca*, I knew the *Altiplano*. But what I didn't know was about the other problems of the Indians in Guatemala. I didn't know the problems the other groups had to holding onto their land. I knew there were lots of other Indians in other parts of the country, because I'd been meeting them in the *finca* since I was a child, but though we all worked together, we didn't know any of the names of the towns they came from, or how they lived, or what they ate. We just imagined that they were like us.
> ~ Rigoberta Menchu, Nobel Peace Prize Winner 1992

ANALYZING AND INTERPRETING LITERATURE

27. **From the context of the passage, what is a *finca*?**

    [A] A farm

    [B] A village or town

    [C] A mountain range

    [D] A house

    [E] It cannot be determined

The correct answer is B.
In the passage, only two Spanish words are used. Since the author describes a group of unrelated people The correct answer is not D. When offered an option like E, typically that is not the correct choice in a reading comprehension exam. Of the three remaining choices, since it talks about a gathering at this location, C is not an appropriate choice. Either A or B could apply, but A is a workplace not a gathering place. Choose B as the best answer - note that it is also mentioned at the end of the paragraph about people living in towns, another clue that this is the best answer.

28. **The author is telling a story about her own life. What is this kind of document called?**

    [A] Autobiography

    [B] Mystery

    [C] Biography

    [D] Narrative

    [E] Romance

The correct answer is A.
A is the type of story where someone talks about their own life. While narrative could be another possible answer, the best answer is A.

ANALYZING AND INTERPRETING LITERATURE

29. Given the information in the passage, the author most likely worked as:

[A] a washer woman

[B] a seamstress

[C] a farmer

[D] a teacher

[E] it cannot be determined from the passage

The correct answer is C.
There are no indications that the woman washed clothes, worked as a seamstress or a teacher. Thus, A, B and D are eliminated. Between choices C and E, you must decide. If you read the book in full, C is the correct answer. But because this is about this passage, you do not have enough information to decide and E is the best selection - a rare occurrence in this exam, but it does happen.

30. The author describes who is the most important. She defines it as:

[A] herself

[B] her family

[C] her community

[D] the rich people that employed them

[E] the *finca*

The correct answer is C.
It is clear that the author says the community is important. It is literally part of the passage. She denounces A (herself) and even to an extent her family (option B); she goes on to talk about the community together, so the best answer is C. D is opposite of the intent of the passage and E is incongruous, though the translation is town that is just a physical location. Community has stronger meaning and is the best answer.

ANALYZING AND INTERPRETING LITERATURE

PASSAGE 8
(Poetry, British, 18th century)

    Tyger! Tyger! burning bright
    In the forests of the night,
    What immortal hand or eye
    Could frame thy fearful symmetry? (line 4)

    In what distant deeps or skies
    Burnt the fire of thine eyes?
    On what wings dare he aspire?
    What the hand dare seize the flame? (line 8)

    And what shoulder, & what art,
    Could twist the sinews of they heart?
    And when thy heart began to beat,
    What dread hand? & what dread feet? (line 12)
       ~Excerpt, William Blake, 1794

31. Which of the topics below is this best description of the poem's main idea?

[A] Strength, as sinews of the heart are strong.

[B] Creationism, and the author asks what immortal being created the tiger.

[C] Flying, because it talks about wings.

[D] Fire, with references to flames and burning forests.

[E] Love, describing the heart and how it beats.

The correct answer is B.
This passage references the first word of each answer, but only one explanation for the excerpt can be correct. Remember this is about the main idea, not just one idea of the passage. If all of these were right, you need to find the option that is the best choice of all the options - one that can be seen in all of the other options. B represents the best choice.

ANALYZING AND INTERPRETING LITERATURE

32. Sinews, in the third stanza, can be best compared to:

[A] thread

[B] a cage

[C] rope

[D] heart strings or emotions

[E] burnt fire, from the second stanza

The correct answer is D.
Sinews are like tendons. They are strong binding fibers. So, A is not correct, nor is E. The closest two options are C and D; however, since this is poetry, sinews are figurative and the meaning is emotions, choice D.

33. Another phrase for "deeps or skies" that would fit in this poem could be:

[A] caves or planes

[B] trees or forests

[C] seas or air

[D] waves or wind

[E] oceans or lakes

The correct answer is C.
In this selection, synonyms - or similar words - need to be used in the same order as the original passage. Knowing this, C is the best option. While D could be considered, the original words do not describe movement, so it is not the best selection.

ANALYZING AND INTERPRETING LITERATURE

34. What is personified in the poem?

[A] A lion

[B] Birds

[C] Candle

[D] A tiger

[E] The sky

The correct answer is D.
This should be a fairly straightforward question, with the correct answer being D.

35. In line 7 of this poem, what word below most nearly means "aspire"?

[A] Soar

[B] Plunge

[C] Scheme

[D] Travel

[E] Admire

The correct answer is A.
Again, look for synonym in the list. Plunge is an antonym. A is the right choice.

ANALYZING AND INTERPRETING LITERATURE

36. **The poet, William Blake, uses all of the following literary tools to convey his message, except:**

   [A] metaphors

   [B] rhymed couplets

   [C] personification

   [D] symbols

   [E] lyrics

The correct answer is C.
For this question, you need to know your literary terms. Look them up if there are any unfamiliar to you. C - personification - is the right answer… it was also hinted in question four for this passage.

ANALYZING AND INTERPRETING LITERATURE

PASSAGE 9
(Prose fiction, British, 19th century)

"Without their visits you cannot hope to shun the path I tread. Expect the first tomorrow night, when the bell tolls One. Expect the second on the next night at the same hour. The third, upon the next night, when the last stroke of Twelve has ceased to vibrate Look to see me no more; and look that, for your own sake, you remember what has passed between us!"

It walked backward from him; and at every step it took, the window raised itself a little, so that, when the apparition reached it, it was wide open.

Scrooge closed the window, and examined the door by which the Ghost had entered. It was double-locked, as he had locked it with his own hands, and the bolts were undisturbed. Scrooge tried to say "Humbug!" but stopped at the first syllable. And being, from the emotion he had undergone, or the fatigues of the day, or his glimpse of the invisible world, or the dull conversation of the Ghost, or the lateness of the hour, much in need of repose, he went straight to bed, without undressing, and fell asleep on the instant.

~Charles Dickens, 1843

37. What quality of the Ghost is the most likely trait that Scrooge dislikes the most?

[A] The Ghost's old fashioned speech bothers Scrooge the most.

[B] The authoritative nature the Ghost takes with Scrooge is the quality disliked the most.

[C] The fact that the Ghost could break into his house is the trait that Scrooge dislikes.

[D] The Ghost is taller than Scrooge, and that bothers him.

[E] Scrooge dislikes that his bedtime was later than usual.

The correct answer is B.
You should eliminate wrong answers. C is wrong because Scrooge checks his house and it is secure. D is wrong as there is no indication about a height difference. E is also not appropriate, though the passage notes he went straight to bed, it mentions no discomfort caused by the ghost for this reason. Between choices A and B, either could be true but the stronger dislike would be B, so that makes it the correct answer.

ANALYZING AND INTERPRETING LITERATURE

38. **The way Scrooge's reaction to the Ghost is portrayed could mean that according to this passage that Scrooge is:**

    [A] tired

    [B] angry

    [C] looking for excuses

    [D] forgetful

    [E] planning to ignore the Ghost

The correct answer is C.
Again, by eliminating the wrong choices, there is nothing that suggests Scrooge is forgetful so it isn't D. While any of the rest are possible, the fact that Scrooge checks around the house and looks for things that could be explanations leads to the most reasonable answer as C.

39. **The Ghost's remarks listed in the passage can most likely be inferred as:**

    [A] a warning to Scrooge

    [B] the Ghost is talking to the wrong person

    [C] Scrooge is hallucinating

    [D] a friend was playing a joke on Scrooge

    [E] no inference can be made

The correct answer is A.
Of the five options, the middle choices - B, C and D - have no support in the passage. As E is not a typical choice for the exam, A is the correct answer.

ANALYZING AND INTERPRETING LITERATURE

40. Scrooge's reaction to the Ghost in this passage leads a reader to conclude:

[A] that Scrooge was just conducting a normal nighttime house-check

[B] when the Ghost comes back for him, Scrooge will go along willingly

[C] even wealthy people like Scrooge lock their houses

[D] that Scrooge does not believe in the supernatural

[E] Scrooge is likely overcome with exhaustion

The correct answer is D.
The first answer is not accurate, as it was not a normal nighttime house check with the ghost. Also, there is no indication that Scrooge will willingly go anywhere with the ghost, so B is wrong. The generalization about wealthy people doesn't apply to the whole passage making that assumption, so C is incorrect. While Scrooge is admittedly tired, the better answer is D, given the extent of reaction to the ghost's presence in his home.

41. The tone of the passage is intended to:

[A] serve as a warning to Scrooge about things he will be shown

[B] serve as a reminder that Scrooge has forgotten appointments

[C] describe how disconcerted Scrooge felt after the warning was given by the Ghost

[D] provide backstory

[E] explain why Scrooge is so stingy

The correct answer is C.
Since the correct answers must be given based on the passage, A is more in line with the full story. B is not what the ghost was saying. A backstory is something that happened to the character in the past, and the ghost talks about the future, so D is incorrect. Nothing explains why Scrooge is stingy, or even that he is (other than the meaning of his name), so C is the correct answer.

ANALYZING AND INTERPRETING LITERATURE

PASSAGE 10
(Prose, non-fiction, American, 20th century)

> Using the Constitution to protect the minorities, James Madison's system of government is largely an attempt to divide and frustrate the majority. Madison envisioned a political system with the broadest possible power base. For example, he rejected the common belief that a democracy could work only in a very small area, arguing that it could succeed in a large country like the United States. A large population spread over a huge area would make it very difficult to force a permanent majority. Such a society would probably divide into varied and fluctuating minorities, making a long lasting majority unlikely. Instead, majorities would be created out of combinations of competing minorities. Thus, any majority would be temporary, and new ones would be elusive. This system, political scientists now term *pluralism*.
>
> ~ Leon Baradat, 1973

42. According to the passage, what is pluralism?

    [A] Majorities created out of combinations of competing minorities

    [B] A new division of political science

    [C] A political system with the smallest possible power base

    [D] A new name for a permanent majority

    [E] The system for democracy to work in a very small area

The correct answer is A.
This is a simple reference to the passage and the correct answer is A.

43. The Constitution mentioned in the first line, in context to this passage, is:

    [A] James Madison's document to create a permanent majority

    [B] the document creating the United States

    [C] the personality of James Madison

    [D] the health of the majority

    [E] instructions on how to create combinations of competing minorities

The correct answer is B.
This question discusses something that should be known outside of context, especially when referencing a President of the United States, and the correct answer is B.

ANALYZING AND INTERPRETING LITERATURE

44. The passage talks about democracy. Another phrase for a democracy is:

[A] the rule of a few over the many

[B] the welfare state

[C] a laissez-faire economy

[D] an elected government system

[E] an appointed government by a monarch

The correct answer is D.
Using definitions of words, the correct answer should be obvious. A defines a monarchy or dictatorship; a welfare state could be socialist in B. A democracy doesn't describe economy, or an appointed government with monarchy, so the correct answer is D.

PASSAGE 11
(Prose non-fiction, British, 21st century)

American black music was going along like an express train. But white cats, after Buddy Holly died and Eddie Cochran died, and Elvis was in the army gone wonky, white American music when I arrived was the Beach Boys and Bobby Vee. They were still stuck in the past. The past was six months ago; it wasn't a long time. But things changed. The Beatles were the milestone. And then they got stuck inside their own cage. "The Fab Four." Hence, eventually, you got the Monkees, all this ersatz stuff. But I think there was a vacuum somewhere in white American music at the time.

When we first got to America and to LA, there was a lot of Beach Boys on the radio, which was pretty funny to us - it was before *Pet Sounds* - it was hot rod songs and surfing songs, pretty lousily played, familiar Chuck Berry licks going on. "Round, round get around / I get around," I though that was brilliant. It was later on, but Brian Wilson had something. "In My Room," "Don't Worry Baby." I was more interested in their B-sides, the ones he slipped in. There was no particular correlation with what we were doing so I could just listen to it on another level. I thought these are very well-constructed songs. I took easily to the pop song idiom. I'd always listened to everything, and America opened it all out - we were hearing records there that were regional hits. We'd get to know local labels and local acts, which is how we came across "Time Is on My Side," in LA, sung by Irma Thomas. It was a B-side of a record on Imperial Records, a label we'd have been aware of because it was independent and successful and based on Sunset Strip.

~Keith Richards, 2010

ANALYZING AND INTERPRETING LITERATURE

45. How many unique singers versus unique bands, respectively, are named in the passage above?

   [A] Seven and Four

   [B] Six and Three

   [C] Eight and Three

   [D] Seven and Three

   [E] Six and Four

The correct answer is D.
This is merely counting. There are Seven singers (Buddy Holly, Eddie Cochran, Elivs, Bobby Vee, Chuck Berry, Brian Wilson, Irma Thomas) and three bands (Beatles, Monkeys, Beach Boys). D The "Fab Four" is referring to the Beatles. (Note the author's group is not named in the passage, and neither is he.)

46. How many songs are referenced in the passage above?

   [A] Two

   [B] Three

   [C] Four

   [D] Five

   [E] Six

The correct answer is C.
Count them - In My Room, Don't Worry Baby and Time Is On My Side. B (note "Round, round get around/I get around" are lyrics and not the name of a song.)

ANALYZING AND INTERPRETING LITERATURE

47. In the context of the selection's first paragraph, how many white singers or groups are named by the author?

[A] Four

[B] Five

[C] Three

[D] Seven

[E] One

The correct answer is D.
The whole passage is about white male singers except Irma Thomas, but her name is in the second paragraph. This question is limited to the first paragraph. Seven singers or bands are named after the author's "white cats" comment. D

48. Given what the author says about the B-side of a record, which of the following sentences is closest to the author's opinion?

[A] The B-side had more creativity and outlets for artists, making it unique.

[B] It was called the B-side because the songs were generally not as good.

[C] Only regional labels took the time to press B-sides.

[D] The B-side was where all the surfing songs were recorded.

[E] Labels were strict about the contents of the B-sides.

The correct answer is A.
You need to read the passage to understand which is the most appropriate. A is the best answer. The others are wrong because B is opposite of what he expresses as his opinion, C is factually not what the author writes, D is the opposite of what he says about the Beach Boys, and E is also the opposite of what the author writes.

ANALYZING AND INTERPRETING LITERATURE

49. When the author talks about the Beatles and says "they got stuck inside their own cage," the author most likely means:

[A] that the Beatles always had to hide in hotels because they were so famous

[B] that successful musical groups could never enjoy the publicity

[C] that the Beatles were trapped on planes all the time

[D] that the Beatles couldn't perform with anyone outside of their four members

[E] the Beatles outgrew the standard previously set for successful musicians, and were trapped in their own famous sensation

The correct answer is E.
For this answer, you need to interpret the author's intention from the context of the passage. The first four options are not supported by the passage at all; E is the best interpretation of the author's phrase.

50. Given the descriptions in the passage, the author's profession is likely:

[A] a roadie

[B] a writer

[C] a singer

[D] a photographer

[E] a teacher

The correct answer is C.
Understanding the author's voice is important. Even if you didn't know that author's name (though you could save time if you did), given the descriptions of what he writes, C is the best and right answer.

ANALYZING AND INTERPRETING LITERATURE

PASSAGE 12
(Prose fiction, British, pre-Ren/Classic)

A marvelous case is it to hear, either the warnings of that he should have voided, or the tokens of that he could not void. For the self night next before his death, the lord Stanley sent a trusty secret messenger unto him at midnight in all the haste, requiring him to rise and ride away with him, for he was disposed utterly no longer to bide; he had so fearful a dream, in which him thought that a boar with his tusks so raced them both by the heads, that the blood ran about both their shoulders. And forasmuch as the protector gave the boar for his cognizance, this dream made so fearful an impression in his heart, that he was thoroughly determined no longer to tarry, but had his horse ready, if the lord Hastings would go with him to ride so far yet the same night, that they should be out of danger ere day. Ay, good lord, quoth the lord Hastings to this messenger, leaneth my lord thy master so much to such trifles, and hath such faith in dreams, which either his own fear fantasieth or do rise in the night's rest by reason of his day thoughts? Tell him it is plain witchcraft to believe in such dreams; which if they were tokens of things to come, why thinketh he not that we might be as likely to make them true by our going if we were caught and brought back (as friends fail fleers), for then had the boar a cause likely to race us with his tusks, as folk that fled for some falsehood, wherefore either is there no peril (nor none there is indeed), or if any be, it is rather in going than biding. And if we should, needs cost, fall in peril one way or other, yet had I livelier that men should see it were by other men's falsehood, than think it were either our own fault or faint heart. And therefore go to thy master, man, and commend me to him, and pray him be merry and have no fear: for I ensure him I am as sure of the man that he wotteth of, as I am of my own hand. God send grace, sir, quoth the messenger, and went his way.

~Sir Thomas More, 1513

51. The beginning of the passage is describing what?

[A] An injury sustained by the main character

[B] A rider that is trying to escape injury

[C] The main character's dream

[D] A witch's story

[E] The boar that the character will grill for dinner

The correct answer is C.
Discounting the incorrect description of what's in the passage (such as in option E and A as well as B), that leaves options C and D. There is no reference to a witch, so the best choice is C. He even states that it is a dream.

ANALYZING AND INTERPRETING LITERATURE

52. What is the cautionary message that the rider gets when he reaches his destination?

[A] Dreams are witchcraft if you believe in them.

[B] Dreams can come true if you believe in them.

[C] God sends His grace.

[D] Those faint of heart do not have dreams.

[E] Men cannot fall for other men's falsehoods.

The correct answer is A.
The rider warns the statement included in A.

53. Did the main character in this passage believe he could out run bad visions?

[A] No, the passage makes it clear you always get what's coming in a dream.

[B] No, dreams mean nothing, so the main character didn't pay any attention to it.

[C] Yes, it was possible to escape bad visions on horseback.

[D] Yes, the main character thought dancing would rid himself of bad dreams.

[E] There is nothing in the passage that assists in answering this question.

The correct answer is C.
Again, the main character gives indications that the correct answer is C. The other options of No are wrong, as is the correct answer given in E. Answer D can be discounted because dancing is not discussed in the passage.

ANALYZING AND INTERPRETING LITERATURE

PASSAGE 13
(Prose fiction, British, 19th century)

> To go into solitude, a man needs to retire as much from his chamber as from society. I am not solitary whilst I read and write, though nobody is with me. But if a man would be alone, let him look at the stars. The rays that come from those heavenly worlds, will separate between him and what he touches. One might think the atmosphere was made transparent with this design, to give man, in the heavenly bodies, the perpetual presence of the sublime. Seen in the streets of cities, how great they are! If the stars should appear one night in a thousand years, how would men believe and adore; and preserve for many generations the remembrance of the city of God which had been shown! But every night come out these envoys of beauty, and light the universe with their admonishing smile.
> ~Ralph Waldo Emerson, 1836

54. The first two lines of this passage imply what?

   [A] A man is never alone.

   [B] A man is always alone.

   [C] A man can be alone if he turns his back on people.

   [D] A man can be alone if he makes his mind focus.

   [E] A man who is lonely is considered alone.

The correct answer is D.
Given this is fiction and nearly a poem, you need to interpret what the author intends. The first two options use those extreme words, so they are not the best choices. The literal description of turning a back on people is not discussed. The difference between lonely and being alone is not discussed, either. So, D is the correct answer you should choose.

ANALYZING AND INTERPRETING LITERATURE

55. Given the whole passage, which of the following is the best match for the author's opinion about nature?

[A] The author prefers to seek to retire in his chamber.

[B] The author sees wonder in the sky and beauty at night.

[C] The author does not like trees.

[D] The author can only see stars one night in a thousand years.

[E] You cannot tell the author's opinion from this passage.

The correct answer is B.
You should realize by now - especially when understanding poems - that it would be extremely rare to select option E as the right answer. Option D is a misstatement of a phrase in the passage. There is no mention of the author even hinting that he does not like trees, so C is incorrect. When considering A or B, A does not resound as strongly as B, which is the right answer.

56. The phrase "light the universe with their admonishing smile" is an example of:

[A] personification

[B] a simile

[C] a metaphor

[D] irony

[E] satire

The correct answer is A.
Remember, the definition of personification is to give an inanimate object the attributes of a human, so A is correct. If you are unfamiliar with the other options in this example, it would be a good idea to look them up and learn them, as at least one of these five will be included on the exam.

ANALYZING AND INTERPRETING LITERATURE

PASSAGE 14
(Poetry, American, 20th century)

> Two roads diverged in a yellow wood,
> And sorry I could not travel both
> And be one traveler, long I stood
> And looked down one as far as I could
> To where it bent in the undergrowth;
>
> Then took the other, as just as fair,
> And having perhaps the better claim,
> Because it was grassy and wanted wear;
> Though as for that the passing there
> Had worn them really about the same,
>
> And both that morning equally lay
> In leaves no step had trodden black.
> Oh, I kept the first for another day!
> Yet knowing how way leads on to way,
> I doubted if I should ever come back.
>
> I shall be telling this with a sigh
> Somewhere ages and ages hence:
> Two roads diverged in a wood, and I—
> I took the one less traveled by,
> And that has made all the difference.
> ~Robert Frost, 1920

57. When the author uses the phrase "wanted wear" in the third stanza, what does that mean?

   [A] It looked just as fair as the other path.

   [B] It was not as inviting.

   [C] The path didn't go the same way as the other one.

   [D] The path was less traveled than the other one.

   [E] You cannot determine what the author means.

The correct answer is D.
There are two possible correct answers. Both B and D are viable options; however, you are looking for the best answer. In the context of the whole poem, the explanation of B does not ring as true since that is the one that the author actually selected. D is the best answer.

ANALYZING AND INTERPRETING LITERATURE

58. The author says that he "took the one less traveled by"; what does that mean?

[A] The other path looked like it was used more.

[B] He did the right thing when others chose the wrong one.

[C] He took the one on the left.

[D] He took the one on the right.

[E] It cannot be determined what the author meant by this short selection.

The correct answer is A.
This is another example of how a question is phrased to make sure you read it accurately. There is no statement about right or left direction, so both C and D are wrong. E is also eliminated as least probable answer because comprehension very rarely provides no correct answer. While B may bear some truth, in particular for the author as given in the end of the poem, A is the best answer.

59. What is another way the author states his path was the "one less traveled by"?

[A] "both that morning equally lay"

[B] "no step had trodden black"

[C] "Somewhere ages and ages hence"

[D] "bent in the undergrowth"

[E] "having perhaps the better claim"

The correct answer is B.
This is another way to look for a synonym, but using a whole phrase. You should be able to narrow it down to D and B; however, B describes what happens when you walk on leaves that haven't been disturbed in a while. It is a parallel description to the straightforward "less traveled" statement, in that it describes the actions and ensuing results. Therefore, B is correct.

ANALYZING AND INTERPRETING LITERATURE

60. What does the author imply since he took the path less traveled?

[A] He has run into fewer people that try to bully him into doing what they want.

[B] Life is tougher getting to see the light.

[C] He was sorry he didn't chose to go the more well-trod path.

[D] He didn't make as much money as the people that took the other path.

[E] His life is better for choosing to go his own path.

The correct answer is E.
Running through the list of options, there is no mention of the author having people force him to make a decision (so A is wrong). B is also not applicable to this passage. There is no expression of remorse as provided in option C anywhere in the passage, so C is not correct. Monetary considerations - making money - are not mentioned either (as in D), so the only option left, which is correct, is E.

PASSAGE 15
(Prose fiction, American, 20th century)

His memories of the Boston Society Contralto were nebulous and musical. She was a lady who sang, sang, sang in the music room on their house on Washington Square - sometimes with guests all about her, the men with their arms folded, balanced breathlessly on the edges of sofas, the women with their hands in their laps, occasionally making little whispers to the men and always clapping very briskly and uttering cooing cries after each song - and she often sang to Anthony alone, in Italian or French or in a strange and terrible dialect...

Oblivious to the social system, he lived for a while alone and unsought in a high room in Beck Hall - a slim dark boy of medium height with a shy sensitive mouth. His allowance was more than liberal. He laid the foundations for a library by purchasing from a wandering bibliophile first editions of Swinburne, Meredith, and Hardy, and a yellowed illegible autograph letter of Keats', finding later he had been amazingly overcharged. He became an exquisite dandy, amassed a rather pathetic collection of silk pajamas, brocaded dressing-gowns, and neckties too flamboyant to wear; in this secret finery he would parade before a mirror in his room or lie stretched in satin along the window-seat looking down on the yard and realizing this clamor, breathless and immediate, in which it seemed he was to never have a part.
~ F. Scott Fitzgerald, 1922

ANALYZING AND INTERPRETING LITERATURE

61. Based on the information in the passage, what is a "contralto"?

[A] A Boston slang term for a high class man

[B] A female singer

[C] A female dancer

[D] A writer

[E] A bibliophile

The correct answer B.
Using the pronouns in the passage, contralto is a female - so A is obviously wrong. While any of the remaining options may be true, in the passage it talks about the woman singing, so B is the correct choice.

62. Based on the information in the passage, an "exquisite dandy" refers to:

[A] the first editions of the books listed in the passage

[B] anyone who wears silk pajamas

[C] a gentleman who has money to spend extravagantly on fancy things

[D] someone who likes to parade before a mirror

[E] someone who likes candy

The correct answer is C.
The term "dandy" references a person, so A is out. E is also out because candy is not mentioned in the passage; it is merely a rhyme for dandy. B is mentioned in the passage that the man like to wear silk pajamas and so is D, when it talks about the mirror. However, you have to look at the whole passage and the thing the man does, so C is the best answer if you do not know what "dandy" means.

ANALYZING AND INTERPRETING LITERATURE

63. Why would the social system be important in this reading selection?

[A] Richer classes don't have dandies, so the main character can't be dandy.

[B] A rich man with no female friends is called a dandy, and it helps explain the story.

[C] The character seems ostracized and that can't happen in certain social classes.

[D] If the main character was of a lower class, he could not live the life described.

[E] No one lives the luxurious life described in the passage.

The correct answer is D.
In this question, it helps to know the meaning of dandy, which you may use from the previous answer if you do not know it. Since the man described in the passage seems to have a lot of money, A cannot be the right answer. E also is not a choice because it uses an extreme phrase - "no one". D is not correct because anyone can be excluded from a group (it also has an extreme contraction of "can't"). Between B and D, there are two reasons why B isn't a good choice. First, no female friends could be read as an extreme description, using "no". Another tip that this may not be the right choice is that if you removed the part of the passage about dandy, the story still works. Therefore, if you don't know that dandies are rarely lower classes, you can reason your way that D is correct.

PASSAGE 16
(Prose fiction, American, 20th century)

> These are morning matters, pictures you dream as the final wave heaves you up on the sand in the bright light and drying air. You remember pressure, and a curved sleep you rested against, soft, like a scallop in its shell. But the air hardens your skin; you stand; you leave the lighted shore to explore some dim headland, and soon you're lost in the leafy interior, intent, remembering nothing.
>
> I still think of that old tomcat, mornings, when I wake. Things are tamer now; I sleep with the window shut. The cats and our rites are gone and my life is changed, but the memory remains of something powerful playing over me. I wake expectant, hoping to see a new thing. If I'm lucky I might be jogged awake by a strange bird call. I dress in a hurry, imagining the yard flapping with auks, or flamingos. This morning it was a wood duck, down at the creek. It flew away.
>
> ~Annie Dillard, 1975 Pulitzer Prize

ANALYZING AND INTERPRETING LITERATURE

64. The tone of the selection is:

[A] reflective

[B] indulgent

[C] indifferent

[D] dishonest

[E] ironic

The correct answer is A.
This is knowing what the different words mean. A is the correct answer. Review the definitions of these words if you don't know them, to make sure they won't trip you up on the exam.

65. The author uses _____ to describe the setting.

[A] personification

[B] ambivalence

[C] satire

[D] allusion

[E] clichés

The correct answer is D.
Definitions are a large part of reading comprehension answer possibilities, as they like to know that you understand more than just what the passage says. D is the correct answer.

ANALYZING AND INTERPRETING LITERATURE

66. **The phrase, "like a scallop in its shell" is an example of:**

    [A] irony

    [B] a simile

    [C] a metaphor

    [D] personification

    [E] euphemism

The correct answer is C.
Again, this is about definitions. When you use the word "like" in a comparison, which is one hint that the phrase is a metaphor. The correct answer is C.

67. **The author describes many of her feelings and situations by focusing the conversation on animals. Based on the information in the passage, one reason could be:**

    [A] animals are comforting and relax the reader

    [B] birds are flighty and the center of her story

    [C] the setting of this story is a farm

    [D] the lead character doesn't have many human friends

    [E] it is the backstory of how animals and nature are always present in the character's life

The correct answer is E.
There are some weigh out options for these answers! A, B, C and D make great leaps if you were to make those conclusions. E is the correct option.

ANALYZING AND INTERPRETING LITERATURE

68. The phrase "the air hardens your skin" within the context of the passage most likely refers to what?

[A] The morning air woke the character up from dreaming.

[B] The scallop shell bed the character sleeps in has opened.

[C] The air dries out the character's skin.

[D] The coldness of the room turns off the brain of the character.

[E] The air turns the character's skin cold when the cat leaves the bed.

The correct answer is A.
This question looks at ensuring you understand the suggestions made by the author. B is totally made up. D is a bit far-fetched, to turn off her brain (what does that have to do with skin?) E gives the impression cats are extremely warm and somehow leaving the bed is related with her description, slightly implausible. A and C remain; but in the context of fiction, A is the better choice.

PASSAGE 17
(Drama, British, 16th century/classical)

> **Bernardo : Welcome, Horatio: welcome, good Marcellus.**
> **Marcellus : What, has this thing appear'd again to-night?**
> **Bernardo : I have seen nothing.**
> **Marcellus : Horatio says 'tis but our fantasy,**
> **And will not let belief take hold of him**
> **Touching this dreaded sight, twice seen of us:**
> **Therefore I have entreated him along**
> **With us to watch the minutes of this night;**
> **That if again this apparition come,**
> **He may approve our eyes and speak to it.**
> **Horatio : Tush, tush, 'twill not appear.**
> **Bernardo : Sit down awhile;**
> **And let us once again assail your ears,**
> **That are so fortified against our story**
> **What we have two nights seen.**
>   **~William Shakespeare, 1599-1602**

ANALYZING AND INTERPRETING LITERATURE

69. **The three men in the play can be said, in this passage:**

[A] to disagree about a ghost that was seen

[B] to disagree that two days ago they saw people meeting "twice seen of us"

[C] that Horatio and Bernardo are trying to persuade Marcellus they saw something

[D] that Horatio and Marcellus are trying to persuade Bernardo they saw something

[E] to meet for a drink for "fortification"

The correct answer is A.
Drama selections need you to pay close attention to the characters and who says what. B is not true - the two men don't disagree about what they saw. C and D do not list the characters correctly about who sees what. E isn't correct at all, so A is the correct answer.

70. **When Marcellus speaks of "approving our eyes", what is he saying?**

[A] Marcellus and Bernardo need glasses.

[B] Bernardo didn't believe what Marcellus saw.

[C] Horatio believes what Marcellus saw.

[D] Horatio should see what Bernardo and Marcellus saw.

[E] Marcellus should believe what Bernardo saw.

The correct answer is D.
You need to review the members of the scene if you got this inaccurate. The only correct choice about who saw what and who needs to see what they saw is D.

ANALYZING AND INTERPRETING LITERATURE

71. When Bernardo says "once again assail your ears", what does he mean?

[A] He wants to repeat himself to Marcellus to make him believe him.

[B] He wants to repeat himself to Horatio to make him believe him.

[C] He wants to repeat himself to help all three of them believe the story.

[D] He wants Marcellus and Horatio to poke holes in the story.

[E] None of these are the meaning of that phrase in the passage.

The correct answer is B.
Pay attention to the characters. That's how these answer choices can be confusing. B is the correct answer.

72. In the context of the passage, entreated means:

[A] invited

[B] engaged

[C] demanded

[D] refused

[E] ignored

The correct answer is A.
Picking the best synonym should get easier at the end of the exam. A is correct.

ANALYZING AND INTERPRETING LITERATURE

PASSAGE 18
(Drama, American, 20th century)

    Edmund : That's foolishness. You know it's only a bad cold.
    Mary : Yes, of course, I know that!
    Edmund : But listen, Mama. I want you to promise me that even if it turns out to be something worse, you'll know I'll soon be alright again, anyway, and don't worry yourself sick, and you'll keep on taking care of yourself -
    Mary : I won't listen when you talk so silly! There's absolutely no reason to talk as if you expect something dreadful! Of course, I promise you I give you my sacred word of honor! But I suppose you're remembering I've promised before on my word of honor.
    Edmund : No!
    Mary : I'm not blaming you, dear. How can you help it? How can any one of us forget? That's what makes it so hard - for all of us. We can't forget.
    Edmund : Mama! Stop it!
    Mary : All right, dear. I didn't beam to be so gloomy. Don't mind me. Here. Let me feel your head. Why, it's nice and cool. You certainly don't have any fever now.

                                          ~Eugene O'Neill, 1955

73. It can be said that this passage of the drama:

    [A] puts American dream against American nightmare

    [B] describes the normal American family

    [C] portrays Americans in a very resilient fashion

    [D] was likely written during a war so obviously has negative overtones

    [E] has the mother remembering the death of another child

The correct answer is E.
You may have read this play, but you have to limit your answers to the passage; therefore, A is not correct. B invites the reader to make assumptions about normal, and that does not usually happen in the exam. There is not enough information in the passage to presume C is correct. The passage is not overly negative, so E is the best answer.

ANALYZING AND INTERPRETING LITERATURE

74. Mary changes the direction of the conversation by:

[A] stopping Edmund from talking by taking his temperature

[B] making Edmund feel badly about the death of his brother

[C] walking out of the room

[D] tucking the covers up to his chin

[E] ignoring him

The correct answer is A.
You need to read the scene to make sure to pick the right answer. A is correct.

75. This portion of the play is a:

[A] monologue

[B] dialogue

[C] soliloquy

[D] entendre

[E] stichomythia

The correct answer is B.
By definition, since there are two people, A and C are incorrect. While D is possible, E is wrong; B is the best choice. Look up the words if you are unfamiliar with them.

76. Mary talks about Edmund expecting something dreadful. What's a literary term for that action?

[A] Oxymoron

[B] Dissonance

[C] Foreshadowing

[D] Stream of consciousness

[E] Understatement

The correct answer is C.
Definitions again! The correct choice is C and by now you should automatically look up any definitions for words that are unfamiliar to you.

ANALYZING AND INTERPRETING LITERATURE

PASSAGE 19
(Prose fiction, British, 18th century)

> But though thus largely indebted to fortune, to nature she had yet greater obligation: her form was elegant, her heart was liberal. Her countenance announced the intelligence of her mind, her complexion varied with every emotion of her foul, and her eyes, the heralds of her speech, now beamed with understanding and now glistened with sensibility.
>
> For the short period of her minority, the management of her fortune and the care of her person, had by the Dean been entrusted to three guardians, among whom her own choice was to settle to her residence: but her mind, saddened by the lots of all her natural friends, coveted to regain its serenity in the quietness of the country, and in the bosom of an aged and maternal counsellor, whom she loved as her mother, and to to whom she had been known from her childhood.
>
> -Fanny Burney, 1782

77. From the context of this passage, which of the following statements is the most likely to be true?

    [A] The main character is poor.

    [B] The main character is an orphan.

    [C] The setting of the story is in England.

    [D] The main character is going to live with her aunt.

    [E] The main character doesn't like to live in town.

The correct answer is B.
The female character seems to have inherited money, so A is not correct. There is no way to know in what country the setting takes place, and remember that all answers are dependent on the passage; so C is incorrect. D is also incorrect because the passage explicitly talks about her wanting to set up her own house. B is the right answer.

ANALYZING AND INTERPRETING LITERATURE

78. In the quote, "her heart was liberal", what is the author trying to express?

[A] The author implies that the main character is of loose morals.

[B] The author implies that while ladylike, she has a wild streak.

[C] The author alludes that the woman is more open than her demeanor.

[D] The author makes it clear that she is alone.

[E] The author shows how she was older than her natural friends.

The correct answer is C.
While this one may seem difficult, if you take each statement apart, The correct answer comes quickly. A is wrong because nowhere does the author talk about morals being questionable. B implies an overly outward exuberance by the main character, and that is overstating what is written. D is simply not accurate, and while there seems to be a difference between her and her friends, nowhere does the passage indicate she is older. C is correct. Also, when the author describes her "heart", it can mean that her inward thoughts, and since her demeanor is so proper, the outward indications of her character, C again is shown to be the right answer.

79. What does the word "minority" mean in the context of the passage?

[A] The woman in the passage is a Native American.

[B] The character is not yet an adult.

[C] The group of people in the story are members of the minority political party.

[D] The character has less money than her friends.

[E] None of the given options explain "minority" in this passage.

The correct answer is B.
This passage does not talk about race or ethnicity or religion; A is wrong. C talks about politics and that is not within the passage, so it, too, is wrong. D is the opposite of what is implied by the author about the main character; and as you have learned, E is likely the wrong choice. Choose B.

ANALYZING AND INTERPRETING LITERATURE

80. What is another word for serenity in this passage?

[A] Peacefulness

[B] Counsellor

[C] Bosom

[D] Rambunctiousness

[E] Prayerful

The correct answer is A.
Another synonym choice - A is correct.

AMERICAN LITERATURE

Description of the Examination
The American Literature examination covers material that is usually taught in a semester survey course (or the equivalent) at the college level. It deals with the prose and poetry written in the United States from colonial times to the present. It is primarily a test of knowledge about literary works — their content, their background, and their authors — but also requires an ability to interpret poetry, fiction, and nonfiction prose, as well as a familiarity with the terminology used by literary critics and historians. The examination emphasizes fiction and poetry and deals to a lesser degree with the essay, drama, and autobiography.

In both coverage and approach, the examination resembles the chronologically organized survey of American literature offered by many colleges. It assumes that candidates have read widely and developed an appreciation of American literature, know the basic literary periods, and have a sense of the historical development of American literature.

The test contains approximately 100 questions to be answered in 90 minutes. Some of these are pretest questions that will not be scored. Any time candidates spend on tutorials and providing personal information is in addition to the actual testing time.

An optional essay section can be taken in addition to the multiple-choice test. The essay section requires that two essays be written during a total time of 90 minutes. For the first essay, a common theme in American literature and a list of major American authors are provided. Candidates are asked to write a well-organized essay discussing the way that theme is handled in works by any two of those authors. For the second essay, candidates are asked to respond to one of two topics — one requiring analysis of a poem, the other requiring analysis of a prose excerpt. In each case, the specific poem or prose excerpt is provided and questions are offered for guidance.

Candidates are expected to write well-organized essays in clear and precise prose. The essay section is graded by faculty at the institution that requests it and is still administered in paper-and-pencil format. There is an additional fee for taking this section, payable to the institution that administers the exam.

Knowledge and Skills Required
Questions on the American Literature examination require candidates to demonstrate one or more of the following abilities in the approximate proportions indicated.

45%-60%   Knowledge of particular literary works, including:
- Authors
- Characters
- Plots
- Setting
- Style
- Themes

25%-40%   Ability to understand and interpret:
- Short poems
- Excerpts from long poems
- Excerpts from prose works

10%-15%   Knowledge of:
- The historical and social settings of specific works
- Relations between literary works
- Relations of specific works to literary traditions
- Influences on authors

AMERICAN LITERATURE

5%-10%   **Familiarity with:**
- Critical terms
- Verse forms
- Literary devices

The subject matter of the American Literature examination is drawn from the following chronological periods. The percentages indicate the approximate percentage of exam questions from each period.

15%   **The Colonial and Early National Period (Beginnings-1830)**

25%   **The Romantic Period (1830-1870)**

20%   **The Period of Realism and Naturalism (1870-1910)**

25%   **The Modernist Period (1910-1945)**

15%   **The Contemporary Period (1945-Present)**

AMERICAN LITERATURE

DIRECTIONS: Read each item and select the best response.

1. *"Does this safari guarantee I come back alive?"* **The reply:** *"We guarantee nothing!"*

    What literary device best describes this quote?

    [A] Foreshadowing

    [B] Call-back

    [C] Science fiction

    [D] Cliffhanger

    [E] Epilogue

2. *Moby Dick's* **Ishmael is an example of what?**

    [A] Antagonist

    [B] Raconteur

    [C] Deus ex Machina

    [D] Red herring

    [E] Prolepsis

3. **What were two major characteristics of the first American literature?**

    [A] Vengefulness and arrogance

    [B] Oral delivery and reverence for the land

    [C] Maudlin and self-pitying egocentrism

    [D] Bellicosity and derision

    [E] Satire and humor

4. **"Assonance" describes:**

    [A] rhyming poetry

    [B] repetition of a letter or sound at the beginning of close words

    [C] a piece of literature with a clear metaphorical meaning.

    [D] a clue used to deceive the reader

    [E] repetition of internal vowel sounds

AMERICAN LITERATURE

5. **Which of the following best describes a parable?**

   [A] A short, entertaining account of some happening, usually using talking animals as characters

   [B] A slow, sad song or poem expressing lamentation

   [C] An extended narrative work expressing universal truths regarding domestic life

   [D] A short, simple story of a familiar occurrence, from which a moral or religious lesson may be drawn

   [E] An oral telling passed down through generations

   "Whirl up, Sea-
   Whirl your pointed pines,
   Splash your great pines
   On our rocks,
   Hurl your green over us-
   Cover us with your pools of fir."

6. **What is the title of the above poem?**

   [A] "Gulls" by William Carlos Williams

   [B] "Nature is what we see" by Emily Dickinson

   [C] "Oread" by Hilda "H.D." Doolittle

   [D] "A Clear Midnight" by Walt Whitman

   [E] "April Rain Song" by Langston Hughes

7. **Which of these sentences best describes the poem?**

   [A] A metaphor, comparing the sea and a forest

   [B] A parable, warning of the dangers inherent in nature

   [C] A ballad, exploring the beauty of creation

   [D] A dirge, a lamentation on something that was lost

   [E] A satire, parodying florid prose styles

8. **The second and third lines contain an example of what poetic device?**

   [A] A slant rhyme

   [B] An epistrophe

   [C] A stanza

   [D] A muse

   [E] An assonance

AMERICAN LITERATURE

9. **What is an untrue statement about theme in literature?**

   [A] It is the central idea of a literary work

   [B] All aspects of a work (plot, characters, etc.) should contribute to the theme in some way

   [C] It is always stated directly in the text

   [D] It can be inferred through close analysis of the text

   [E] It is often open to interpretation

10. **Jack Kerouac was credited with giving a voice to which cultural movement?**

    [A] Hipsters

    [B] Generation X

    [C] Pacifist and conscientious objectors

    [D] The Beat Generation

    [E] Hippy culture

"The thousand injuries of Fortunato I had borne as best I could, but when he ventured on insult I vowed revenge."

11. **This quote begins what famous short story?**

    [A] Murders in the Rue Morgue

    [B] A Sound of Thunder

    [C] The Cask of Amontillado

    [D] An Occurrence at Owl Creek Bridge

    [E] The Story of an Hour

12. **Arthur Miller's *The Crucible* parallels which historical event?**

    [A] The Cold War

    [B] The fall of the Berlin Wall

    [C] Sen. McCarthy's House un-American Activities Committee hearings

    [D] The Persian Gulf War

    [E] The Great Depression

AMERICAN LITERATURE

13. In *The Scarlet Letter*, Hester Prynne must wear the titular letter after she is found guilty of…

    [A] Murder

    [B] Theft

    [C] Prostitution

    [D] Adultery

    [E] Witchcraft

14. Who wrote "A Good Man is Hard to Find"?

    [A] Ernest Hemingway

    [B] Nathaniel Hawthorne

    [C] John Updike

    [D] Flannery O'Connor

    [E] Zora Neal Hurston

15. Neil Simon won the Pulitzer Prize for which play?

    [A] Biloxi Blues

    [B] The Sunshine Boys

    [C] Brighton Beach Memoirs

    [D] Lost in Yonkers

    [E] The Odd Couple

16. Which of the following novels features an African American protagonist?

    [A] The Invisible Man

    [B] Gone With the Wind

    [C] To Kill a Mockingbird

    [D] The Age of Innocence

    [E] A Good Man is Hard To Find

17. In Mark Twain's *Adventures of Huckleberry Finn*, what is the name of Huckleberry's primary traveling companion?

    [A] Boo

    [B] Jim

    [C] Tom

    [D] George

    [E] Pap

18. "Prolepsis" is another term for what literary device?

    [A] Flash-forward

    [B] Frame story

    [C] MacGuffin

    [D] Comic relief

    [E] Protagonist

AMERICAN LITERATURE

19. The title of *To Kill a Mockingbird* refers to:

    [A] a Biblical passage.

    [B] a poem by Robert Burns

    [C] a line spoken in the novel by Atticus Finch.

    [D] a Shakespearian sonnet.

    [E] a Southern proverb.

20. "Mark Twain" was the pen name of which author?

    [A] August Wilson

    [B] Samuel Clemens

    [C] Horace Greeley

    [D] Nathaniel Hawthorne

    [E] Thomas Paine

so much depends
upon

a red wheel
barrow

glazed with rain
water

beside the white
chickens.

21. Who authored the above poem?

    [A] Walt Whitman

    [B] William Carlos Williams

    [C] Robert Frost

    [D] Wallace Stevens

    [E] Emily Dickinson

22. The poem's curious format makes use of what poetic technique?

    [A] Free verse

    [B] Slant

    [C] Enjambment

    [D] Metaphor

    [E] Haiku

AMERICAN LITERATURE

23. **This poem is a prime example of what literary movement?**

    [A] Imagism

    [B] Realism

    [C] Avant-garde

    [D] Absurdism

    [E] Post-modernism

24. **Ezra Pound is also famous for which poetry collection?**

    [A] The Waste Land

    [B] Ripostes

    [C] Four Quartets

    [D] Absalom, Absalom

    [E] A Further Range

25. **What occurs at the end of John Steinbeck's *Of Mice and Men*?**

    [A] Lenny runs away from home, leaving George morose

    [B] George is acquitted of all charges after a lengthy legal battle

    [C] George shoots Lenny to spare him a painful lynching

    [D] Candy dies, leaving George a sizable inheritance

    [E] The farm becomes insolvent, leaving the ranch hands unemployed

26. **The short story collection *The Things They Carried* depicts what war?**

    [A] The Civil War

    [B] World War II

    [C] The Korean War

    [D] The Vietnam War

    [E] World War I

27. **Raymond Chandler is best known for his work in what literary genre?**

    [A] Science fiction

    [B] Historical fiction

    [C] Mystery

    [D] Horror

    [E] Magical realism

28. **American colonial writers were primarily:**

    [A] naturalists

    [B] romanticists

    [C] neoclassicists

    [D] realists

    [E] atheists

AMERICAN LITERATURE

29. Herman Melville's *Moby Dick* is an example of what literary movement?

    [A] Romanticism

    [B] Americanism

    [C] Magical Realism

    [D] Neoclassicism

    [E] Allegory

30. Mark Twain's *Adventures of Tom Sawyer* takes places during which period in American history?

    [A] Antebellum South

    [B] Manifest Destiny

    [C] The Civil War

    [D] Reconstruction

    [E] Jim Crow

31. Who is the protagonist of Ernest Hemingway's *For Whom the Bell Tolls?*

    [A] Tom Joad

    [B] Robert Jordan

    [C] Santiago

    [D] Nick Carraway

    [E] Jake Barnes

32. Which elements are least applicable to all types of poetry?

    [A] Setting and audience

    [B] Theme and tone

    [C] Pattern and diction

    [D] Diction and rhyme scheme

    [E] Plot and historicity

33. What was an early alternative title for *The Great Gatsby*?

    [A] Trimalchio in West Egg

    [B] The Spectacular Gatsby

    [C] The Star-Spangled Banner

    [D] Satyricon

    [E] Citizen Gatsby

34. Which short story was not written by William Faulkner?

    [A] Red Leaves

    [B] Dry September

    [C] Uncle Willy

    [D] To Build a Fire

    [E] Barn Burning

AMERICAN LITERATURE

35. **Which play by Eugene O'Neill did not win the Pulitzer Prize for Drama?**

    [A] The Iceman Cometh

    [B] Anna Christie

    [C] Long Day's Journey Into Night

    [D] Beyond the Horizon

    [E] Strange Interlude

36. **Who is the protagonist of Zora Neale Hurston's *Their Eyes Were Watching God*?**

    [A] Tituba

    [B] Janie Crawford

    [C] Calpurnia

    [D] Maude Atkinson

    [E] Phoebe Watson

37. **In *The Glass Menagerie*, which character possesses the titular collection?**

    [A] Amanda

    [B] Laura

    [C] Blanche

    [D] Steven

    [E] Stella

38. **E. E. Cummings was best known for writing poetry in what style?**

    [A] Romantic

    [B] Absurdist

    [C] Elegy

    [D] Pastoral

    [E] Avant-Garde

"I'll tell you God's truth." His right hand suddenly ordered divine retribution to stand by. "I am the son of some wealthy people in the middle-west--all dead now. I was brought up in America but educated at Oxford because all my ancestors have been educated there for many years. It is a family tradition."

39. **Which American literary character describes himself with the above quote?**

    [A] Atticus Finch

    [B] Rabbit Angstrom

    [C] Jay Gatsby

    [D] Ignatius Reilley

    [E] Philip Marlowe

AMERICAN LITERATURE

40. **What occurs at the end of Richard Wright's *Native Son*?**

    [A] Bigger escapes the city with the help of his brother, Buddy.

    [B] Bigger defends himself in court, and his fate is left ambiguous.

    [C] Jack betrays Bigger to the police.

    [D] Bigger is convicted of murder, eventually accepting his fate.

    [E] Bigger's gang is killed in a firefight, leaving him the only survivor.

41. **Which author wrote *A Raisin in the Sun*?**

    [A] Ida B. Wells

    [B] Lorraine Hansbury

    [C] Langston Hughes

    [D] Richard Wright

    [E] Toi Derracotte

42. **Which Native American author wrote *House Made of Dawn*?**

    [A] N. Scott Momaday

    [B] Sherman Alexie

    [C] Louise Erdrich

    [D] Clarence Alexander

    [E] Sandra Birdsell

43. **What autobiographical event does Kurt Vonnegut describe in his novel, *Slaughterhouse-Five*?**

    [A] His mother's suicide

    [B] The sinking of the USS Indianapolis

    [C] The bombing of Dresden

    [D] His time publishing short stories in Playboy Magazine

    [E] His addiction to morphine

*"By now, pull in your ladder road behind you
And put a sign up CLOSED to all but me.
Then make yourself at home. The only field
Now left's no bigger than a harness gall.
First there's the children's house of make-believe,
Some shattered dishes underneath a pine,
The plaything's in the playhouse of the children.
Weep for what little things could make them glad.
Then for the house that is no more a house,
But only a belilaced cellar hole,
Now slowly closing like a dent in dough.
This was no playhouse but a house in earnest.*

AMERICAN LITERATURE

44. The excerpt is written in what meter?

[A] Iambic pentameter

[B] Free

[C] Enjambed

[D] Quantitative

[E] Pyrrhic

45. Who wrote the above excerpt?

[A] Walt Whitman

[B] Henry David Thoreau

[C] Robert Frost

[D] Joyce Carol Oates

[E] Wallace Stevens

46. What does the author think about the "children's playhouse" mentioned in the excerpt?

[A] It's a real, physical location, now destroyed by the ravages of time.

[B] It was a flight of fancy, now gone because the children have matured.

[C] It was a lie, and it is important to understand it as such.

[D] It was imagined, but the joy the children felt there made it real.

[E] It was a poor substitution for a real house.

47. *"My father brought to conversations a cavernous capacity for caring that dismayed strangers."*

What poetic device does this quote display?

[A] Assonance

[B] Unreliable narrator

[C] Censure

[D] Alliteration

[E] Hyperbole

48. O. Henry's works are known for what two features?

[A] Witty narration and twist endings

[B] Nature imagery and social themes

[C] Neoclassical prose and extensive dialogue

[D] Poetic interludes and political allegory

[E] Tragic characters and abrupt conclusions

AMERICAN LITERATURE

49. Which poem contains the line *"I have measured out my life in coffee spoons"*?

[A] "Song of Myself" by Walt Whitman

[B] "The Love Song of J. Alfred Prufrock" by T. S. Eliot

[C] "Middle Passage" by Robert Hayden

[D] "To My Dear and Loving Husband" by Ann Bradstreet

[E] "Memories of West Street and Lepke" by Robert Lowell

50. Which of these writers is not associated with the Southern Gothic style?

[A] Harry Crews

[B] Cormac McCarthy

[C] Erskine Caldwell

[D] Harriet Beecher Stowe

[E] William Faulkner

51. Studs Terkel is primarily remembered as a chronicler of…

[A] Race relations and the Civil Rights movement

[B] Oral histories of the common man

[C] The rise of political parties in the United States

[D] Governmental corruption in Chicago

[E] Sports culture in the American Midwest.

52. What is a "red herring"?

[A] An attack on someone's character

[B] A piece of information that misleads the reader

[C] A fallacious argument

[D] An objective for a character to fulfill

[E] A primary antagonist

53. What is the setting of the novel, *Native Son*?

[A] The Bronx

[B] Atlanta, Georgia

[C] Chicago's South Side

[D] Pre-Civil War Mississippi

[E] The Cherokee Indian Reservation

AMERICAN LITERATURE

54. *In Medias Res* describes a story that:

   [A] ends suddenly

   [B] ends somber note

   [C] is written in the present tense

   [D] begins in the middle of a sequence of events

   [E] is very old

55. Theodore Dreiser is best associated with which American city?

   [A] St. Louis

   [B] Chicago

   [C] Boston

   [D] New York

   [E] Philadelphia

56. In *The Old Man and the Sea*, the protagonist struggles with what kind of fish?

   [A] Swordfish

   [B] Shark

   [C] Marlin

   [D] Musky

   [E] Sailfish

57. "The New Colossus" by Emma Lazarus is an example of what type of poetic form?

   [A] Iambic pentameter

   [B] Free verse

   [C] Allegory

   [D] Ballad

   [E] Sonnet

58. What is the name of the foreign-born harpooner Ishmael befriends in *Moby Dick*?

   [A] Pequod

   [B] Kokovoko

   [C] Queequeg

   [D] Starbuck

   [E] Santiago

59. *The Piano Lesson* is part of August Wilson's:

   [A] Pittsburgh Cycle

   [B] Millennium Trilogy

   [C] Roots Saga

   [D] Chicago Trilogy

   [E] Pulitzer Plays

AMERICAN LITERATURE

60. What was the name of the fictional county in which William Faulkner set many of his works?

    [A] Lafayette

    [B] Hannibal

    [C] Yoknapatawpha

    [D] Arkham

    [E] Flathead

61. Booker T. Washington's autobiography, *Up From Slavery*, contains a speech he'd written containing what primary message?

    [A] African American social equality will be accomplished by any means necessary.

    [B] The economic factors behind slavery have proven insurmountable.

    [C] Blacks must reconnect with their African roots.

    [D] White and black Americans must work together to develop commercial and industrial opportunities for both communities.

    [E] Until white Americans accept the reality of their privileged position, no progress can be made.

62. What American orator was noted for both their staunch abolitionism and support of women's rights?

    [A] Frederick Douglass

    [B] Ida B. Wells

    [C] Langston Hughes

    [D] Dred Scott

    [E] Margaret Mitchell

63. Charles W. Chestnutt's *The House Behind the Cedars* deals with what central theme?

    [A] Woman's suffrage and emancipation

    [B] Race relations in the post-Civil War South

    [C] The role of religion in American colonial society

    [D] Class immobility for the working poor

    [E] The grieving process after losing a loved one

AMERICAN LITERATURE

64. Which of these stories is considered an early piece of American feminist literature?

    [A] The Yellow Wallpaper

    [B] The Lottery

    [C] A Good Man is Hard to Find

    [D] Where Are You Going, Where Have You Been?

    [E] I Know Why the Caged Bird Sings

65. In Mark Twain's *Adventures of Huckleberry Finn*, the King and the Duke are:

    [A] slave owners

    [B] confidence men

    [C] aristocrats

    [D] boat workers

    [E] tradesmen

66. *A Raisin in the Sun* gets its title from what poem?

    [A] A Dream Deferred

    [B] I Know Why The Caged Bird Sings

    [C] Dreams

    [D] from Citizen, I

    [E] A Negro Love Song

"They were hungry, and they were fierce. And they had hoped to find a home, and they found only hatred. Okies--the owners hated them because the owners knew they were soft and the Okies strong, that they were fed and the Okies hungry; and perhaps the owners had heard from their grandfathers how easy it is to steal land from a soft man if you are fierce and hungry and armed. The owners hated them."

67. Which novel contains the above passage?

    [A] A Farewell to Arms

    [B] Absalom, Absalom

    [C] Oil!

    [D] The Grapes of Wrath

    [E] The Adventures of Augie March

68. Which novel exposed the horrid working conditions of Chicago meat packers?

    [A] Upton Sinclair's *The Jungle*

    [B] Mike Royko's *Boss*

    [C] Langston Hughes's *Not Without Laughter*

    [D] Carl Sandburg's *The People, Yes*

    [E] Theodore Dreiser's *An American Tragedy*

AMERICAN LITERATURE

69. **Which Upton Sinclair novel became highly controversial for its motel sex scene?**

    [A] The Jungle

    [B] The Brass Check

    [C] Sylvia

    [D] Oil!

    [E] Between Two Worlds

70. **Which Revolutionary era work was directly inspired by Thomas Paine's *Common Sense*?**

    [A] Benjamin Franklin's "The Way to Wealth"

    [B] John Adams's autobiography

    [C] The Declaration of Independence

    [D] Freneau's "On the Causes of Political Degeneracy"

    [E] Crevecoeur's *Letters from an American Farmer*

71. **Which of Edgar Allen Poe's short stories is considered to be the first popular piece of detective fiction?**

    [A] The Mystery of Marie Roget

    [B] Murders in the Rue Morgue

    [C] The Purloined Letter

    [D] The Fall of the House of Usher

    [E] The Tell-Tale Heart

72. **Mark Twain's *Adventures of Tom Sawyer* takes place in what fictional town?**

    [A] St. Petersburg

    [B] Hannibal

    [C] Arkham

    [D] Joliet

    [E] Springfield

73. **"Climax" describes what part of a story?**

    [A] The ending

    [B] The falling action

    [C] The point of highest tension

    [D] The resolution

    [E] The call to action

74. **What was the "unpardonable sin" committed by Ethan Brand in Nathaniel Hawthorn's short story?**

    [A] Loss of faith in a Christian God

    [B] Murder

    [C] The hubris of setting oneself above God

    [D] To value intellect over brotherhood

    [E] Any sin committed without repentance

AMERICAN LITERATURE

75. **Which of these authors achieved great success with an abolitionist novel?**

    [A] Harriet Beecher Stowe

    [B] Louisa May Alcott

    [C] Sarah Orne Jewett

    [D] Rebecca Harding Davis

    [E] Mary Wilkins Freeman

76. **Which of the following is not a characteristic of a fable?**

    [A] Animals that talk and feel like humans

    [B] Happy solutions to human dilemmas

    [C] Teaches a moral or standard for behavior

    [D] Illustrates specific people or groups without directly naming them

    [E] Passed down orally from generation to generation

77. **In Henry James's *Daisy Miller*, the title character dies as a result of:**

    [A] suicide, specifically by ingesting poison

    [B] tuberculosis, contracted while sailing

    [C] "Roman Fever", caught after spending a night in the Colosseum

    [D] complications during the birth of her son

    [E] a beating she receives from Winterbourne

78. **"I would prefer not to" is a common refrain from what literary character?**

    [A] Nick Carraway

    [B] Bartleby

    [C] Ethan Brand

    [D] Tom Sawyer

    [E] Bigger Thomas

79. **"So it goes" is a phrase repeated often in which novel?**

    [A] Slaughterhouse-Five

    [B] A Confederacy of Dunces

    [C] The Old Man and the Sea

    [D] East of Eden

    [E] The Road

AMERICAN LITERATURE

80. **Which literary movement is noted for its early exploration of the inner lives of women and female desires?**

    [A] Romantic

    [B] Weird

    [C] Gothic

    [D] Realist

    [E] Neoclassical

81. ***The Grapes of Wrath* is a powerful indictment of the Great Depression, focusing its most aggressive critique on:**

    [A] illegal immigrants who took jobs away from American farmers

    [B] the greed of the upper class, specifically bankers

    [C] Roosevelt's New Deal, which failed spectacularly

    [D] religious institutions that exploited a desperate working class

    [E] irresponsible Wall Street moneylenders

82. **Who wrote *How I Learned to Drive?***

    [A] Tony Kushner

    [B] Paula Vogel

    [C] August Wilson

    [D] Amy Freed

    [E] David Lyndsay-Abaire

83. **Which colonial American author did not write in an autobiographical style?**

    [A] Edward Taylor

    [B] Benjamin Franklin

    [C] Samson Occom

    [D] Mary Rowlandson

    [E] Elizabeth Ashbridge

84. ***The Great Gatsby* was written as a satire and critique of what era in American history?**

    [A] The Roaring 20s

    [B] The Red Scare

    [C] Manifest Destiny

    [D] The New Deal

    [E] The Great Depression

85. **Truman Capote was strongly identified with what social scene?**

    [A] Working class laborers

    [B] New York social elite

    [C] East coast academia

    [D] Far left political intelligentsia

    [E] Religious scholars

AMERICAN LITERATURE

86. H. P. Lovecraft became a seminal figure in which literary subgenre?

   [A] Gothic fiction

   [B] High fantasy

   [C] Hardboiled mystery

   [D] Weird fiction

   [E] Political satire

87. William S. Borroughs was considered a major voice for which artistic movement?

   [A] Postmodern

   [B] Horror

   [C] Surreal

   [D] Modern

   [E] Pop

88. Margaret Mitchell's *Gone with the Wind* ends with:

   [A] Scarlett selling the homestead to pay her debts

   [B] Rhett abandoning Scarlett

   [C] Scarlett's daughter dying of fever, leaving her in mourning

   [D] Rhett and Scarlett marry

   [E] the Civil War's cessation, leaving the family hopeful

89. Which term best describes the form of the following poetic excerpt?

   Because I could not stop for Death -
   He kindly stopped for me -
   The Carriage held but just Ourselves -
   And Immortality.

   We slowly drove - He knew no haste
   And I had put away
   My labor and my leisure too,
   For His Civility -

   We passed the School, where Children strove
   At Recess - in the Ring -
   We passed the Fields of Gazing Grain -
   We passed the Setting Sun –

   [A] Ballad

   [B] Lyrical

   [C] Gothic

   [D] Rhyming

   [E] Imagist

90. Who wrote the above poem?

   [A] Harriet Beecher Stowe

   [B] Edgar Allen Poe

   [C] Emily Dickinson

   [D] Sylvia Plath

   [E] Mabel Loomis Todd

AMERICAN LITERATURE

91. **The poem characterizes Death using what poetic technique?**

    [A] Allegory

    [B] Metaphor

    [C] Personification

    [D] Simile

    [E] Synecdoche

92. **Tim O'Brien is most famous for which short story collection?**

    [A] The Things They Carried

    [B] The Good War

    [C] The Guns of August

    [D] The Rising Sun

    [E] The Golden Apples

93. **Which is the best definition of *vers libre*?**

    [A] Poetry that consists of an unaccented syllable followed by an accented one

    [B] Short lyrical poetry with an instructive purpose

    [C] Poetry that does not have a uniform pattern of rhythm

    [D] Poetry that tells a story and has a plot

    [E] Overly romantic or sentimental prose

94. ***Deus ex Machina* occurs in a story that:**

    [A] is short

    [B] continues after the main characters have died

    [C] is religious in tone

    [D] is resolved by new forces not introduced earlier in the story

    [E] is overly complicated

95. **What becomes of the titular item in John Steinbeck's *The Pearl*?**

    [A] It is sold off, bringing much wealth to the family

    [B] It is stolen by trackers who pursue Kino over the mountains

    [C] It is lost when a large wave shakes Kino's boat

    [D] It is thrown back into the sea after the death of Kino's son

    [E] It is smashed to dust by Kino's wife, Juana

96. **"Satire" describes:**

    [A] broad comedy

    [B] intensely political literature

    [C] humor intended to critique

    [D] an ironic turn of events

    [E] esoteric writing

AMERICAN LITERATURE

97. Which of the following is the best definition of imagism?

   [A] A poetic style that makes use of florid prose and universal themes

   [B] A movement in poetry characterized by precise images, free verse, and suggestion over complete statement

   [C] A counter-movement in literature rejecting postmodern surrealism

   [D] A style of prose that focuses largely on the divinity of nature

   [E] A satirical kind of poetry that lampooned the inscrutable style of the intellectual elite

98. What is "sprung rhythm"?

   [A] Rhythm designed to mimic natural speech

   [B] Meter consisting of five-syllable poetic feet

   [C] Poetry that suggests a musical cadence

   [D] Avant-garde rhythm, in a strange meter

   [E] Exuberant rhythm designed to suggest joy

*"Sing we for love and idleness,
Naught else is worth the having.*

*Though I have been in many a land,
There is naught else in living.*

*And I would rather have my sweet,
Though rose-leaves die of grieving,*

*Than do high deeds in Hungary
To pass all men's believing."*

99. What is the main message of this poem, Ezra Pound's "An Immortality"?

   [A] Though love is nice, it cannot last.

   [B] You must travel the world to find what makes you happy.

   [C] Great deeds make a man immortal.

   [D] Love is all that matters in life.

   [E] In the end, all things are forgotten.

100. What is the rhyme scheme of this poem?

   [A] abcbdbeb

   [B] aabbccdd

   [C] ababcdcd

   [D] abcbabcb

   [E] ababcdcd

AMERICAN LITERATURE

ANSWER KEY

Question Number	Correct Answer	Your Answer
1	A	
2	B	
3	C	
4	E	
5	D	
6	C	
7	A	
8	B	
9	C	
10	D	
11	C	
12	C	
13	D	
14	D	
15	D	
16	A	
17	B	
18	A	
19	C	
20	B	
21	B	
22	C	
23	A	
24	B	
25	C	
26	D	
27	C	
28	C	
29	A	
30	A	
31	B	
32	A	
33	A	
34	D	
35	A	

Question Number	Correct Answer	Your Answer
36	B	
37	B	
38	E	
39	C	
40	D	
41	B	
42	A	
43	C	
44	A	
45	C	
46	D	
47	D	
48	A	
49	B	
50	D	
51	B	
52	B	
53	C	
54	D	
55	B	
56	C	
57	E	
58	C	
59	A	
60	C	
61	D	
62	A	
63	B	
64	A	
65	B	
66	A	
67	D	
68	A	
69	D	
70	C	

Question Number	Correct Answer	Your Answer
71	B	
72	A	
73	C	
74	D	
75	A	
76	B	
77	C	
78	B	
79	A	
80	C	
81	B	
82	B	
83	A	
84	A	
85	B	
86	D	
87	A	
88	B	
89	B	
90	C	
91	C	
92	A	
93	C	
94	D	
95	D	
96	C	
97	B	
98	A	
99	B	
100	A	

AMERICAN LITERATURE

RATIONALES

1. *Does this safari guarantee I come back alive?" The reply: "We guarantee nothing!"* **What literary device best describes this quote?**

    [A] Foreshadowing

    [B] Call-back

    [C] Science fiction

    [D] Cliffhanger

    [E] Epilogue

The correct answer is A.
The quote from Bradbury's "A Sound of Thunder" heightens the tension of the story, suggesting things will go wrong in the future. The quote is from a sci-fi story, but "science fiction" is not a literary device. The quote is placed at the opening of the story so it cannot be a cliffhanger, epilogue, or call-back.

2. *Moby Dick's* **Ishmael is an example of what?**

    [A] Antagonist

    [B] Raconteur

    [C] Deus ex Machina

    [D] Red herring

    [E] Prolepsis

The correct answer is B.
The prose of the book is from Ishmael's telling, making him the narrator or raconteur. He supports Ahab's quest, albeit reluctantly, so he can't be characterized as an antagonist. The terms from C, D, and E could not apply in this context.

AMERICAN LITERATURE

3. **What were two major characteristics of the first American literature?**

   [A] Vengefulness and arrogance

   [B] Oral delivery and reverence for the land

   [C] Maudlin and self-pitying egocentrism

   [D] Bellicosity and derision

   [E] Satire and humor

The correct answer is C.
This characteristic can be seen in Captain John Smith's work, as well as William Bradford, and Michael Wigglesworth's works.

4. **"Assonance" describes:**

   [A] rhyming poetry

   [B] repetition of a letter or sound at the beginning of close words

   [C] a piece of literature with a clear metaphorical meaning.

   [D] a clue used to deceive the reader

   [E] repetition of internal vowel sounds

The correct answer is E.
Assonance - in poetry, the repetition of the sound of a vowel or diphthong in no rhyming stressed syllables near enough to each other for the echo to be discernible.

AMERICAN LITERATURE

5. Which of the following best describes a parable?

[A] A short, entertaining account of some happening, usually using talking animals as characters

[B] A slow, sad song or poem expressing lamentation

[C] An extended narrative work expressing universal truths regarding domestic life

[D] A short, simple story of a familiar occurrence, from which a moral or religious lesson may be drawn

[E] An oral telling passed down through generations

The correct answer is D.
Parables are accessible even to illiterate listeners, and even if they contain fantastic elements, they are always framed around the familiar. Answer A would best describe a fable, B a dirge, C a variety of story forms, and while parables were often told orally, that is not the primary definition of a parable, so E is too vague.

"Whirl up, Sea-
Whirl your pointed pines,
Splash your great pines
On our rocks,
Hurl your green over us-
Cover us with your pools of fir."

6. What is the title of the above poem?

[A] "Gulls" by William Carlos Williams

[B] "Nature is what we see" by Emily Dickinson

[C] "Oread" by Hilda "H.D." Doolittle

[D] "A Clear Midnight" by Walt Whitman

[E] "April Rain Song" by Langston Hughes

The correct answer is C.
The poem is by Hilda Doolittle. The other answers contain similar imagery or subject matter, but they are incorrect.

AMERICAN LITERATURE

7. Which of these sentences best describes the poem?

[A] A metaphor, comparing the sea and a forest

[B] A parable, warning of the dangers inherent in nature

[C] A ballad, exploring the beauty of creation

[D] A dirge, a lamentation on something that was lost

[E] A satire, parodying florid prose styles

The correct answer is A.
The poem strikes a clear metaphorical connection between the natural sea and forest, though it intentionally does not indicate which the "correct" interpretation is. It contains little in common with a parable or dirge, nor does its joyousness characterize it as a ballad. It is also not satirical or comedic.

8. The second and third lines contain an example of what poetic device?

[A] A slant rhyme

[B] An epistrophe

[C] A stanza

[D] A muse

[E] An assonance

The correct answer is B.
An epistrophe is where multiple lines in a poem end with the same word. Since both lines end with "pines", it is an epistrophe.

AMERICAN LITERATURE

9. **What is an untrue statement about theme in literature?**

   [A] It is the central idea of a literary work

   [B] All aspects of a work (plot, characters, etc.) should contribute to the theme in some way

   [C] It is always stated directly in the text

   [D] It can be inferred through close analysis of the text

   [E] It is often open to interpretation

The correct answer is C.
Theme is rarely stated directly in a text (though some authors get away with doing so, usually in service of comedy). Theme is almost always inferred through analysis of the text, specifically the aspects mentioned in answer B, which means many readers can interpret theme in different ways.

10. **Jack Kerouac was credited with giving a voice to which cultural movement?**

    [A] Hipsters

    [B] Generation X

    [C] Pacifist and conscientious objectors

    [D] The Beat Generation

    [E] Hippy culture

The correct answer is D.
Kerouac was known as a counter-culture icon, and the groups mentioned in A, B, C and E drew much inspiration from him. But Kerouac's clearest connection is to the Beat movement, which he is sometimes credited with personally starting.

AMERICAN LITERATURE

11. *"The thousand injuries of Fortunato I had borne as best I could, but when he ventured on insult I vowed revenge."* **This quote begins what famous short story?**

    [A] Murders in the Rue Morgue

    [B] A Sound of Thunder

    [C] The Cask of Amontillado

    [D] An Occurrence at Owl Creek Bridge

    [E] The Story of an Hour

    The correct answer is C.
    The quote begins Poe's eponymous short story. The other answers do not contain the line.

12. **Arthur Miller's *The Crucible* parallels which historical event?**

    [A] The Cold War

    [B] The fall of the Berlin Wall

    [C] Sen. McCarthy's House un-American Activities Committee hearings

    [D] The Persian Gulf War

    [E] The Great Depression

    The correct answer is C.
    Miller wrote The Crucible as a direct response to the "red scare" and its tactics that he felt were akin to witch hunting. The events mentioned in A, B, D, and E all met their share of criticism, satire and parable, but Miller's pet cause was McCarythyism.

AMERICAN LITERATURE

13. In *The Scarlet Letter*, Hester Prynne must wear the titular letter after she is found guilty of…

   [A] Murder

   [B] Theft

   [C] Prostitution

   [D] Adultery

   [E] Witchcraft

The correct answer is D.
Prynne's extramarital affair forms the backbone of the story. She commits no murder or theft, and though she is sometimes compared to a prostitute in the story, that is not what brands her with the letter. She is not associated with witchcraft.

14. Who wrote "A Good Man is Hard to Find"?

   [A] Ernest Hemingway

   [B] Nathaniel Hawthorne

   [C] John Updike

   [D] Flannery O'Connor

   [E] Zora Neal Hurston

The correct answer is D.
The story was written by Flanner O'Connor in 1955.

AMERICAN LITERATURE

15. Neil Simon won the Pulitzer Prize for which play?

[A] Biloxi Blues

[B] The Sunshine Boys

[C] Brighton Beach Memoirs

[D] Lost in Yonkers

[E] The Odd Couple

The correct answer is D.
Simon won the Pulitzer for Lost in Yonkers in 1991. The others have won Tony awards and other awards, but no Pulitzer's.

16. Which of the following novels features an African American protagonist?

[A] The Invisible Man

[B] Gone With the Wind

[C] To Kill a Mockingbird

[D] The Age of Innocence

[E] A Good Man is Hard To Find

The correct answer is A.
The Invisible Man, which is sometimes confused with the sci-fi novel of the same name, features an African American man coping with his feelings of inadequacy in a white society. B and C's answers both feature prominent African American characters, but they are not the protagonists of the novels. D and E's answers make little mention of race.

AMERICAN LITERATURE

17. In Mark Twain's *Adventures of Huckleberry Finn,* what is the name of Huckleberry's primary traveling companion?

    [A] Boo

    [B] Jim

    [C] Tom

    [D] George

    [E] Pap

The correct answer is B.
Jim is the escaped slave who travels with Huck. The other names come from famous black characters in other literary works (except Boo, who is a Caucasian man in To Kill a Mockingbird).

18. "Prolepsis" is another term for what literary device?

    [A] Flash-forward

    [B] Frame story

    [C] MacGuffin

    [D] Comic relief

    [E] Protagonist

The correct answer is A.
Prolepsis is the Greek term for a flashforward that's sometimes used in academic circles. It does not describe a frame story, MacGuffin, etc.

AMERICAN LITERATURE

19. The title of *To Kill a Mockingbird* refers to:

[A] A Biblical passage.

[B] A poem by Robert Burns

[C] A line spoken in the novel by Atticus Finch.

[D] A Shakespearian sonnet.

[E] A Southern proverb.

The correct answer is C.
Atticus tells Scout it is a sin to kill a mockingbird in the novel, referencing the book's themes of innocence and persecution. It has no connection to the Bible or Shakespeare, and Of Mice and Men is the book with a title taken from a Burns poem. The saying has achieved some popularity, but only after the publication of the novel.

20. "Mark Twain" was the pen name of which author?

[A] August Wilson

[B] Samuel Clemens

[C] Horace Greeley

[D] Nathaniel Hawthorne

[E] Thomas Paine

The correct answer is B.
Clemens wrote under the name Mark Twain, which he began using during his time working riverboats. The other authors did not use pseudonyms.

AMERICAN LITERATURE

*so much depends
upon*

*a red wheel
barrow*

*glazed with rain
water*

*beside the white
chickens.*

21. Who authored the above poem?

[A] Walt Whitman

[B] William Carlos Williams

[C] Robert Frost

[D] Wallace Stevens

[E] Emily Dickinson

The correct answer is B.
The poem was written by William Carlos Williams in 1923.

22. The poem's curious format makes use of what poetic technique?

[A] Free verse

[B] Slant

[C] Enjambment

[D] Metaphor

[E] Haiku

The correct answer is C.
An enjambment is when a sentence is split between two lines without punctuation. "Red Wheelbarrow" is heavily enjambed. A, B, D, and E would not refer to structure so much as content. Williams himself denied any metaphor in the poem, and it does not meet the syllable count to make it a haiku.

AMERICAN LITERATURE

23. This poem is a prime example of what literary movement?

[A] Imagism

[B] Realism

[C] Avant-garde

[D] Absurdism

[E] Post-modernism

The correct answer is A.
Williams was considered a seminal Imagist. The poem is considered modernist, as it slightly predates the post-modern movement, and its non-traditional structure lends it some similarities with avant-garde and absurist styles, it is primarily recognized as an imagist poem.

24. Ezra Pound is also famous for which poetry collection?

[A] The Waste Land

[B] Ripostes

[C] Four Quartets

[D] Absalom, Absalom

[E] A Further Range

The correct answer is B.
Pound published Ripostes in 1912.

AMERICAN LITERATURE

25. What occurs at the end of John Steinbeck's *Of Mice and Men*?

[A] Lenny runs away from home, leaving George morose

[B] George is acquitted of all charges after a lengthy legal battle

[C] George shoots Lenny to spare him a painful lynching

[D] Candy dies, leaving George a sizable inheritance

[E] The farm becomes insolvent, leaving the ranch hands unemployed

The correct answer is C.
Lenny accidentally kills a woman with his clumsy strength, prompting a lynch mob of farmers to chase him down. George executes Lenny to spare him this. Lenny does run away, but George quickly finds him. There is no legal battle or inheritance involved in the novel's climax, and the farm remains functional at the story's end, though still in dire straights.

26. The short story collection *The Things They Carried* depicts what war?

[A] The Civil War

[B] World War II

[C] The Korean War

[D] The Vietnam War

[E] World War I

The correct answer is D.
The book makes references to other wars, but it takes place solely in Vietnam during the war.

AMERICAN LITERATURE

27. Raymond Chandler is best known for his work in what literary genre?

[A] Science fiction

[B] Historical fiction

[C] Mystery

[D] Horror

[E] Magical realism

The correct answer is C.
Chandler is known as a master of detective fiction. He did not delve into sci-fi, historical fiction, or magic realism. His stories sometimes contained violence, but were never classified as horror.

28. American colonial writers were primarily:

[A] naturalists

[B] romanticists

[C] neoclassicists

[D] realists

[E] atheists

The correct answer is C.
The early colonists had been schooled in England, and even though their writing became quite American in content, their emphasis on clarity and balance in their language remained British. This literature reflects the lives of the early colonists, such as William Bradford's excerpts from The Mayflower Compact, Anne Bradstreet's poetry, and William Byrd's journal, A History of the Dividing Line.

AMERICAN LITERATURE

29. Herman Melville's *Moby Dick* is an example of what literary movement?

    [A] Romanticism

    [B] Americanism

    [C] Magical Realism

    [D] Neoclassicism

    [E] Allegory

The correct answer is A.
Moby Dick is primarily a Romantic novel, it presents an earnest adventurousness and a very sanitized and appealing view of the whaling industry, and its central struggle between Ahab and whale is played as operatic and broad. The book has sometimes been considered an allegory, but "allegory" is not a literary movement. Nor is "Americanist", though the novel is American. The whale is often compared to mythological creatures but is never stated to be expressly magical, and while the book contains aspects linking it to Shakespeare or various Greek tragedies, it's best recognized as a Romantic work and not a Neoclassical one.

30. Mark Twain's *Adventures of Tom Sawyer* takes places during which period in American history?

    [A] Antebellum South

    [B] Manifest Destiny

    [C] The Civil War

    [D] Reconstruction

    [E] Jim Crow

The correct answer is A.
The novel is set in the Antebellum era, predating the Civil War, Reconstruction, and Jim Crow. It also comes long after the push west that was Manifest Destiny.

AMERICAN LITERATURE

31. Who is the protagonist of Ernest Hemingway's *For Whom the Bell Tolls?*

[A] Tom Joad

[B] Robert Jordan

[C] Santiago

[D] Nick Carraway

[E] Jake Barnes

The correct answer is B.
Jake Barnes and Santiago appear only in Hemingway's The Sun Also Rises and Old Man and the Sea, respectively. Nick Carraway and Tom Joad are not featured in Hemingway stories.

32. Which elements are least applicable to all types of poetry?

[A] Setting and audience

[B] Theme and tone

[C] Pattern and diction

[D] Diction and rhyme scheme

[E] Plot and historicity

The correct answer is A.
Setting and audience are important elements of narrative, but there are many poems in which the setting and audience are unimportant.

AMERICAN LITERATURE

33. What was an early alternative title for *The Great Gatsby*?

   [A] Trimalchio in West Egg

   [B] The Spectacular Gatsby

   [C] The Star-Spangled Banner

   [D] Satyricon

   [E] Citizen Gatsby

The correct answer is A.
F. Scott Fitzgerald was keen on drawing parallels between Gatsby and the freedman-turned-aristocrat Trimalchio character from Satyricon. He never considered the name Satyricon however, so D is invalid. B, C, and E were never suggested by Fitzgerald.

34. Which short story was not written by William Faulkner?

   [A] Red Leaves

   [B] Dry September

   [C] Uncle Willy

   [D] To Build a Fire

   [E] Barn Burning

The correct answer is D.
"To Build a Fire" is a Jack London story, the others are all Faulkner.

AMERICAN LITERATURE

35. Which play by Eugene O'Neill did not win the Pulitzer Prize for Drama?

[A] The Iceman Cometh

[B] Anna Christie

[C] Long Day's Journey Into Night

[D] Beyond the Horizon

[E] Strange Interlude

The correct answer is A.
Faulkner won four Pulitzers for Drama, the most of any playwright and an unprecedented achievement, but he did not win for Iceman. It was nominated for several theater awards, but no Pulitzer. Answers B, C, D, and E all contain Pulitzer plays.

36. Who is the protagonist of Zora Neale Hurston's *Their Eyes Were Watching God?*

[A] Tituba

[B] Janie Crawford

[C] Calpurnia

[D] Maude Atkinson

[E] Phoebe Watson

The correct answer is B.
Janie Crawford is the protagonist of the story.

AMERICAN LITERATURE

37. **In *The Glass Menagerie*, which character possesses the titular collection?**

[A] Amanda

[B] Laura

[C] Blanche

[D] Steven

[E] Stella

The correct answer is B.
Laura is the introverted daughter of the family who finds solace in her collection of glass figurines. The mother, Amanda, is contemptuous of Laura's obsession. The names from answers C, D, and E come from Tennessee Williams's A Streetcar Named Desire and are not featured in Glass Menagerie.

38. **E. E. Cummings was best known for writing poetry in what style?**

[A] Romantic

[B] Absurdist

[C] Elegy

[D] Pastoral

[E] Avant-Garde

The correct answer is E.
Cummings occasionally wrote love poems, but his work overall was never characterized as primarily romantic. Absurdism refers to a style that eschews functionality and direct interpretation, avant-garde is the far more appropriate description.

AMERICAN LITERATURE

"I'll tell you God's truth." His right hand suddenly ordered divine retribution to stand by. "I am the son of some wealthy people in the middle-west--all dead now. I was brought up in America but educated at Oxford because all my ancestors have been educated there for many years. It is a family tradition."

39. Which American literary character describes himself with the above quote?

[A] Atticus Finch

[B] Rabbit Angstrom

[C] Jay Gatsby

[D] Ignatius Reilley

[E] Philip Marlowe

The correct answer is C.
The line is spoken by Jay Gatsby, describing his own (invented) past.

40. What occurs at the end of Richard Wright's *Native Son*?

[A] Bigger escapes the city with the help of his brother, Buddy.

[B] Bigger defends himself in court, and his fate is left ambiguous.

[C] Jack betrays Bigger to the police.

[D] Bigger is convicted of murder, eventually accepting his fate.

[E] Bigger's gang is killed in a firefight, leaving him the only survivor.

The correct answer is D.
The novel deals directly with the social dysfunction that turns black men towards crime, but it does not spare Bigger, who is jailed for murder and eventually accepts that he will be executed.

AMERICAN LITERATURE

41. Which author wrote *A Raisin in the Sun*?

[A] Ida B. Wells

[B] Lorraine Hansbury

[C] Langston Hughes

[D] Richard Wright

[E] Toi Derracotte

The correct answer is B.
Lorraine Hansbury wrote the play in 1959.

42. Which Native American author wrote *House Made of Dawn*?

[A] N. Scott Momaday

[B] Sherman Alexie

[C] Louise Erdrich

[D] Clarence Alexander

[E] Sandra Birdsell

The correct answer is A.
Momaday published the novel in 1968.

AMERICAN LITERATURE

43. **What autobiographical event does Kurt Vonnegut describe in his novel, *Slaughterhouse-Five*?**

    [A] His mother's suicide

    [B] The sinking of the USS Indianapolis

    [C] The bombing of Dresden

    [D] His time publishing short stories in Playboy Magazine

    [E] His addiction to morphine

The correct answer is C.
Vonnegut survived the bombing of Dresden in much the same way as the novel's protagonist does in the book, by hiding in a cellar with several other POWs. His mother's suicide is described in the novel Breakfast of Champions and not Slaughterhouse, as is his time being published in porn magazines. He has no connection to the USS Indianapolis, nor was he ever addicted to morphine.

AMERICAN LITERATURE

"By now, pull in your ladder road behind you
And put a sign up CLOSED to all but me.
Then make yourself at home. The only field
Now left's no bigger than a harness gall.
First there's the children's house of make-believe,
Some shattered dishes underneath a pine,
The plaything's in the playhouse of the children.
Weep for what little things could make them glad.
Then for the house that is no more a house,
But only a belilaced cellar hole,
Now slowly closing like a dent in dough.
This was no playhouse but a house in earnest.

44. The excerpt is written in what meter?

   [A] Iambic pentameter

   [B] Free

   [C] Enjambed

   [D] Quantitative

   [E] Pyrrhic

The correct answer is A.
Frost's "Directive" is written with five iambs (stressed-unstressed syllables) per line, though it does shirk this formula in spots. It uses enjambment but only sparingly, and could not be characterized as free, quantitive, or pyrrhic prose.

45. Who wrote the above excerpt?

   [A] Walt Whitman

   [B] Henry David Thoreau

   [C] Robert Frost

   [D] Joyce Carol Oates

   [E] Wallace Stevens

The correct answer is C.
Robert Frost wrote the poem in 1946.

AMERICAN LITERATURE

46. What does the author think about the "children's playhouse" mentioned in the excerpt?

[A] It's a real, physical location, now destroyed by the ravages of time.

[B] It was a flight of fancy, now gone because the children have matured.

[C] It was a lie, and it is important to understand it as such.

[D] It was imagined, but the joy the children felt there made it real.

[E] It was a poor substitution for a real house.

The correct answer is D.
The poem's tone is bittersweet, especially the last line of the excerpt, which entreats you to weep for this lost children's refuge. Frost's work is often characterized by sentimentality. The more cynical answers in A, B, C, and E would rarely apply to any Frost poem.

47. *"My father brought to conversations a cavernous capacity for caring that dismayed strangers."* **What poetic device does this quote display?**

[A] Assonance

[B] Unreliable narrator

[C] Censure

[D] Alliteration

[E] Hyperbole

The correct answer is D.
John Updike uses several hard K sounds in the quote, perhaps for humorous intent. Since they are placed at the beginnings of words, they would be considered alliteration and not assonance, so A is invalid. We do not have enough evidence from the quote to suggest B or E is true.

AMERICAN LITERATURE

48. O. Henry's works are known for what two features?

[A] Witty narration and twist endings

[B] Nature imagery and social themes

[C] Neoclassical prose and extensive dialogue

[D] Poetic interludes and political allegory

[E] Tragic characters and abrupt conclusions

The correct answer is A.
Henry was beloved for his warmth and humor. His work contains some of the elements listed in B, C, D, and E, but they are not primary features of his work.

49. Which poem contains the line *"I have measured out my life in coffee spoons"*?

[A] "Song of Myself" by Walt Whitman

[B] "The Love Song of J. Alfred Prufrock" by T. S. Eliot

[C] "Middle Passage" by Robert Hayden

[D] "To My Dear and Loving Husband" by Ann Bradstreet

[E] "Memories of West Street and Lepke" by Robert Lowell

The correct answer is B.
The line is from Eliot's "Prufrock".

50. Which of these writers is not associated with the Southern Gothic style?

[A] Harry Crews

[B] Cormac McCarthy

[C] Erskine Caldwell

[D] Harriet Beecher Stowe

[E] William Faulkner

The correct answer is D.
All the names on this list save Stowe are strongly associated with southern gothic writing. Stowe is primarily known for her abolitionist literature.

AMERICAN LITERATURE

51. Studs Terkel is primarily remembered as a chronicler of…

[A] Race relations and the Civil Rights movement

[B] Oral histories of the common man

[C] The rise of political parties in the United States

[D] Governmental corruption in Chicago

[E] Sports culture in the American Midwest.

The correct answer is B.
Terkel occasionally wrote political works in a more journalistic vein, but his greatest works, such as The Good War, make extensive use of edited transcripts of interviews with average Americans.

52. What is a "red herring"?

[A] An attack on someone's character

[B] A piece of information that misleads the reader

[C] A fallacious argument

[D] An objective for a character to fulfill

[E] A primary antagonist

The correct answer is B.
Red herrings are often employed by mystery or suspense writers to prevent the reader from anticipating upcoming developments.

AMERICAN LITERATURE

53. What is the setting of the novel, *Native Son*?

[A] The Bronx

[B] Atlanta, Georgia

[C] Chicago's South Side

[D] Pre-Civil War Mississippi

[E] The Cherokee Indian Reservation

The correct answer is C.
The novel is set entirely in Chicago's South Side.

54. *In Medias Res* describes a story that:

[A] ends suddenly

[B] ends somber note

[C] is written in the present tense

[D] begins in the middle of a sequence of events

[E] is very old

The correct answer is D.
A story that begins In Media Res is one that "jumps straight to the action", as if were.

55. Theodore Dreiser is best associated with which American city?

[A] St. Louis

[B] Chicago

[C] Boston

[D] New York

[E] Philadelphia

The correct answer is B.
Dreiser worked for the Chicago Globe for many years, and his novels Sister Carrie and The Desire Trilogy feature Chicago as a primary setting. He did write for the St. Louis Globe but he never lived in or depicted the city.

AMERICAN LITERATURE

56. In *The Old Man and the Sea*, **the protagonist struggles with what kind of fish?**

[A] Swordfish

[B] Shark

[C] Marlin

[D] Musky

[E] Sailfish

The correct answer is C.
Santiago is stated to wrestle for several days with a massive marlin, larger than most sharks.

57. "The New Colossus" by Emma Lazarus is an example of what type of poetic form?

[A] Iambic pentameter

[B] Free verse

[C] Allegory

[D] Ballad

[E] Sonnet

The correct answer is E.
Lazarus's poem is a sonnet in two stanzas. The poem makes use of iambic pentameter, but that does not fully characterize its overall style. It does not use free verse or allegory (it metaphorically compares the State of Liberty to the Colossus of Rhodes, but this is not allegorical), and though it is a hopeful piece, it lacks the romantic themes and lyrical style that would characterize it as a ballad.

AMERICAN LITERATURE

58. What is the name of the foreign-born harpooner Ishmael befriends in *Moby Dick*?

   [A] Pequod

   [B] Kokovoko

   [C] Queequeg

   [D] Starbuck

   [E] Santiago

The correct answer is C.
Queequeg is a Polynesian harpooner whom Ishmael befriends in the novel. Answer A refers to the name of the ship they sail on, and D refers to another character in the book, who is neither foreign nor a great friend of Ishmael's. E refers to the protagonist of Hemingway's Old Man and the Sea and B refers to Queequeg's fictional home island.

59. *The Piano Lesson* is part of August Wilson's:

   [A] Pittsburgh Cycle

   [B] Millennium Trilogy

   [C] Roots Saga

   [D] Chicago Trilogy

   [E] Pulitzer Plays

The correct answer is A.
Wilson has set ten plays in his hometown of Pittsburgh, with Piano Lesson being among the most famous.

AMERICAN LITERATURE

60. What was the name of the fictional county in which William Faulkner set many of his works?

[A] Lafayette

[B] Hannibal

[C] Yoknapatawpha

[D] Arkham

[E] Flathead

The correct answer is C.
A refers to the real county in Mississippi which Faulkner based his works on. B is the fictional setting of Mark Twain's Tom Sawyer, and D was a country invented by Lovecraft.

61. Booker T. Washington's autobiography, *Up From Slavery*, contains a speech he'd written containing what primary message?

[A] African American social equality will be accomplished by any means necessary.

[B] The economic factors behind slavery have proven insurmountable.

[C] Blacks must reconnect with their African roots.

[D] White and black Americans must work together to develop commercial and industrial opportunities for both communities.

[E] Until white Americans accept the reality of their privileged position, no progress can be made.

The correct answer is D.
Washington was controversial within the black community for his advocacy of entrepreneurship over voting rights for blacks, and his belief that Jim Crow laws were not a priority for the black community. Answer A could more readily be ascribed to Civil Rights leader Malcolm X, and B's defeatist stance would never be uttered by Washington. He made few prominent mentions of African roots (such a concept would be more appealing to black Americans in the 1960s, long after Washington's time), and his diplomatic attitude towards white Americans meant he was unlikely to criticize their privileged position.

AMERICAN LITERATURE

62. What American orator was noted for both their staunch abolitionism and support of women's rights?

[A] Frederick Douglass

[B] Ida B. Wells

[C] Langston Hughes

[D] Dred Scott

[E] Margaret Mitchell

The correct answer is A.
Douglass believed in freedom for all, including women and racial minorities. B and E refer to women with strong feminist and racial themes in their works, but neither can be considered abolitionist since both lived long after the slavery was banned. C never made any strong statements about women's liberation, nor did D.

63. Charles W. Chestnutt's *The House Behind the Cedars* deals with what central theme?

[A] Woman's suffrage and emancipation

[B] Race relations in the post-Civil War South

[C] The role of religion in American colonial society

[D] Class immobility for the working poor

[E] The grieving process after losing a loved one

The correct answer is B.
Chestnut was a noted black author and activist, themes of race appear often in his work. Religious and class-related issues do appear in the book, but race is by far the novel's primary concern.

AMERICAN LITERATURE

64. Which of these stories is considered an early piece of American feminist literature?

[A] The Yellow Wallpaper

[B] The Lottery

[C] A Good Man is Hard to Find

[D] Where Are You Going, Where Have You Been?

[E] I Know Why the Caged Bird Sings

The correct answer is A.
All of these stories are written by women, most of whom are also accepted as feminists. But "Wallpaper" is the only early one (1892), the others having been written decades later.

65. In Mark Twain's *Adventures of Huckleberry Finn*, the King and the Duke are:

[A] slave owners

[B] confidence men

[C] aristocrats

[D] boat workers

[E] tradesmen

The correct answer is B.
Both men never reveal their names, insisting that they are lost European royalty. They run several scams with Huck and Jim's aid. They claim to be aristocrats but this is a ruse.

66. *A Raisin in the Sun* gets its title from what poem?

[A] A Dream Deferred

[B] I Know Why The Caged Bird Sings

[C] Dreams

[D] from Citizen, I

[E] A Negro Love Song

The correct answer is A.
The title comes from "A Dream Deferred", written by Langston Hughes in 1951.

AMERICAN LITERATURE

"They were hungry, and they were fierce. And they had hoped to find a home, and they found only hatred. Okies--the owners hated them because the owners knew they were soft and the Okies strong, that they were fed and the Okies hungry; and perhaps the owners had heard from their grandfathers how easy it is to steal land from a soft man if you are fierce and hungry and armed. The owners hated them."

67. Which novel contains the above passage?

   [A] A Farewell to Arms

   [B] Absalom, Absalom

   [C] Oil!

   [D] The Grapes of Wrath

   [E] The Adventures of Augie March

The correct answer is D.
Steinbeck's Grapes of Wrath helped familiarize average Americans with the term "Okies", describing the Oklahoma migrant farmers who make up much of the novel's cast.

68. Which novel exposed the horrid working conditions of Chicago meat packers?

   [A] Upton Sinclair's The Jungle

   [B] Mike Royko's Boss

   [C] Langston Hughes's Not Without Laughter

   [D] Carl Sandburg's The People, Yes

   [E] Theodore Dreiser's An American Tragedy

The correct answer is A.
Upton Sinclair was a notorious muckraker, and The Jungle was among his biggest early successes, describing the brutal exploitation of meat packers in unsafe conditions. Dreiser, Royko and Sandburg also wrote about unfair conditions in Chicago, but never about meat packing.

AMERICAN LITERATURE

69. Which Upton Sinclair novel became highly controversial for its motel sex scene?

[A] The Jungle

[B] The Brass Check

[C] Sylvia

[D] Oil!

[E] Between Two Worlds

The correct answer is D.
Oil! was banned in some areas for its depiction of a sexual encounter. Sinclair fought to bring the case to trial, and greatly increased the book's infamy, making it a bestseller.

70. Which Revolutionary era work was directly inspired by Thomas Paine's *Common Sense*?

[A] Benjamin Franklin's "The Way to Wealth"

[B] John Adams's autobiography

[C] The Declaration of Independence

[D] Freneau's "On the Causes of Political Degeneracy"

[E] Crevecoeur's Letters from an American Farmer

The correct answer is C.
The Declaration was directly influenced by Thomas Paine and the political culture he created. The pamphlet's direct, accessible style appealed even to illiterate listeners, and provided the framework for the Declaration's similarly direct messaging.

AMERICAN LITERATURE

71. Which of Edgar Allen Poe's short stories is considered to be the first popular piece of detective fiction?

[A] The Mystery of Marie Roget

[B] Murders in the Rue Morgue

[C] The Purloined Letter

[D] The Fall of the House of Usher

[E] The Tell-Tale Heart

The correct answer is B.
"Rue Morgue" introduced detective fiction into popular culture. Poe used his Dupin protagonist in other stories, such as in "Marie Roget" and "Purloined Letter", but they both came after "Morgue". D and E both refer to Poe stories with aspects of mystery, but they could not be considered detective works in earnest.

72. Mark Twain's *Adventures of Tom Sawyer* takes place in what fictional town?

[A] St. Petersburg

[B] Hannibal

[C] Arkham

[D] Joliet

[E] Springfield

The correct answer is A.
St. Petersburg was Mark Twain's stand in for the real town of Hannibal, Missouri, where Twain lived.

AMERICAN LITERATURE

73. "Climax" describes what part of a story?

   [A] The ending

   [B] The falling action

   [C] The point of highest tension

   [D] The resolution

   [E] The call to action

The correct answer is C.
Climaxes precede the falling action and come long after the call to action. A climax usually involves some form of resolution, but the terms are not synonymous – some works feature a climactic scene that is "resolved" shortly after. Climaxes also come towards the end of a story, but they are not necessarily endings themselves.

74. What was the "unpardonable sin" committed by Ethan Brand in Nathaniel Hawthorn's short story?

   [A] Loss of faith in a Christian God

   [B] Murder

   [C] The hubris of setting oneself above God

   [D] To value intellect over brotherhood

   [E] Any sin committed without repentance

The correct answer is D.
The title character in "Ethan Brand" claims he has committed "the sin of an intellect that triumphed over the sense of brotherhood with man and reverence for God, and sacrificed everything to its own mighty claims!" The character claims his intellect has surpassed his love of God, but since he welcomes divine retribution, he has not lost faith as yet.

AMERICAN LITERATURE

75. Which of these authors achieved great success with an abolitionist novel?

[A] Harriet Beecher Stowe

[B] Louisa May Alcott

[C] Sarah Orne Jewett

[D] Rebecca Harding Davis

[E] Mary Wilkins Freeman

The correct answer is A.
Stowe's Uncle Tom's Cabin is a quintessential piece of abolitionist literature, and is by far Stowe's most recognized work.

76. Which of the following is not a characteristic of a fable?

[A] Animals that talk and feel like humans

[B] Happy solutions to human dilemmas

[C] Teaches a moral or standard for behavior

[D] Illustrates specific people or groups without directly naming them

[E] Passed down orally from generation to generation

The correct answer is B.
Fables do not present a happy solution to a human dilemma. A fable is a short tale with animals, humans, gods, or even inanimate objects as characters. Fables often conclude with a moral, delivered in the form of an epigram (a short, witty, and ingenious statement in verse).

AMERICAN LITERATURE

77. In Henry James's *Daisy Miller*, the title character dies as a result of:

[A] suicide, specifically by ingesting poison

[B] tuberculosis, contracted while sailing

[C] "Roman Fever", caught after spending a night in the Colosseum

[D] complications during the birth of her son

[E] a beating she receives from Winterbourne

The correct answer is C.
Daisy's dalliance with a dashing Italian causes her to spend the night in the Colosseum, where she is found by an irate Winterbourne. Despite his protests, she spends the night in the arena and falls ill. She is never beaten by Winterbourne, nor does she catch tuberculosis or give birth. Her death can be considered the result of youthful negligence on her part, but not suicide.

78. "I would prefer not to" is a common refrain from what literary character?

[A] Nick Carraway

[B] Bartleby

[C] Ethan Brand

[D] Tom Sawyer

[E] Bigger Thomas

The correct answer is B.
Bartleby utters the line many times in Melville's "Bartleby the Scrivener", reflecting the character's unwillingness to interact on even the most basic level.

AMERICAN LITERATURE

79. "So it goes" is a phrase repeated often in which novel?

[A] Slaughterhouse-Five

[B] A Confederacy of Dunces

[C] The Old Man and the Sea

[D] East of Eden

[E] The Road

The correct answer is A.
Kurt Vonnegut's Slaughterhouse-Five features a race of alien creatures who use the phrase "so it goes" when describing the predestined nature of reality. B's title has a similar sardonic style to Vonnegut's work, but does not contain the repeated line. C, D and E could be described as similarly fatalistic, but they likewise do not contain the line.

80. Which literary movement is noted for its early exploration of the inner lives of women and female desires?

[A] Romantic

[B] Weird

[C] Gothic

[D] Realist

[E] Neoclassical

The correct answer is C.
Gothic literature included women in an influential way, featuring them as both villains and protagonists and exploring many feminine desires. Authors like Mary Shelley and Charlotte Bronte expounded on women's stories in the genre known as Female Gothic. Romantic and neoclassical stories featured women, but usually as side-characters. Realist and weird fiction are not noted for a preponderance of women.

AMERICAN LITERATURE

81. ***The Grapes of Wrath*** **is a powerful indictment of the Great Depression, focusing its most aggressive critique on:**

[A] illegal immigrants who took jobs away from American farmers

[B] the greed of the upper class, specifically bankers

[C] Roosevelt's New Deal, which failed spectacularly

[D] religious institutions that exploited a desperate working class

[E] irresponsible Wall Street moneylenders

The correct answer is B.
Steinbeck said "I want to put a tag of shame on the greedy bastards who are responsible for [the Depression]." The tragic odyssey of the Joad family is set into motion by a defaulted bank loan, and bankers play a recurring villainous role in the story.

82. Who wrote *How I Learned to Drive*?

[A] Tony Kushner

[B] Paula Vogel

[C] August Wilson

[D] Amy Freed

[E] David Lyndsay-Abaire

The correct answer is B.
Paula Vogel wrote the play in

AMERICAN LITERATURE

83. Which colonial American author did not write in an autobiographical style?

   [A] Edward Taylor

   [B] Benjamin Franklin

   [C] Samson Occom

   [D] Mary Rowlandson

   [E] Elizabeth Ashbridge

The correct answer is A.
Taylor's work was primarily metaphysical poetry. B, C, D, and E were all noted for their extremely autobiographical works.

84. *The Great Gatsby* **was written as a satire and critique of what era in American history?**

   [A] The Roaring 20s

   [B] The Red Scare

   [C] Manifest Destiny

   [D] The New Deal

   [E] The Great Depression

The correct answer is A.
Gatsby is the quintessential depiction and indictment of the decadent Roaring 20s, predating the Red Scare, Great Depression, and New Deal, and coming long after Manifest Destiny.

AMERICAN LITERATURE

85. Truman Capote was strongly identified with what social scene?

[A] Working class laborers

[B] New York social elite

[C] East coast academia

[D] Far left political intelligentsia

[E] Religious scholars

The correct answer is B.
Capote was a noted socialite, making New York history with his Black and White Ball. Though he came from a working class background, he became infamous as a New York elite. He wanted little to do with academia, politics, or religion.

86. H. P. Lovecraft became a seminal figure in which literary subgenre?

[A] Gothic fiction

[B] High fantasy

[C] Hardboiled mystery

[D] Weird fiction

[E] Political satire

The correct answer is D.
Lovecraft was regular contributor to the influential Weird Tales literary magazine, which published many of his best known works. His works contain Gothic and fantastic influences but are not wholly within either genre. He never wrote satire or detective fiction.

AMERICAN LITERATURE

87. William S. Borroughs was considered a major voice for which artistic movement?

   [A] Postmodern

   [B] Horror

   [C] Surreal

   [D] Modern

   [E] Pop

The correct answer is A.
Burroughs is viewed as one of the great American postmodernists. His stories contain surreal and horrific elements, but always in service of overarching postmodernism. Pop art is related to postmodern, but Burroughs was never claimed as a pop artist.

88. Margaret Mitchell's *Gone with the Wind* ends with:

   [A] Scarlett selling the homestead to pay her debts

   [B] Rhett abandoning Scarlett

   [C] Scarlett's daughter dying of fever, leaving her in mourning

   [D] Rhett and Scarlett marry

   [E] the Civil War's cessation, leaving the family hopeful

The correct answer is B.
After several tragedies rock the family, Rhett decides he must leave Atlanta to find the dignified South he knew as a young man. He abandons Scarlett.

AMERICAN LITERATURE

89. Which term best describes the form of the following poetic excerpt?

Because I could not stop for Death -
He kindly stopped for me -
The Carriage held but just Ourselves -
And Immortality.

We slowly drove - He knew no haste
And I had put away
My labor and my leisure too,
For His Civility -

We passed the School, where Children strove
At Recess - in the Ring -
We passed the Fields of Gazing Grain -
We passed the Setting Sun –

[A] Ballad

[B] Lyrical

[C] Gothic

[D] Rhyming

[E] Imagist

The correct answer is B.
Dickinson's poem is considered a prime example of lyrical poetry, such that it has often been set to music. It lacks the sentimentality of a ballad and shares some macabre aspects of a Gothic poem, but lacks the grandeur of the style. It contains rhymes but is hardly a "rhyming poem", and it lacks the precise description of an imagist work.

AMERICAN LITERATURE

90. Who wrote the above poem?

   [A] Harriet Beecher Stowe

   [B] Edgar Allen Poe

   [C] Emily Dickinson

   [D] Sylvia Plath

   [E] Mabel Loomis Todd

The correct answer is C.
Dickinson's piece was published in 1890.

91. The poem characterizes Death using what poetic technique?

   [A] Allegory

   [B] Metaphor

   [C] Personification

   [D] Simile

   [E] Synecdoche

The correct answer is C.
The abstract concept of death is characterized as a human figure. This could be argued to create an allegory or metaphor, but the actual device that creates these interpretations is personification.

AMERICAN LITERATURE

92. Tim O'Brien is most famous for which short story collection?

[A] The Things They Carried

[B] The Good War

[C] The Guns of August

[D] The Rising Sun

[E] The Golden Apples

The correct answer is A.
O'Brien published the collection in 1990. It's considered one of the greatest pieces of Vietnam War literature.

93. Which is the best definition of *vers libre*?

[A] Poetry that consists of an unaccented syllable followed by an accented one

[B] Short lyrical poetry with an instructive purpose

[C] Poetry that does not have a uniform pattern of rhythm

[D] Poetry that tells a story and has a plot

[E] Overly romantic or sentimental prose

The correct answer is C.
Vers libre eschews meter, rhythm, and other restraints to better mimic actual speech. Content such as plot or romance can be present but they are not necessary to be vers libre. A describes iambic pentameter, which is anathema to vers libre.

AMERICAN LITERATURE

94. *Deus ex Machina* occurs in a story that:

[A] is short

[B] continues after the main characters have died

[C] is religious in tone

[D] is resolved by new forces not introduced earlier in the story

[E] is overly complicated

The correct answer is D.
Deus ex machina occurs when a story is quickly resolved by the introduction of new elements, such as gods solving the plot via magic. B would better describe a saga, and while the term has origins in religious Greek theater, stories that feature deus ex machina are not necessarily religious in tone.

95. What becomes of the titular item in John Steinbeck's *The Pearl?*

[A] It is sold off, bringing much wealth to the family

[B] It is stolen by trackers who pursue Kino over the mountains

[C] It is lost when a large wave shakes Kino's boat

[D] It is thrown back into the sea after the death of Kino's son

[E] It is smashed to dust by Kino's wife, Juana

The correct answer is D.
The Pearl's chief theme is greed. Kino's desire to keep the pearl causes trackers to chase the family, eventually causing the death of his son. He throws the pearl into the sea shortly after. Juana wishes to destroy the pearl, but never does so.

AMERICAN LITERATURE

96. "Satire" describes:

   [A] broad comedy

   [B] intensely political literature

   [C] humor intended to critique

   [D] an ironic turn of events

   [E] esoteric writing

The correct answer is C.
Satire is often overtly comedic, ironic, and political, but much great satire has been understated and apolitical.

97. Which of the following is the best definition of imagism?

   [A] A poetic style that makes use of florid prose and universal themes

   [B] A movement in poetry characterized by precise images, free verse, and suggestion over complete statement

   [C] A counter-movement in literature rejecting postmodern surrealism

   [D] A style of prose that focuses largely on the divinity of nature

   [E] A satirical kind of poetry that lampooned the inscrutable style of the intellectual elite

The correct answer is B.
Precision was the goal of many imagists, who sought to evoke grander themes with tight, precise descriptions. A almost describes the opposite of imagist poetry, and while some imagists expressed dissatisfaction with postmodernism, others were great fans.

AMERICAN LITERATURE

98. What is "sprung rhythm"?

[A] Rhythm designed to mimic natural speech

[B] Meter consisting of five-syllable poetic feet

[C] Poetry that suggests a musical cadence

[D] Avant-garde rhythm, in a strange meter

[E] Exuberant rhythm designed to suggest joy

The correct answer is A.
Sprung rhythm makes use of stressed syllables and varied syllable counts to create aesthetically pleasing, "realistic" poetry.

"Sing we for love and idleness,
Naught else is worth the having.

Though I have been in many a land,
There is naught else in living.

And I would rather have my sweet,
Though rose-leaves die of grieving,

Than do high deeds in Hungary
To pass all men's believing."

99. What is the main message of this poem, Ezra Pound's "An Immortality"?

[A] Though love is nice, it cannot last.

[B] You must travel the world to find what makes you happy.

[C] Great deeds make a man immortal.

[D] Love is all that matters in life.

[E] In the end, all things are forgotten.

The correct answer is B.
Pound was a noted romantic, and very well-traveled. These aspects of his life are reflected in the poem.

AMERICAN LITERATURE

100. What is the rhyme scheme of this poem?

[A] abcbdbeb

[B] aabbccdd

[C] ababcdcd

[D] abcbabcb

[E] ababcdcd

The correct answer is A.
The poem features an unusual rhyme patter, with only the B rhyme being repeated

COLLEGE COMPOSITION

Description of the Examination

The CLEP College Composition examinations assess writing skills taught in most first-year college composition courses. Those skills include analysis, argumentation, synthesis, usage, ability to recognize logical development and research. The exams cannot cover every skill (such as keeping a journal or peer editing) required in many first-year college writing courses. Candidates will, however, be expected to apply the principles and conventions used in longer writing projects to two timed writing assignments and to apply the rules of standard written English.

College Composition contains approximately 50 multiple-choice items to be answered in approximately 50 minutes and two essays to be written in 70 minutes (with 30 minutes to write the first essay and 40 minutes to read the two sources and write the second essay), for a total of approximately 120 minutes testing time. Essays must be typed on the computer.

The actual examination contains multiple-choice items and two mandatory, centrally scored essays. The essays are scored twice a month by college English faculty from throughout the country via an online scoring system. Each of the two essays is scored independently by two different readers, and the scores are then combined. This combined score is weighted approximately equally with the score from the multiple-choice section. These scores are then combined to yield the candidate's score. The resulting combined score is reported as a single score between 20 and 80. Separate scores are not reported for the multiple-choice and essay sections.

Knowledge and Skills Required

The subject matter of the College Composition examination is drawn from the following topics. The percentages next to the main topics indicate the approximate percentage of exam questions on that topic for the 50 multiple-choice items.

10% **Conventions of Standard English**
- measures the awareness of logical, structural and grammatical relationships within sentences. Questions relate to syntax, punctuation, concord/agreement, modifiers, active versus passive voice and additional areas

40% **Revision Skills**
- measures revision skills in the context of early essays, such as organization, level of detail, awareness of audience or tone, sentence variety and structure, main ideas, transitions, point of views

25% **Ability to Use Source Material**
- measures familiarity with basic reference and research skills via the use of reference materials, evaluation of sources, integration of resources and documentation

25% **Rhetorical Analysis**
- measures ability to analyze writing primarily using passage based questions reviewing appeals, tone, structure, rhetorical effects

COLLEGE COMPOSITION

There are 50 questions that you must answer in less than 50 minutes. Then, there are essay questions that you must answer in a timed fashion: the first essay has 30 minutes and the second essay has 40 minutes to read two passages and complete and essay.

Remember, your goals for this test are those questions you answer accurately; it is not based on how many are incorrect. Take your time, and good luck.

DIRECTIONS: Read each item carefully, paying attention to the underlined portions. If there is an error, it will be underlined. Assume that elements of the sentence not underlined are correct. If there is an error, select the one underlined part and enter that letter on the answer sheet. If there is no error, choose E

1. On a long day in October, the rain <u>fell</u> so hard that it <u>causes</u> flooding all <u>along</u> the highway, <u>bringing</u> traffic to a stop. <u>No error</u>.

   [A] fell

   [B] causes

   [C] along

   [D] bringing

   [E] No error

2. <u>Their</u> attempts are almost always comical, not <u>being able</u> to move supplies without <u>loosing</u> at least one package on the <u>route</u>. <u>No error.</u>

   [A] Their

   [B] being able

   [C] loosing

   [D] route

   [E] No error

3. At least two of the seven <u>defendents</u> <u>want</u> a delay, <u>saying</u> they need more time <u>to prepare</u> for trial. <u>No error</u>.

   [A] defendents

   [B] want

   [C] saying

   [D] to prepare

   [E] No eror

4. The surfer <u>was bit</u> by a shark, but <u>got</u> his revenge when he <u>caught</u> him and <u>ate</u> it for dinner. <u>No error</u>

   [A] was bit

   [B] got

   [C] caught

   [D] ate

   [E] No error

5. A portrait of a <u>women</u> <u>had been</u> painted onto an iceberg, which was precariously <u>perched</u> on the edge of a melting <u>piece</u> of glacier. <u>No error</u>

   [A] women

   [B] had been

   [C] perched

   [D] piece

   [E] No error

REVISION SKILLS
Read the following paragraph and answer the questions that follow.

    There was a steaming mist in all the hollows, and it roamed in its forlornness up the hill, like an evil spirit, seeking rest and finding none. A clammy and intensely cold mist, it made its way through the air in ripples that visibly followed and overspread one another, as the waves of an unwholesome sea might do. It was dense enough to shut out everything from the light of the coach-lamps but these its own workings, and a few yards of road; and the reek of the laboring horses steamed into it, as if they had made it at all.

6. The description of this scene gives the impression that it is:

   [A] an oppressive journey.

   [B] an enlightening route.

   [C] a contemplative traveling discussion.

   [D] an entertaining troupe making way to the next show.

   [E] None of these things is true.

7. What is the main idea of this passage?

   [A] Weather sets the stage in any narrative.

   [B] The coach horses were not up to the task of the road.

   [C] It was a dark and cold night, relatively unsuitable for travel.

   [D] One of the coach-lamps was unlit, making it difficult to see.

   [E] An English countryside scene is perfect for a scary setting.

8. The author's purpose is to:

   [A] Inform

   [B] Entertain

   [C] Persuade

   [D] Narrate

   [E] Analyze

COLLEGE COMPOSITION

Read the following passage and answer the questions that follow.

    Everyone called him Pop Eye. Even in those days when I was a skinny thirteen-year-old I thought he probably knew about his nickname but didn't care. His eyes were too interested in what lay up ahead to notice us barefoot kids.
    He looked like someone who had seen or known great suffering and hadn't been able to forget it. His large eyes in his large head stuck out further than anyone else's - like they wanted to lave the surface of his face. They made you think of someone who can't get out the house quickly enough.
    Pop Eye wore the same white linen suit every day. His trousers snagged onto hi sony knees in the sloppy heat. Some days he wore a clown's nose. His nose was already big. he didn't need that red light bulb. But for reasons we couldn't think of he wore the red nose on certain days that may have meant something to him. We never saw him smile. And on those days he wore the clowns nose you found yourself looking away because you never saw such sadness.

9. **What is the main idea of the passage?**

   [A] The main character was a generally sad man, disinterested in the scene around him.

   [B] The main character cannot remember the thirteen-year-old kid.

   [C] The physical appearance of the main character was awkward.

   [D] The main character was so poor that he only had one suit.

   [E] None of these represent the main idea of the passage.

10. **From the passage, one can infer that:**

    [A] Pop Eye is surrounded by family.

    [B] Pop Eye works as a clown.

    [C] The narrator is related to Pop Eye.

    [D] Pop Eye lives a lonely life.

    [E] The narrator has done well for himself.

COLLEGE COMPOSITION

11. What is the author's purpose in writing this passage?

    [A] To entertain

    [B] To narrate

    [C] To describe

    [D] To persuade

    [E] To make demands

12. The author implies that :

    [A] the main character had secret talents.

    [B] the main character had great sadness.

    [C] the narrator was related to the main character.

    [D] the main character was generally neat and tidy.

    [E] the narrator was homeless.

Read the following passage excerpted from Biography.com and choose the best answer to the questions that follow.

> A prolific artist, Austrian composer Wolfgang Mozart created a string of operas, concertos, symphonies and sonatas that profoundly shaped classical music. Over the years, Mozart aligned himself with a variety of European venues and patrons, composing hundreds of works that included sonatas, symphonies, masses, concertos and operas, marked by vivid emotion and sophisticated textures.
>
> During the time when he worked for Archbishop Hieronymus von Colleredo, young Mozart had the opportunity to work in several different musical genres composing symphonies, string quartets, sonatas and serenades and a few operas. He developed a passion for violin concertos producing what came to be the only five he wrote. In 1776, he turned his efforts toward piano concertos, culminating in the Piano Concerto Number 9 in E flat major in early 1777. In Salzburg in 1779, Wolfgang Amadeus Mozart produced a series of church works, including the Coronation Mass. He also composed another opera for Munich, Ideomeneo in 1781.

13. Who is the target audience of this passage?

    [A] Artists.

    [B] Austrians.

    [C] Catholics.

    [D] A person interested in classical music.

    [E] None of these are accurate.

14. **What is the main idea of the previous passage?**

   [A] Mozart had a sister that also performed with him.

   [B] Mozart's father was his promoter.

   [C] The Catholic church was supportive of Mozart's talent.

   [D] Many operas and other pieces were composed by Mozart before he was 25 years old.

   [E] The rapid development and appreciation of Mozart's music.

15. **What is the author's purpose in writing this?**

   [A] To describe

   [B] To narrate

   [C] To entertain

   [D] To inform

   [E] To argue

16. **From reading this passage, we can conclude that:**

   [A] Mozart wrote several complex pieces of music at a young age.

   [B] There were not many composers as young and talented as Mozart.

   [C] There was a special relationship between the Catholic church and Mozart's family.

   [D] There were not as many composers in Austria as other countries.

   [E] None of these are accurate.

17. **Which of the following is not a musical genre?**

   [A] Opera

   [B] Sonnet

   [C] Symphony.

   [D] Concerto.

   [E] Quartet.

COLLEGE COMPOSITION

Read the following paragraph and answer the questions that follow.

(1) Outside, the late afternoon sun slanted down in the yard, throwing into gleaming brightness the dogwood trees that were solid masses of white blossoms against the background of new green. (2) The twins' horses were hitched in the driveway, big animals, red as their masters' hair; and around the horses' legs quarreled the pack of lean, nervous possum hounds that accompanied Stuart and Brent wherever they went. (3) A little aloof, as became and aristocrat, lay a black-spotted carriage dog, puzzle on paws, patiently waiting for the boys to go home to supper.

18. What is the main idea of this passage?

   [A] The passage is describing an afternoon outdoor setting.

   [B] The twins had very poised animals.

   [C] Certain concessions should be made for dogs.

   [D] The difficulties of travel in thick blossoming forests.

   [E] None of these covey the main idea of the passage.

19. What is the author's main purpose?

   [A] To inform

   [B] To entertain

   [C] To describe

   [D] To narrate

   [E] To record

20. What type of sentence is the second sentence?

   [A] Simple

   [B] Compound

   [C] Complex

   [D] Complex-Compound

   [E] Dependent clause

COLLEGE COMPOSITION

Read the following paragraph from Wikipedia and answer the question that follows.

Isaac Newton built the first practical reflecting telescope and developed a theory of colour based on the observation that a prism decomposes white light into the many colors of the visible spectrum. He formulated an empirical law of cooling, studied the speed of sound, and introduced the notion of a Newtonian fluid. In addition to his work on calculus, as a mathematician Newton contributed to the study of power series, generalized the binomial theorem to non-integer exponents, developed a method for approximating the roots of a function, and classified most of the cubic plane curves.

21. What is the main idea of this passage?

    [A] Power series is an important part of scientific discovery.

    [B] Fluid engineering is about the empirical law of cooling.

    [C] Through telescopes, scientists have made discoveries that have helped many people.

    [D] Newton was a mathematician and a scientist.

    [E] None of the above.

Read the following paragraph from *Popular Mechanics* and answer the question that follows.

We've been finding planets beyond our solar system for two decades now, but there are good reasons why it's taken so long to find the first forming world. For one thing, Stephanie Sallum says, planets spend only a brief period of their long lives in formation. Simply looking at the the odds, "it's unlikely that you'll come across a planet when it's still forming," she says.

22. The author's purpose is to

    [A] Describe

    [B] Inform

    [C] Persuade

    [D] Narrate

    [E] Summarize

Read the following paragraph from National Geographic and answer the question.

So far, more than 150 countries – from Sudan to Suriname and from Kiribati to Kyrgyzstan – have outlined for United Nations negotiators just how, when, and by how much each would cut carbon dioxide over the next several decades. If an agreement is reached, it would mark the first serious global commitment to reduce the pollution that is warming the planet, souring the oceans, and causing seas to rise.

23. What type of organizational pattern is the author using?

   [A] Comparison and Contrast

   [B] Generalization

   [C] Cause and Effect

   [D] Simple Listing

   [E] Analogy

Read the following paragraph from *Antiques and Fine Art* and answer the following question.

> Since the colonial period, the Atlantic Ocean has operated both as a barrier between America and Europe and as a conduit for international exchanges of peoples, goods, and ideas. It spurred commerce and enterprise that was the basis for both national economic activity and personal fortune. The activities in America's great harbors and port cities also supported the nation's cultural development, prompting the rise of schools of maritime and landscape painting, as well as portraiture.

24. Which organizational pattern does the author use?

   [A] Comparison and Contrast

   [B] Simple Listing

   [C] Cause and Effect

   [D] Definition

   [E] Description

Read the following quote and answer the following question.

> "I don't think about whether people will remember me or not. I've been an okay person. I've learned a lot. I've taught people a thing or two. That's what's important."
> – Julia Child

25. The quote primarily:

   [A] describes.

   [B] informs.

   [C] entertains.

   [D] narrates.

   [E] lists.

26. Addressing someone absent or something inhuman as though present and able to respond describes a figure of speech known as:

   [A] personification

   [B] synecdoche

   [C] metonymy

   [D] apostrophe

   [E] rhetorical strategy

COLLEGE COMPOSITION

ABILITY TO USE SOURCE MATRIAL
Read the following paragraphs and answer the questions that follows.

    At the end of the period, the artistic temperament of the painter undergoes a profound modification; it reflects a set of assimilated romantic ideas, expands the grandeur of classical art, and, while in the early works the love for the antique style throughout the popular subjects with inanimate edifice with the classic treatment as well as characterless, mythological subjects in the frescoes. The painter's figures assume heroic proportions, exude solemn expressions, and everything seems to come alive in a life more lush, more monumental and simple at the same time...

    Overall, we find an artist's determined personality, animated by a continuous and rapid progress, the result of a clear conscience and scrupulous study fiery aspects of reality with which can be sympathized, of an intense search of technical development, the assimilation of many and beautiful expressions of art. So he states, from the beginning of his artistic activity, a teacher of exceptional importance, which rises with noble means and personal and solid, without resorting to defiant rage, the glitz, the stylism that characterize so remarkable part of the art of his time.

    Serra, Luigi. Domenico Zampieri detto Il Domenichino. Rome: Casa Editrice del Bollettino d'Arte, Del Ministero Della P. Istruzione. 1909. pp11-12.

27. Where does the excerpt originate?

    [A] Webster's Dictionary

    [B] Luigi Serra

    [C] Domenico Zampieri

    [D] World Book Encyclopedia

    [E] Wikipedia

28. In the second paragraph, the second sentence can best be described as:

    [A] compound.

    [B] complex.

    [C] run-on.

    [D] a fragment.

    [E] compound-complex.

29. This, H. (2006). Food for Tomorrow? How the Scientific Discipline of Molecular Gastronomy Could Change the Way We Eat. *EMBO Reports*, 7(11), 1062-1066.

    In the citation, 1062 provides what information?

    [A] Date printed

    [B] Date accessed

    [C] First page of reference

    [D] Last page of reference

    [E] None of these are correct

COLLEGE COMPOSITION

30. **In the citation above, the (11) refers to:**

    [A] the eleventh article in the magazine.

    [B] the eleventh article published by this author.

    [C] there are eleven articles on gastronomy in this issue.

    [D] there are eleven authors.

    [E] This is the eleventh issue in the series, in volume seven.

31. **In the *EMBO* citation above, 7 refers to what?**

    [A] The number of volumes this has magazine has published in 2006.

    [B] How many articles have discussed gastronomy in the magazine's history

    [C] The seventh report for this issue.

    [D] Pagination.

    [E] Tagnemics

32. **Bernstein, M. (2002). 10 tips on writing the living Web. *A List Apart: For People Who Make Websites, 149*. Retrieved from http://www.alistapart.com/articles/writeliving is a citation example of a:**

    [A] newspaper.

    [B] book.

    [C] online periodical.

    [D] abstract.

    [E] none of these selections are accurate.

33. **2. Weinstein, "Plato's *Republic*," 452–53.**

    This is an example of:

    [A] note style.

    [B] duplicate style.

    [C] bibliography.

    [D] APA style.

    [E] MLA style.

COLLEGE COMPOSITION

34. Kossinets, Gueorgi, and Duncan J. Watts. "Origins of Homophily in an Evolving Social Network." *American Journal of Sociology* 115 (2009): 405–50. Accessed February 28, 2010. doi:10.1086/599247.

    Which style is this?

    [A] MLA

    [B] APA

    [C] Chicago

    [D] New York

    [E] None of these

35. Maxmen, Amy. "How Ebola Found Fertile Ground in Sierra Leone's Chaotic Capital." National Geographic. 27 January, 2015. Web. 16 November, 2015.

    This is an example of what kind of citation format?

    [A] MLA

    [B] APA

    [C] Chicago

    [D] Turabian

    [E] None of these

36. In the citation above, what does 27 January 2015 reference?

    [A] Reference date

    [B] Publication date

    [C] Editing date

    [D] Web upload date

    [E] None of these

37. Treverton, Gregory F. "The Changed Target." *Intelligence for an Age of Terror*. Cambridge: Cambridge UP, 2009. 24-25. Print. What does print reference?

    [A] Magazine article

    [B] Newspaper article

    [C] Printed web source

    [D] Book

    [E] None of these

RHETORICAL ANALYSIS
Read the following paragraph from the *National Independent Schools Magazine* and answer the questions that follow.

> The bias against introverted students is embedded in our educational system: years of unrelenting focus on cooperative learning, thinking aloud, and talking-as-learning, with grades for class participation, required public speaking (often now as a disproportionate pedagogical focus displacing more traditional

forms of scholarship and substantive mastery), and a pervasive, almost normative, value placed on being social and well liked, particularly in a large-group context. In sum, the classroom focus is now too often on "doing," in sacrifice to "thinking."

38. What is meant by the word "un- relenting" in the first sentence?

    [A] Continuing

    [B] Protective

    [C] Pervasive

    [D] Cautious

    [E] Reckless

39. What is the author's tone?

    [A] Aseptic

    [B] Analytical

    [C] Disbelieving

    [D] Disapproving

    [E] Scornful

40. What type of organizational pattern is the author using?

    [A] Classification

    [B] Explanation

    [C] Comparison and Contrast

    [D] Cause and Effect

    [E] Entertaining

41. Who would be the intended audience of this excerpt?

    [A] Politicians, for funding purposes.

    [B] Social workers, for counseling purposes.

    [C] Teachers, for refocusing efforts.

    [D] Parents, for normative adjustments.

    [E] None of these are applicable.

Read the following passage from Roll of Thunder, Hear My Cry and answer the questions that follow.

My youngest brother paid no attention to me. Grasping more firmly his newspaper-wrapped notebook and his tin-can lunch of cornbread and oil sausages, he continued to concentrate on the dusty road. He lagged several feet behind my other brothers, Stacey and Christopher-John, and me, attempting to keep the rusty Mississippi dust from swelling with each step and drifting back upon his shiny black shoes and the cuffs of his corduroy pants by lifting each foot high before setting it gently down again. Always meticulously neat, six-year-old Little Man never allowed dirt or tears or stains to mar anything he owned. Today was no exception.

"You keep it up and make us late for school, Mama's

gonna wear you out," I threatened, pulling with exasperation at the high collar of the Sunday dress Mama had made me wear for the first day of school - as if that event were something special. It seemed to me that showing up at school all on a bright August-like October morning made for running the cool forest trails and wading barefoot in the forest pond was concession enough; Sunday clothing was asking too much. Christopher-John and Stacey were not too pleased about the clothing or school either. Only Little Man, just beginning his school career, found the prospects of both intriguing.

42. What is the meaning of the word "meticulously" in the next to last sentence in the first paragraph?

    [A] Many

    [B] Very

    [C] Exceptionally

    [D] Rarely

    [E] Fairly

43. What is the overall organizational pattern used in this passage?

    [A] Generalization

    [B] Cause and Effect

    [C] Addition

    [D] Descriptive

    [E] Informational

44. What is the author's tone?

    [A] Disbelieving

    [B] Exasperated

    [C] Informative

    [D] Optimistic

    [E] None of these are correct.

Read the following passage from Pride and Prejudice and answer the questions that follow.

Mr. Bennet was so odd a mixture of quick parts, sarcastic humour, reserve, and caprice, that the experience of three-and-twenty years had been insufficient to make his wife understand his character. Her mind was less difficult to develop. She was a woman of mean understanding, little information, and uncertain temper. When she was discontented, she fancied herself nervous. The business of her life was to get her daughters married; its solace was visiting and news.

Mr. Bennet was among the earliest of those who waited on Mr. Bingley. He had always intended to visit him, though to the last always assuring his wife that he should not go; and till the evening after the visit was paid she had no knowledge of it. It was then disclosed in the following manner. Observing his second daughter employed in trimming a hat, he suddenly addressed her with:

"I hope Mr. Bingley will like it, Lizzy."

45. What is the overall organizational pattern of this passage?

   [A] Generalization

   [B] Cause and Effect

   [C] Addition

   [D] Summary

   [E] Informational

46. What is the meaning of the phrase "uncertain temper" in the third sentence?

   [A] Hot tempered

   [B] Quixotic emotions

   [C] Unusually morose

   [D] Generally happy

   [E] None of these apply

47. What is the organizational pattern of the second paragraph?

   [A] Cause and Effect

   [B] Classification

   [C] Addition

   [D] Explanation

   [E] None of these things

Read the following passage from Wuthering Heights and answer the questions that follow.

Before passing the threshold, I pause to admire a quantity of grotesque carving lavished over the front, and especially about the principal door; above which, among a wilderness of crumbling griffins and shameless little boys, I detected the date '1500,' and the name 'Hareton Earnshaw.' I would have made a few comments, and requested a short history of the plane from the surly owner; but his attitude at the door appeared to demand my speedy entrance, or complete departure, and I had no desire to aggregate his impatience previous to inspecting the penetralium.

48. What is the author's overall organizational pattern?

   [A] Classification

   [B] Cause and Effect

   [C] Definition

   [D] Comparison and Contrast

   [E] None of these things

COLLEGE COMPOSITION

49. **The author's tone in the passage is one of:**

    [A] Inquisition

    [B] Excitement

    [C] Surliness

    [D] Concern

    [E] Impatience

50. **The most similar way to rephrase "I had no desire to aggregate his impatience" in context of the passage would be:**

    [A] I wanted to keep him happy

    [B] I didn't want to make him mad

    [C] I didn't want to stay around

    [D] I wanted him to quickly inspect the penetralium

    [E] None of these are approximations

COLLEGE COMPOSITION

PRACTICE TEST ESSAY 1

As a reminder, you have 30 minutes to compose your essay and type it on the computer.

Directions: Write an essay in which you discuss the extent to which you agree or disagree with the statement below. Support your discussion with specific reasons and examples from your reading, experience or observations.

Topic: *Beauty is in the eye of the beholder.*

Readers will assign scores based on a matrix, or scoring guide. Here is an example outline of how both student essays will be graded on a six point scale.

SCORE OF 6 - The 6 essay presents a thesis that is coherent and well-developed. The writer's ideas are detailed, intelligent, and thoroughly elaborated. The writer's use of language and structure is correct and meaningful.

SCORE OF 5 - The 5 essay presents a thesis and offers persuasive support. The writer's ideas are usually new, mature, and thoroughly developed. A command of language and a variety of structures are evident.

SCORE OF 4 - The 4 essay presents a thesis and frequently offers a plan of development, which is usually demonstrated. The writer offers sufficient details to achieve the purpose of the essay. There is capable use of language and varied sentence structure. Errors in sentence structure and usage don't interfere with the writer's main purpose.

SCORE OF 3 - The 3 essay gives a thesis and offers a plan of development, which is usually demonstrated. The writer gives support that leans toward generalized statements or a listing. Overall, the support in a 3 essay is neither adequate nor coherent enough to be convincing. There are errors in sentence structure and usage that frequently interfere with the writer's ability to state the purpose.

SCORE OF 2 - The 2 essay usually states a thesis. The writer offers support that may be incomplete. Simple and disconnected sentence structure is present. Mistakes in grammar and usage often thwart the writer's ability to state the purpose.

SCORE OF 1 - The 1 essay has a thesis that is pointless or poorly articulated. Support is shallow. The language is muddled and confusing. Many mistakes in grammar and usage.

COLLEGE COMPOSITION

PRACTICE TEST ESSAY 2

As a reminder, you have 40 minutes to read these two passages and type your essay on the computer.

Directions: Write an essay in which you incorporate the two sources of information provided below. You must use both sources and you must use appropriate citation for both sources using the author's last name, the title or by any other means that adequately identifies it. Support your discussion with specific reasons and examples from your reading, experience or observations.

Assignment: Read the following sources carefully. Then write an essay in which you develop a position on whether people or communities express devotion differently.

Introduction: Devotion, according to Oxford's Dictionary, is "love, loyalty or enthusiasm for a person, activity, or cause."

Source 1: Shakespeare, William. *Romeo and Juliet.* England: 1595.

"But, soft! what light through yonder window breaks?
It is the east, and Juliet is the sun.
Arise, fair sun, and kill the envious moon,
Who is already sick and pale with grief,
That thou, her maid, art far more fair than she.
Be not her maid, since she is envious;
Her vestal livery is but sick and green
And none but fools do wear it; cast it off.
It is my lady, O, it is my love!
Oh, that she knew she were!"

Source 2: Heller, Joseph. "Catch 22." United States: 1961.

"What is a country? A country is a piece of land surrounded on all sides by boundaries, usually unnatural."

COLLEGE COMPOSITION

ANSWER KEY

Question Number	Correct Answer	Your Answer	Question Number	Correct Answer	Your Answer	Question Number	Correct Answer	Your Answer
1	B		18	A		35	A	
2	C		19	C		36	B	
3	A		20	D		37	D	
4	A		21	D		38	A	
5	A		22	B		39	D	
6	A		23	C		40	D	
7	C		24	A		41	C	
8	D		25	B		42	C	
9	A		26	A		43	D	
10	D		27	B		44	B	
11	C		28	C		45	A	
12	B		29	C		46	B	
13	D		30	E		47	D	
14	E		31	A		48	E	
15	D		32	C		49	A	
16	A		33	B		50	B	
17	B		34	C				

COLLEGE COMPOSITION

EXPLANATIONS

CONVENTIONS OF STANDARD WRITTEN ENGLISH
DIRECTIONS: Read each item carefully, paying attention to the underlined portions. If there is an error, it will be underlined. Assume that elements of the sentence not underlined are correct. If there is an error, select the one underlined part and enter that letter on the answer sheet. If there is no error, choose E.

1. On a long day in October, the rain <u>fell</u> so hard that it <u>causes</u> flooding all <u>along</u> the highway, <u>bringing</u> traffic to a stop. <u>No error</u>.

    [A] fell

    [B] causes

    [C] along

    [D] bringing

    [E] No error

The correct answer is B.
Causes should be caused, as the sentence is written in the past tense.

2. <u>Their</u> attempts are almost always comical, not <u>being able</u> to move supplies without <u>loosing</u> at least one package on the <u>route</u>. <u>No error</u>.

    [A] Their

    [B] being able

    [C] loosing

    [D] route

    [E] No error

The correct answer is C.
The underlined word has one too many 'O's, and should be written as losing.

COLLEGE COMPOSITION

3. At least two of the seven <u>defendents</u> <u>want</u> a delay, <u>saying</u> they need more time <u>to prepare</u> for trial. <u>No error</u>.

   [A] defendents

   [B] want

   [C] saying

   [D] to prepare

   [E] No eror

The correct answer is A.
The word listed is misspelled frequently, and is correctly spelled defendants.

4. The surfer <u>was bit</u> by a shark, but <u>got</u> his revenge when he <u>caught</u> him and <u>ate</u> it for dinner. <u>No error</u>

   [A] was bit

   [B] got

   [C] caught

   [D] ate

   [E] No error

The correct answer is A.
The correct answer is A as the appropriate past conjugation is was bitten.

COLLEGE COMPOSITION

5. A portrait of a <u>women</u> <u>had been</u> painted onto an iceberg, which was precariously <u>perched</u> on the edge of a melting <u>piece</u> of glacier. <u>No error</u>

   [A] women

   [B] had been

   [C] perched

   [D] piece

   [E] No error

The correct answer is A.
The underlined word should be singular, woman, as indicated by the verb tense as well as the lead-in "a" (plural would be the).

REVISION SKILLS
Read the following paragraph and answer the questions that follow.

> There was a steaming mist in all the hollows, and it roamed in its forlornness up the hill, like an evil spirit, seeking rest and finding none. A clammy and intensely cold mist, it made its way through the air in ripples that visibly followed and overspread one another, as the waves of an unwholesome sea might do. It was dense enough to shut out everything from the light of the coach-lamps but these its own workings, and a few yards of road; and the reek of the laboring horses steamed into it, as if they had made it at all.

6. The description of this scene gives the impression that it is:

   [A] an oppressive journey.

   [B] an enlightening route.

   [C] a contemplative traveling discussion.

   [D] an entertaining troupe making way to the next show.

   [E] None of these things is true.

The correct answer is A.
Choice B is incorrect because there are no descriptive words that indicate "enlightening". C is incorrect as there is no discussion, and D is also incorrect in that there is no reference whatsoever to justify this is true.

COLLEGE COMPOSITION

7. **What is the main idea of this passage?**

[A] Weather sets the stage in any narrative.

[B] The coach horses were not up to the task of the road.

[C] It was a dark and cold night, relatively unsuitable for travel.

[D] One of the coach-lamps was unlit, making it difficult to see.

[E] An English countryside scene is perfect for a scary setting.

The correct answer is C.
While all options may be true, the only one that is correct on a high level without excluding other pieces of the narrative makes C the best answer.

8. **The author's purpose is to:**

[A] Inform

[B] Entertain

[C] Persuade

[D] Narrate

[E] Analyze

The correct answer is D.
The author is simply narrating the setting for the action of the plot.

COLLEGE COMPOSITION

Read the following passage and answer the questions that follow.

> Everyone called him Pop Eye. Even in those days when I was a skinny thirteen-year-old I thought he probably knew about his nickname but didn't care. His eyes were too interested in what lay up ahead to notice us barefoot kids.
>
> He looked like someone who had seen or known great suffering and hadn't been able to forget it. His large eyes in his large head stuck out further than anyone else's - like they wanted to lave the surface of his face. They made you think of someone who can't get out the house quickly enough.
>
> Pop Eye wore the same white linen suit every day. His trousers snagged onto hi sony knees in the sloppy heat. Some days he wore a clown's nose. His nose was already big. he didn't need that red light bulb. But for reasons we couldn't think of he wore the red nose on certain days that may have meant something to him. We never saw him smile. And on those days he wore the clowns nose you found yourself looking away because you never saw such sadness.

9. What is the main idea of the passage?

   [A] The main character was a generally sad man, disinterested in the scene around him.

   [B] The main character cannot remember the thirteen-year-old kid.

   [C] The physical appearance of the main character was awkward.

   [D] The main character was so poor that he only had one suit.

   [E] None of these represent the main idea of the passage.

The correct answer is A.
While options B through D are correct according to the passage, the overall idea is encompassed in A.

10. From the passage, one can infer that:

    [A] Pop Eye is surrounded by family.

    [B] Pop Eye works as a clown.

    [C] The narrator is related to Pop Eye.

    [D] Pop Eye lives a lonely life.

    [E] The narrator has done well for himself.

The correct answer is D.
No other options are supported by information in the passage.

COLLEGE COMPOSITION

11. What is the author's purpose in writing this passage?

[A] To entertain

[B] To narrate

[C] To describe

[D] To persuade

[E] To make demands

The correct answer is C.
The author does describe the scene more than any other options. The author sets the scene for future plot development.

12. The author implies that :

[A] the main character had secret talents.

[B] the main character had great sadness.

[C] the narrator was related to the main character.

[D] the main character was generally neat and tidy.

[E] the narrator was homeless.

The correct answer is B.
This fact is directly stated in the last paragraph.

COLLEGE COMPOSITION

Read the following passage excerpted from Biography.com and choose the best answer to the questions that follow.

> A prolific artist, Austrian composer Wolfgang Mozart created a string of operas, concertos, symphonies and sonatas that profoundly shaped classical music. Over the years, Mozart aligned himself with a variety of European venues and patrons, composing hundreds of works that included sonatas, symphonies, masses, concertos and operas, marked by vivid emotion and sophisticated textures.
>
> During the time when he worked for Archbishop Hieronymus von Colleredo, young Mozart had the opportunity to work in several different musical genres composing symphonies, string quartets, sonatas and serenades and a few operas. He developed a passion for violin concertos producing what came to be the only five he wrote.   In 1776, he turned his efforts toward piano concertos, culminating in the Piano Concerto Number 9 in E flat major in early 1777. In Salzburg in 1779, Wolfgang Amadeus Mozart produced a series of church works, including the Coronation Mass. He also composed another opera for Munich, Ideomeneo in 1781.

13. Who is the target audience of this passage?

    [A] Artists.

    [B] Austrians.

    [C] Catholics.

    [D] A person interested in classical music.

    [E] None of these are accurate.

The correct answer is D.
While the other options use listed words in the selection, the answer most correct is D.

COLLEGE COMPOSITION

14. What is the main idea of the previous passage?

[A] Mozart had a sister that also performed with him.

[B] Mozart's father was his promoter.

[C] The Catholic church was supportive of Mozart's talent.

[D] Many operas and other pieces were composed by Mozart before he was 25 years old.

[E] The rapid development and appreciation of Mozart's music.

The correct answer is E.
While all of the items are facts and listed in the context of the passage, the overall main idea is expressed in E.

15. What is the author's purpose in writing this?

[A] To describe

[B] To narrate

[C] To entertain

[D] To inform

[E] To argue

The correct answer is D.
The author is providing the reader with information about musicality and progress of Mozart's development.

16. From reading this passage, we can conclude that:

[A] Mozart wrote several complex pieces of music at a young age.

[B] There were not many composers as young and talented as Mozart.

[C] There was a special relationship between the Catholic church and Mozart's family.

[D] There were not as many composers in Austria as other countries.

[E] None of these are accurate.

The correct answer is A.
Options B through D express opinions not supported in the passage.

COLLEGE COMPOSITION

17. Which of the following is not a musical genre?

[A] Opera

[B] Sonnet

[C] Symphony.

[D] Concerto.

[E] Quartet.

The correct answer is B.
A Sonnet is a poem form while a Sonota is a musical form. This correct form is directly listed in the passage.

Read the following paragraph and answer the questions that follow.

(1)Outside, the late afternoon sun slanted down in the yard, throwing into gleaming brightness the dogwood trees that were solid masses of white blossoms against the background of new green. (2)The twins' horses were hitched in the driveway, big animals, red as their masters' hair; and around the horses' legs quarreled the pack of lean, nervous possum hounds that accompanied Stuart and Brent wherever they went. (3)A little aloof, as became and aristocrat, lay a black-spotted carriage dog, puzzle on paws, patiently waiting for the boys to go home to supper.

18. What is the main idea of this passage?

[A] The passage is describing an afternoon outdoor setting.

[B] The twins had very poised animals.

[C] Certain concessions should be made for dogs.

[D] The difficulties of travel in thick blossoming forests.

[E] None of these covey the main idea of the passage.

The correct answer is A.
Option B is not true, as the dogs were quarreling around the horses' legs; Option C is not conveyed in the passage; Option D is not relayed int he passage anywhere about the group traveling.

COLLEGE COMPOSITION

19. What is the author's main purpose?

[A] To inform

[B] To entertain

[C] To describe

[D] To narrate

[E] To record

The correct answer is C.
The author is simply describing the scene.

20. What type of sentence is the second sentence?

[A] Simple

[B] Compound

[C] Complex

[D] Complex-Compound

[E] Dependent clause

The correct answer is D.
A semi-colon is even used, which is typical to conjoin to complex sentences. With the use of conjunctions (and), this also makes it compound.

COLLEGE COMPOSITION

Read the following paragraph from Wikipedia and answer the question that follows.

> **Isaac Newton built the first practical reflecting telescope and developed a theory of colour based on the observation that a prism decomposes white light into the many colors of the visible spectrum. He formulated an empirical law of cooling, studied the speed of sound, and introduced the notion of a Newtonian fluid. In addition to his work on calculus, as a mathematician Newton contributed to the study of power series, generalized the binomial theorem to non-integer exponents, developed a method for approximating the roots of a function, and classified most of the cubic plane curves.**

21. What is the main idea of this passage?

[A] Power series is an important part of scientific discovery.

[B] Fluid engineering is about the empirical law of cooling.

[C] Through telescopes, scientists have made discoveries that have helped many people.

[D] Newton was a mathematician and a scientist.

[E] None of the above.

The correct answer is D.
While the first three options are correct, the fourth gives a higher-level viewpoint of the overall passage.

COLLEGE COMPOSITION

Read the following paragraph from *Popular Mechanics* and answer the question that follows.

> We've been finding planets beyond our solar system for two decades now, but there are good reasons why it's taken so long to find the first forming world. For one thing, Stephanie Sallum says, planets spend only a brief period of their long lives in formation. Simply looking at the the odds, "it's unlikely that you'll come across a planet when it's still forming," she says.

22. The author's purpose is to

    [A] Describe

    [B] Inform

    [C] Persuade

    [D] Narrate

    [E] Summarize

The correct answer is B.
Option B is correct in that the discussion is about the new discovery of plants and the reasons that it has been hard to discover.

Read the following paragraph from National Geographic and answer the question.

> So far, more than 150 countries – from Sudan to Suriname and from Kiribati to Kyrgyzstan – have outlined for United Nations negotiators just how, when, and by how much each would cut carbon dioxide over the next several decades. If an agreement is reached, it would mark the first serious global commitment to reduce the pollution that is warming the planet, souring the oceans, and causing seas to rise.

23. What type of organizational pattern is the author using?

    [A] Comparison and Contrast

    [B] Generalization

    [C] Cause and Effect

    [D] Simple Listing

    [E] Analogy

The correct answer is C.
The author lists some causes and effects for fighting global warming.

COLLEGE COMPOSITION

Read the following paragraph from *Antiques and Fine Art* and answer the following question.

    Since the colonial period, the Atlantic Ocean has operated both as a barrier between America and Europe and as a conduit for international exchanges of peoples, goods, and ideas. It spurred commerce and enterprise that was the basis for both national economic activity and personal fortune. The activities in America's great harbors and port cities also supported the nation's cultural development, prompting the rise of schools of maritime and landscape painting, as well as portraiture.

24. Which organizational pattern does the author use?

    [A] Comparison and Contrast

    [B] Simple Listing

    [C] Cause and Effect

    [D] Definition

    [E] Description

The correct answer is A.
Since the author is demonstrating differences between America and Europe around the Atlantic Ocean, the correct answer is (A).

Read the following quote and answer the following question.

    "I don't think about whether people will remember me or not. I've been an okay person. I've learned a lot. I've taught people a thing or two. That's what's important." – Julia Child

25. The quote primarily:

    [A] describes.

    [B] informs.

    [C] entertains.

    [D] narrates.

    [E] lists.

The correct answer is B.
Since the quote telling us how Julia Child saw her life, the correct answer here is (B).

COLLEGE COMPOSITION

26. Addressing someone absent or something inhuman as though present and able to respond describes a figure of speech known as:

[A] personification

[B] synecdoche

[C] metonymy

[D] apostrophe

[E] rhetorical strategy

The correct answer is A.
Personification is taking something inhuman and giving it personal traits (such as responding).

ABILITY TO USE SOURCE MATERIAL
Read the following paragraphs and answer the questions that follows.

At the end of the period, the artistic temperament of the painter undergoes a profound modification; it reflects a set of assimilated romantic ideas, expands the grandeur of classical art, and, while in the early works the love for the antique style throughout the popular subjects with inanimate edifice with the classic treatment as well as characterless, mythological subjects in the frescoes. The painter's figures assume heroic proportions, exude solemn expressions, and everything seems to come alive in a life more lush, more monumental and simple at the same time…

Overall, we find an artist's determined personality, animated by a continuous and rapid progress, the result of a clear conscience and scrupulous study fiery aspects of reality with which can be sympathized, of an intense search of technical development, the assimilation of many and beautiful expressions of art. So he states, from the beginning of his artistic activity, a teacher of exceptional importance, which rises with noble means and personal and solid, without resorting to defiant rage, the glitz, the stylism that characterize so remarkable part of the art of his time.

Serra, Luigi. Domenico Zampieri detto Il Domenichino. Rome: Casa Editrice del Bollettino d'Arte, Del Ministero Della P. Istruzione. 1909. pp11-12.

COLLEGE COMPOSITION

28. Where does the excerpt originate?

[A] Webster's Dictionary

[B] Luigi Serra

[C] Domenico Zampieri

[D] World Book Encyclopedia

[E] Wikipedia

The correct answer is B.
It is listed as the source directly below the passage, and in the format, Serra is the author. Zampieri is the subject of the material.

28. In the second paragraph, the second sentence can best be described as:

[A] compound.

[B] complex.

[C] run-on.

[D] a fragment.

[E] compound-complex.

The correct answer is C.
The correct answer is C which is just a fact that you need to know when answering questions in this section.

29. This, H. (2006). Food for Tomorrow? How the Scientific Discipline of Molecular Gastronomy Could Change the Way We Eat. *EMBO Reports*, 7(11), 1062-1066.

   In the citation, 1062 provides what information?

   [A] Date printed

   [B] Date accessed

   [C] First page of reference *

   [D] Last page of reference

   [E] None of these are correct

The correct answer is C.
The first page of the reference cited.

30. In the citation above, the (11) refers to:

   [A] the eleventh article in the magazine.

   [B] the eleventh article published by this author.

   [C] there are eleven articles on gastronomy in this issue.

   [D] there are eleven authors.

   [E] This is the eleventh issue in the series, in volume seven.

The correct answer is E.
The citation for the correct issue in the correctly listed volume.

31. In the *EMBO* citation above, 7 refers to what?

   [A] The number of volumes this has magazine has published in 2006

   [B] How many articles have discussed gastronomy in the magazine's history

   [C] The seventh report for this issue

   [D] Pagination

   [E] Tagnemics

The correct answer is A.

COLLEGE COMPOSITION

as it lists the correct volume from the original citation.

32. **Bernstein, M. (2002). 10 tips on writing the living Web.** *A List Apart: For People Who Make Websites, 149.* **Retrieved from http://www.alistapart.com/articles/writeliving is a citation example of a:**

    [A] newspaper.

    [B] book.

    [C] online periodical.

    [D] abstract.

    [E] none of these selections are accurate.

The correct answer is C.
Option C is correct, which should be evident not only by the title but also the website listed in the citation.

33. **2. Weinstein, "Plato's *Republic*," 452–53.**

    This is an example of:

    [A] note style.

    [B] duplicate style.

    [C] bibliography.

    [D] APA style.

    [E] MLA style.

The correct answer is B.
The correct answer is B as if it was any of the others, it would have a complete first and last name as well as place of publication and year.

COLLEGE COMPOSITION

34. Kossinets, Gueorgi, and Duncan J. Watts. "Origins of Homophily in an Evolving Social Network." *American Journal of Sociology* 115 (2009): 405–50. Accessed February 28, 2010. doi:10.1086/599247.

    Which style is this?

    [A] MLA

    [B] APA

    [C] Chicago

    [D] New York

    [E] None of these

The correct answer is C.
The year comes later in Chicago format and the second name is listed in first name last name order.

35. Maxmen, Amy. "How Ebola Found Fertile Ground in Sierra Leone's Chaotic Capital." National Geographic. 27 January, 2015. Web. 16 November, 2015.

    This is an example of what kind of citation format?

    [A] MLA

    [B] APA

    [C] Chicago

    [D] Turabian

    [E] None of these

The correct answer is A.
The above example is a clear representation of MLA citation format. These are facts, the differences between citation types that should be known for the test.

COLLEGE COMPOSITION

36. In the citation above, what does 27 January 2015 reference?

    [A] Reference date

    [B] Publication date

    [C] Editing date

    [D] Web upload date

    [E] None of these

The correct answer is B.
In MLA this area is for the publication date. The reference date comes at the end. Any editing or version dates would come after the title with an editor's name.

37. Treverton, Gregory F. "The Changed Target." *Intelligence for an Age of Terror*. Cambridge: Cambridge UP, 2009. 24-25. Print. What does print reference?

    [A] Magazine article

    [B] Newspaper article

    [C] Printed web source

    [D] Book

    [E] None of these

The correct answer is D.
The "print" gives that fact.

COLLEGE COMPOSITION

RHETORICAL ANALYSIS
Read the following paragraph from the *National Independent Schools Magazine* and answer the questions that follow.

The bias against introverted students is embedded in our educational system: years of unrelenting focus on cooperative learning, thinking aloud, and talking-as-learning, with grades for class participation, required public speaking (often now as a disproportionate pedagogical focus displacing more traditional forms of scholarship and substantive mastery), and a pervasive, almost normative, value placed on being social and well liked, particularly in a large-group context. In sum, the classroom focus is now too often on "doing," in sacrifice to "thinking."

38. What is meant by the word "un- relenting" in the first sentence?

    [A] Continuing

    [B] Protective

    [C] Pervasive

    [D] Cautious

    [E] Reckless

The correct answer is A
You should be able to be determined this through careful reading of the passage. This is a key to succeeding in this section, being able to analyze and replace words with similar meanings.

39. What is the author's tone?

    [A] Aseptic

    [B] Analytical

    [C] Disbelieving

    [D] Disapproving

    [E] Scornful

The correct answer is D.
The author uses words that show disapproval of bias against introverted students throughout the passage.

COLLEGE COMPOSITION

40. What type of organizational pattern is the author using?

[A] Classification

[B] Explanation

[C] Comparison and Contrast

[D] Cause and Effect

[E] Entertaining

The correct answer is D.
The author mentions the things that are being pushed onto children that may not learn best in that style and has clearly stated "bias against" - this would be most correctly listed as effect and cause, but is the best option as it is not typical to list "effect and cause" in choices.

41. Who would be the intended audience of this excerpt?

[A] Politicians, for funding purposes.

[B] Social workers, for counseling purposes.

[C] Teachers, for refocusing efforts.

[D] Parents, for normative adjustments.

[E] None of these are applicable.

The correct answer is C.
There is no mention of funding or politics; there is no mention of social workers or counseling; there is no mention of parents or adjustments. Though any of these groups and purposes may be targeted, we can only answer questions based on the information presented in the selections within the test. Be sure to not bring outside information into answering questions.

COLLEGE COMPOSITION

Read the following passage from Roll of Thunder, Hear My Cry and answer the questions that follow.

> My youngest brother paid no attention to me. Grasping more firmly his newspaper-wrapped notebook and his tin-can lunch of cornbread and oil sausages, he continued to concentrate on the dusty road. He lagged several feet behind my other brothers, Stacey and Christopher-John, and me, attempting to keep the rusty Mississippi dust from swelling with each step and drifting back upon his shiny black shoes and the cuffs of his corduroy pants by lifting each foot high before setting it gently down again. Always meticulously neat, six-year-old Little Man never allowed dirt or tears or stains to mar anything he owned. Today was no exception.
> "You keep it up and make us late for school, Mama's gonna wear you out," I threatened, pulling with exasperation at the high collar of the Sunday dress Mama had made me wear for the first day of school - as if that event were something special. It seemed to me that showing up at school all on a bright August-like October morning made for running the cool forest trails and wading barefoot in the forest pond was concession enough; Sunday clothing was asking too much. Christopher-John and Stacey were not too pleased about the clothing or school either. Only Little Man, just beginning his school career, found the prospects of both intriguing.

42. What is the meaning of the word "meticulously" in the next to last sentence in the first paragraph?

    [A] Many

    [B] Very

    [C] Exceptionally

    [D] Rarely

    [E] Fairly

The correct answer is C.
While B and E may be correct, it is not emphatic enough and the other options are not applicable or opposite.

COLLEGE COMPOSITION

43. **What is the overall organizational pattern used in this passage?**

   [A] Generalization

   [B] Cause and Effect

   [C] Addition

   [D] Descriptive

   [E] Informational

The correct answer is D.
The author describes the scene of the children walking down the dirt road.

44. **What is the author's tone?**

   [A] Disbelieving

   [B] Exasperated

   [C] Informative

   [D] Optimistic

   [E] None of these are correct.

The correct answer is B.
The sister is the narrator for this passage and she actually uses the word "exasperation" in the first sentence of the second paragraph.

COLLEGE COMPOSITION

Read the following passage from Pride and Prejudice and answer the questions that follow.

> Mr. Bennet was so odd a mixture of quick parts, sarcastic humour, reserve, and caprice, that the experience of three-and-twenty years had been insufficient to make his wife understand his character. Her mind was less difficult to develop. She was a woman of mean understanding, little information, and uncertain temper. When she was discontented, she fancied herself nervous. The business of her life was to get her daughters married; its solace was visiting and news.
>
> Mr. Bennet was among the earliest of those who waited on Mr. Bingley. He had always intended to visit him, though to the last always assuring his wife that he should not go; and till the evening after the visit was paid she had no knowledge of it. It was then disclosed in the following manner. Observing his second daughter employed in trimming a hat, he suddenly addressed her with:
>
> "I hope Mr. Bingley will like it, Lizzy."

45. What is the overall organizational pattern of this passage?

   [A] Generalization

   [B] Cause and Effect

   [C] Addition

   [D] Summary

   [E] Informational

The correct answer is A.
Because it was a description of the generalities with both Mr. as well as Mrs. Bennet. There is no cause and effect described, and C as well as D are not correct. E may be a tempting choice, but it is not relaying information - when data and facts (such as science) are given, that is when it's appropriate to select informational.

COLLEGE COMPOSITION

46. What is the meaning of the phrase "uncertain temper" in the third sentence?

[A] Hot tempered

[B] Quixotic emotions

[C] Unusually morose

[D] Generally happy

[E] None of these apply

The correct answer is B.
Answer A may seem a likely choice, except temper is not being used literally in this passage. C and D give one extreme or another, and that is not what is implied in the context of the passage either.

47. What is the organizational pattern of the second paragraph?

[A] Cause and Effect

[B] Classification

[C] Addition

[D] Explanation

[E] None of these things

The correct answer is D.
By selecting D, the explanation is how the second paragraph is organized, the reader shows that he or she understood that the narrator is providing explanation as to why Mr. Bennet didn't previously tell his wife about visiting Mr. Bingley and then why he did.

COLLEGE COMPOSITION

Read the following passage from Wuthering Heights and answer the questions that follow.

> Before passing the threshold, I pause to admire a quantity of grotesque carving lavished over the front, and especially about the principal door; above which, among a wilderness of crumbling griffins and shameless little boys, I detected the date '1500,' and the name 'Hareton Earnshaw.' I would have made a few comments, and requested a short history of the plane from the surly owner; but his attitude at the door appeared to demand my speedy entrance, or complete departure, and I had no desire to aggregate his impatience previous to inspecting the penetralium.

48. What is the author's overall organizational pattern?

   [A] Classification

   [B] Cause and Effect

   [C] Definition

   [D] Comparison and Contrast

   [E] None of these things

The correct answer is E.
The offered answers for organizational pattern of the passage are not correct; therefore, answer E is correct.

49. The author's tone in the passage is one of:

   [A] Inquisition

   [B] Excitement

   [C] Surliness

   [D] Concern

   [E] Impatience

The correct answer is A.
The speaker actually says a few comments would have been made about what is seen in the room. Answer B is not conveyed in the passage. C, D, and E are words used to describe the male's attitude in the passage, so they could be immediately eliminated.

COLLEGE COMPOSITION

50. **The most similar way to rephrase "I had no desire to aggregate his impatience" in context of the passage would be:**

    [A] I wanted to keep him happy

    [B] I didn't want to make him mad

    [C] I didn't want to stay around

    [D] I wanted him to quickly inspect the penetralium

    [E] None of these are approximations

The correct answer is B.
The correct rephrasing is B for most accurately representing a rephrased sentence. While A may be true from analysis, it is not correct syntax to match the phrase pulled from the passage. C and D are just not correct choices (D actually skips part of the sentence and tricks a reader moving too quickly by using the ending of the actual paragraph - make sure you read carefully!)

COLLEGE COMPOSITION MODULAR

Description of the Examination
The CLEP College Composition examinations assess writing skills taught in most first-year college composition courses. Those skills include analysis, argumentation, synthesis, usage, ability to recognize logical development and research. The exams cannot cover every skill (such as keeping a journal or peer editing) required in many first-year college writing courses. Candidates will, however, be expected to apply the principles and conventions used in longer writing projects to two timed writing assignments and to apply the rules of standard written English.

College Composition contains approximately 50 multiple-choice items to be answered in approximately 50 minutes and two essays to be written in 70 minutes (with 30 minutes to write the first essay and 40 minutes to read the two sources and write the second essay), for a total of approximately 120 minutes testing time. Essays must be typed on the computer. The actual examination contains multiple-choice items and two mandatory, centrally scored essays. The essays are scored twice a month by college English faculty from throughout the country via an online scoring system. Each of the two essays is scored independently by two different readers, and the scores are then combined. This combined score is weighted approximately equally with the score from the multiple-choice section. These scores are then combined to yield the candidate's score. The resulting combined score is reported as a single scared score between 20 and 80. Separate scores are not reported for the multiple-choice and essay sections.

The College Composition Modular exam allows institutions to administer and/or score test-takers' essays after approximately 90 multiple choice questions are completed in 90 minutes (with the two essay questions to be completed in 70 minutes to complete both essay answers), for a total of approximately 160 minutes. The knowledge and skills assessed are the same as those measured by College Composition, but the format and timing allow a more extended indirect assessment of test-takers' knowledge and skills. The percentages of exam questions on each topic are the same in the College Composition exam as well as this sample College Composition Modular sample test.

Knowledge and Skills Required
The subject matter of the College Composition examination is drawn from the following topics. The percentages next to the main topics indicate the approximate percentage of exam questions on that topic for the multiple-choice items.

10% Conventions of Standard English
- measures the awareness of logical, structural and grammatical relationships within sentences. Questions relate to syntax, punctuation, concord/agreement, modifiers, active versus passive voice and additional areas

40% Revision Skills
- measures revision skills in the context of early essays, such as organization, level of detail, awareness of audience or tone, sentence variety and structure, main ideas, transitions, point of views
- Modular format includes questions that require sentence restructuring/word replacement to improve comprehension

25% Ability to Use Source Material
- measures familiarity with basic reference and research skills via the use of reference materials, evaluation of sources, integration of resources and documentation

25% Rhetorical Analysis
- measures ability to analyze writing primarily using passage based questions reviewing appeals, tone, structure, rhetorical effects

<u>**On the next page, the sample test begins.**</u> **There are 90 questions that you must answer in less than 90 minutes. Then, there are essay questions that you must answer in a timed fashion: the first essay has 30 minutes and the second essay has 40 minutes to read two passages and complete and essay.**

Remember, your goals for this test are those questions you answer accurately; it is not based on how many are incorrect. Take your time, and good luck.

CONVENTIONS OF STANDARD WRITTEN ENGLISH

DIRECTIONS: Read each item carefully, paying attention to the underlined portions. If there is an error, it will be underlined. Assume that elements of the sentence not underlined are correct. If there is an error, select the one underlined part and enter that letter on the answer sheet. If there is no error, choose E.

1. A <u>fearful</u> man, all in grey, <u>were</u> down by the river <u>standing</u> by the bunches of <u>rushes</u>. <u>No error</u>.

   [A] fearful

   [B] were

   [C] standing

   [D] rushes

   [E] No error

2. When our group of <u>friends</u> goes to Italy next year, we will be <u>seeing</u> many of the <u>countries</u> famous <u>landmarks</u>. <u>No error</u>.

   [A] friends

   [B] seeing

   [C] countries

   [D] landmarks

   [E] No error

3. <u>Their</u> are no walls high enough, no <u>valleys</u> deep enough, <u>to</u> keep the warriors <u>from</u> attacking the city. <u>No error</u>.

   [A] Their

   [B] valleys

   [C] to

   [D] from

   [E] No error

4. <u>Whenever</u> the phone rings, the dog <u>likes</u> to run to the front door to <u>see</u> who <u>has come</u> to visit. <u>No error</u>

   [A] Whenever

   [B] likes

   [C] see

   [D] has come

   [E] No error

5. <u>Every one</u> must pass <u>through</u> Vanity Fair in order to get to the <u>celestial</u> city and receive <u>their</u> three golden eggs. <u>No error</u>

   [A] Every one

   [B] through

   [C] celestial

   [D] their

   [E] No error

6. Suffering <u>has been</u> stronger than all other teaching, and <u>have</u> taught me to understand what <u>your</u> heart <u>use</u> to be. <u>No error</u>

   [A] has been

   [B] have

   [C] your

   [D] use

   [E] No error

7. The loneliest moment in <u>someone's</u> life is when they are watching <u>their</u> <u>hole</u> world fall apart, and all they can do is <u>stare</u> blankly. <u>No error</u>

   [A] someone's

   [B] their

   [C] hole

   [D] stare

   [E] No error

8. I have not <u>broken</u> your heart - you have <u>broke</u> it; and in <u>breaking</u> it, you <u>have</u> broken mine. <u>No error</u>

   [A] broken

   [B] broke

   [C] breaking

   [D] have

   [E] No error

Mr. Smith gave instructions for the painting to be hung on the wall. And then it leaped forth before his eyes: the little cottages on the river, the white clouds floating over the valley and the green of the towering mountain ranges which were seen in the distance. The painting was so vivid that it seemed almost real. Mr. Smith was now absolutely certain that the painting had been worth money.

9. From the last sentence, one can infer that:

   [A] the painting was expensive.

   [B] the painting was cheap.

   [C] Mr. Smith was considering purchasing the painting.

   [D] Mr. Smith thought the painting was too expensive and decided not to purchase it.

   [E] None of these things is true.

10. What is the main idea of this passage?

   [A] The painting that Mr. Smith purchased is expensive.

   [B] Mr. Smith purchased a painting.

   [C] Mr. Smith was pleased with the quality of the painting he had purchased.

   [D] The painting depicted cottages and valleys.

   [E] Mr. Smith was looking to buy some paintings.

11. The author's purpose is to:

   [A] Inform

   [B] Entertain

   [C] Persuade

   [D] Narrate

   [E] Analyze

   One of the most difficult problems plaguing American education is the assessment of teachers. No one denies that teachers ought to be answerable for what they do, but what exactly does that mean? The Oxford American Dictionary defines accountability as: the obligation to give a reckoning or explanation for one's actions.
   Does a student have to learn for teaching to have taken place? Historically, teaching has not been defined in this restrictive manner; the teacher was thought to be responsible for the quantity and quality of material covered and the way in which it was presented. However, some definitions of teaching now imply that students must learn in order for teaching to have taken place.
   As a teacher who tries my best to keep current on all the latest teaching strategies, I believe that those teachers who do not bother even to pick up an educational journal every once in a while should be kept under close watch. There are many teachers out there who have been teaching for decades and refuse to change their ways even if research has proven that their methods are outdated and ineffective. There is no place in the profession of teaching for these types of individuals. It is time that the American educational system clean house, for the sake of our children.

12. What is the main idea of the passage?

   [A] Teachers should not be answerable for what they do.

   [B] Teachers who do not do their job should be fired.

   [C] The author is a good teacher.

   [D] Assessment of teachers is a serious problem in society today.

   [E] Defining accountability.

13. From the passage, one can infer that:

    [A] The author considers herself a good teacher.

    [B] Poor teachers will be fired.

    [C] Students have to learn for teaching to take place.

    [D] The author will be fired.

    [E] All of these are characteristics of fables

14. What is the author's purpose in writing the passage on the previous page?

    [A] To entertain

    [B] To narrate

    [C] To describe

    [D] To persuade

    [E] To make demands

15. The author states that teacher assessment is a problem for:

    [A] Elementary schools

    [B] Secondary schools

    [C] American education

    [D] Families

    [E] Teachers

Disciplinary practices have been found to affect diverse areas of child development such as the acquisition of moral values, obedience to authority, and performance at school. Even though the dictionary has a specific definition of the word "discipline," it is still open to interpretation by people of different cultures.

There are four types of disciplinary styles: assertion of power, withdrawal of love, reasoning, and permissiveness. Assertion of power involves the use of force to discourage unwanted behavior. Withdrawal of love involves making the love of a parent conditional on a child's good behavior. Reasoning involves persuading the child to behave one way rather than another. Permissiveness involves allowing the child to do as he or she pleases and face the consequences of his/her actions.

16. Name the four types of disciplinary styles.

    [A] Reasoning, power assertion, morality, and permissiveness.

    [B] Morality, reasoning, permissiveness, and withdrawal of love.

    [C] Withdrawal of love, permissiveness, power, and reasoning.

    [D] Permissiveness, morality, reasoning, and power assertion.

    [E] Explore, Inform, Entertain, Persuade.

17. **What is the main idea of the previous passage?**

    [A] Different people have different ideas of what discipline is.

    [B] Permissiveness is the most widely used disciplinary style.

    [C] Most people agree on their definition of discipline.

    [D] There are four disciplinary styles.

    [E] Child development needs to focus on obedience to authority.

18. **What is the author's purpose in writing this?**

    [A] To describe

    [B] To narrate

    [C] To entertain

    [D] To inform

    [E] To argue

19. **From reading this passage, we can conclude that:**

    [A] The author is a teacher.

    [B] The author has many children.

    [C] The author has written a book about discipline.

    [D] The author has done a lot of research on discipline.

    [E] The author has at least two siblings.

20. **What does the technique of reasoning involve?**

    [A] Persuading the child to behave in a certain way.

    [B] Allowing the child to do as he/she pleases.

    [C] Using force to discourage unwanted behavior.

    [D] Making love conditional on good behavior.

    [E] Distracting the child in order to get them to behave appropriately.

Each underlined portion of sentences 21-23 contains one or more errors in grammar, usage, mechanics, or sentence structure. Circle the choice that best corrects the error without changing the meaning of the original sentence. Choice E may repeat the underlined portion. Select the identical phrase if you find no error.

21. **Walt Whitman was famous for <u>his composition, *Leaves of Grass*, serving as a nurse during the Civil War, and a devoted son.</u>**

    [A] Leaves of Grass, his service as a nurse during the Civil War, and a devoted son.

    [B] composing Leaves of Grass, serving as a nurse during the Civil War, and being a devoted son.

    [C] his composition, Leaves of Grass, his nursing during the Civil War, and his devotion as a son.

    [D] serving as a nurse during the civil war, being a devoted son and Leaves of Grass.

    [E] his composition, Leaves of Grass, serving as a nurse during the Civil War, and a devoted son.

22. **There were <u>fewer pieces</u> of evidence presented during the second trial.**

    [A] fewer peaces

    [B] less peaces

    [C] less pieces

    [D] not as many peaces

    [E] fewer pieces

23. **Wally <u>groaned, "Why</u> do I have to do an oral interpretation <u>of "The Raven."</u>**

    [A] groaned "Why … of 'The Raven'?"

    [B] groaned "Why … of "The Raven"?

    [C] groaned "Why … of "The Raven?"

    [D] groaned, "Why … of "The Raven."

    [E] groaned, "Why… of *The Raven*?"

Microbiology is the study of tiny organisms that can only be seen through a magnifying glass or microscope. Scientists have used microbiology to help prevent and cure certain diseases. It has also been important in the development of new and better foods.

24. What is the main idea of this passage?

[A] Microbiology has been used to prevent and cure certain diseases.

[B] Through microbiology, scientists have made discoveries that have helped many people.

[C] Microbiology is the study of tiny organisms.

[D] It is necessary to have a magnifying glass or microscope when engaged in a microbiological study.

[E] none of the above.

Many people insist on wearing "real" fur coats even though artificial furs have been available for over 30 years. It is cruel to torture animals just to be fashionable. Save an animal by wearing artificial fur coats instead of "real" ones.

25. The author's purpose is to

[A] Desccribe

[B] Inform

[C] Persuade

[D] Narrate

[E] Summarize

Plants are very versatile living organisms. They are constantly adapting to survive in their environments. Some plants have grown spines to protect themselves from herbivores. Plants that grow in cold regions grow close to the ground to avoid harsh winds.

26. What type of organizational pattern is the author using?

[A] Cause and Effect

[B] Generalization

[C] Comparison and Contrast

[D] Simple Listing

[E] Analogy

Rembrandt and Van Gogh were two Dutch painters. Both were from wealthy families. Both showed incredible talent at a young age. Van Gogh did not begin to paint seriously until he was twenty-seven. Rembrandt, on the other hand, had already completed many paintings by that age.

27. Which organizational pattern does the author use?

   [A] Comparison and Contrast

   [B] Simple Listing

   [C] Cause and Effect

   [D] Definition

   [E] Description

   Charles Lindbergh had no intention of becoming a pilot. He was enrolled in the University of Wisconsin until a flying lesson changed the entire course of his life. He began his career as a pilot by performing daredevil stunts at fairs

28. The author wrote this paragraph primarily to:

   [A] describe

   [B] inform

   [C] entertain

   [D] narrate

   [E] analyze

29. Addressing someone absent or something inhuman as though present and able to respond describes a figure of speech known as:

   [A] personification

   [B] synecdoche

   [C] metonymy

   [D] apostrophe

   [E] rhetorical strategy

Read the following paragraph and answer the questions below, selecting the best choice of the options presented.

   (1) It was a cold and windy night. (2) Everyone was close around the fire in order to keep warm. (3) It was lonely for the little boy, who waited for his mother to bring him a marshmallow to toast on a stick. (4) His sister died just weeks ago and he really missed her.

30. In sentence (2), a better way to phrase "was close" could be:

   [A] huddled

   [B] gather

   [C] stood

   [D] left from

   [E] none of these options are better

31. In sentence (4), the author is describing what emotion?

   [A] hunger

   [B] happiness

   [C] coldness

   [D] sadness

   [E] anger

   As she mused the pitiful vision of her mother's life laid its spell on the very quick of her being—that life of commonplace sacrifices closing in final craziness. She trembled as she heard again her mother's voice saying constantly with foolish insistence: Derevaun Seraun! Derevaun Seraun!

   **[Derevaun Seraun means "The end of pleasure is pain!" (Gaelic)]

32. The following passage is written from which point of view?

   [A] First person, narrator

   [B] Second person, direct address

   [C] Third person, omniscient

   [D] First person, omniscient

   [E] First person, direct address

33. To understand the origins of a word, one must study the:

   [A] synonyms

   [B] inflections

   [C] phonetics

   [D] etymology

   [E] epidemiology

34. Which is the best definition for syntax?

   [A] The specific order of word choices by an author to create a particular mood or feeling in the reader

   [B] Writing that explains something thoroughly

   [C] The background or exposition for a short story or drama

   [D] Word choices that help teach a truth or moral

   [E] Proper elocution

35. Which is the least true statement concerning an author's literary tone?

   [A] Tone is partly revealed through the selection of details.

   [B] Tone is the expression of the author's attitude toward his or her subject.

   [C] Tone can be expressed in a variety of ways by an author.

   [D] Tone in literature corresponds to the tone of voice a speaker uses.

   [E] Tone in literature is usually satiric or angry.

36. Regarding the study of poetry, which elements are least applicable to all types of poetry?

   [A] Setting and audience

   [B] Theme and tone

   [C] Pattern and diction

   [D] Diction and rhyme scheme

   [E] Words and symbols

**There is no frigate like a book
To take us lands away,
Nor any coursers like a page
Of prancing poetry;
This traverse may the poorest take
Without oppress of toll;
How frugal is the chariot
That bears the human soul!**

37. How many types of transport types does the author incorporate?

   [A] two

   [B] three

   [C] four

   [D] five

   [E] none

38. If the words 'frigate, coursers, and chariot' were replaced with synonyms, what would the best choice of the following options include?

   [A] Train, car, carriage

   [B] Train, horse, carriage

   [C] Ship, car, carriage

   [D] Ship, car, train

   [E] Ship, horse, carriage

39. What is a good paraphrase of "To take us lands away" that Ms. Dickinson writes in this poem?

   [A] War makes it unsafe to travel, so we can just read about places.

   [B] Poems will drive us to save our souls.

   [C] Books can engage us to see new things

   [D] Authors can show us how to go on vacation.

   [E] It shows poems are short and fun.

Tyger! Tyger! burning bright
In the forests of the night,
What immortal hand or eye
Could frame thy fearful symmetry?

In what distant deeps or skies
Burnt the fire of thine eyes?
On what wings dare he aspire?
What the hand dare seize the flame?

And what shoulder, & what art,
Could twist the sinews of they heart?
And when thy heart began to beat,
What dread hand? & what dread feet?

40. Sinews, in the third stanza, can be best compared to:

   [A] thread.

   [B] a cage.

   [C] rope.

   [D] heart strings or emotions.

   [E] burnt fire, from the second stanza.

41. Another phrase for "deeps or skies" that would fit in this poem could be:

   [A] caves or planes.

   [B] trees or forests.

   [C] seas or air.

   [D] waves or wind.

   [E] oceans or lakes.

42. In line 7 of this poem, what word below most nearly means "aspire"?

   [A] Soar.

   [B] Plunge.

   [C] Scheme.

   [D] Travel.

   [E] Admire.

These are morning matters, pictures you dream as the final wave heaves you up on the sand in the bright light and drying air. You remember pressure, and a curved sleep you rested against, soft, like a scallop in its shell. But the air hardens your skin; you stand; you leave the lighted shore to explore some dim headland, and soon you're lost in the leafy interior, intent, remembering nothing.

I still think of that old tomcat, mornings, when I wake. Things are tamer now; I sleep with the window shut. The cats and our rites are gone and my life is changed, but the memory remains of something powerful playing over me. I wake expectant, hoping to see a new thing. If I'm lucky I might be jogged awake by a strange bird call. I dress in a hurry, imagining the yard flapping with auks, or flamingos. This morning it was a wood duck, down at the creek. It flew away.

43. The phrase, "like a scallop in its shell" is an example of:

    [A] an irony.

    [B] a simile.

    [C] a metaphor.

    [D] personification.

    [E] euphemism.

44. The phrase "the air hardens your skin" within the context of the passage most likely refers to what?

    [A] The morning air woke the character up from dreaming.

    [B] The scallop shell bed the character sleeps in has opened.

    [C] The air dries out the character's skin.

    [D] The coldness of the room turns off the brain of the character.

    [E] The air turns the character's skin cold when the cat leaves the bed.

One of the most difficult problems plaguing American education is the assessment of teachers. No one denies that teachers ought to be answerable for what they do, but what exactly does that mean? The Oxford American Dictionary defines accountability as: the obligation to give a reckoning or explanation for one's actions.

Does a student have to learn for teaching to have taken place? Historically, teaching has not been defined in this restrictive manner; the teacher was thought to be responsible for the quantity and quality of material covered and the way in which it was presented. However, some definitions of teaching now imply that students must learn in order for teaching to have taken place.

As a teacher who tries my best to keep current on all the latest teaching strategies, I believe that those teachers who do not bother even to pick up an educational journal every once in a while should be kept under close watch. There are many teachers out there who have been teaching for decades and refuse to change their ways even if research has proven that their methods are outdated and ineffective. There is no place in the profession of teaching for these types of individuals. It is time that the American educational system clean house, for the sake of our children

45. Where does the author get her definition of "accountability?"

    [A] Webster's Dictionary

    [B] Encyclopedia Brittanica

    [C] Oxford Dictionary

    [D] World Book Encyclopedia

    [E] Wikipedia

46. In the second paragraph, the second sentence can best be described as:

    [A] compound.

    [B] complex.

    [C] run-on.

    [D] a fragment.

    [E] compound-complex.

47. Taite, Richard. "Five Things to Know About Recovery from Alcohol." *Psychology Today.* Web. (https://www.psychologytoday.com/blog/ending-addiction-good/201510/five-things-know-about-recovery-alcohol-or-drugs) October 16, 2015.

    In the citation, 16 October 2015 provides what information?

    [A] Date printed

    [B] Date accessed

    [C] Date placed on the Internet

    [D] Date the last person accessed it

    [E] None of these are correct

48. Nelson, MD., Lewis S et al. Addressing the Opioid Epidemic. *JAMA.* 13 October 2015; 314(14): 1453-1454.

    The (14) refers to:

    [A] the fourteenth article in the magazine.

    [B] the fourteenth article published by this author.

    [C] there are fourteen articles on opioids in this issue.

    [D] there are fourteen authors.

    [E] This is the fourteenth issue in the series, in volume 314.

49. In the *JAMA* citation previously, 1454-1454 refers to what?

    [A] The number of issues this has magazine has published.

    [B] How many articles have discussed opioids in the magazine's history.

    [C] Page numbers for this citation.

    [D] Ongoing page numbers for the table of contents in this magazine.

    [E] Tagnemics

50. The word 'print' at the end of a citation is a reference for:

   [A] the article is from a newspaper.

   [B] the article is from a book.

   [C] the article is from a periodical.

   [D] the article was not accessed online.

   [E] none of these selections are accurate.

51. Ciottone, Gregory et al. Disaster Medicine, Second Edition. Elsevier, digital. September 24, 2015. ISBN-13: 978-0323286657

   The "et al" refers to:

   [A] no hard cover copy is available.

   [B] the content is digital only.

   [C] this has been published in the United States.

   [D] that Ciottone is the editor.

   [E] more than one author should be listed.

52. Serra, Luigi. Domencio Zampieri, detto Il Domenichino. E. Calzone, ed. 1909. Princeton University.

   Who is the editor?

   [A] Serra Luigi

   [B] Luigi Serra

   [C] E. Calzone

   [D] Domenico Zampieri

   [E] Domenichino

53. Cattong, Bruce. "Grant and Lee: A Study in Contrasts." *The Bedford Reader.* 9th ed. Ed. X. J. Kennedy et al. Boston: Bedford/St. Martin's, 2006. 258-61. Print. This is an example of what kind of citation format?

   [A] MLA

   [B] APA

   [C] Chicago

   [D] Turabian

   [E] None of these

54. Aloise-Young, P. A. (1993). The development of self-presentation: Self-promotion in 6- to 10- year-old children. *Social Cognition, II*, 201-222. This is an example of what kind of citation?

[A] MLA

[B] APA

[C] Chicago

[D] Turabian

[E] None of these

55. Smith, John Maynard. "The Origin of Altruism." *Nature* 393 (1998): 639-40. This is an example of which kind of citation?

[A] MLA

[B] APA

[C] Chicago

[D] Turabian

[E] None of these

"(1)These good folk, who have only just begun to think and act for themselves, are slow as yet to grasp the changed conditions which should attach them to these theories. (2)They have only reached those ideas which conduce to economy and to physical welfare; in the future, if some one else carries on this work of mine, they will come to understand the principles that serve to uphold and preserve public order and justice. (3)As a matter of fact, it is not sufficient to be an honest man, you must appear to be honest in the eyes of others. (4)Society does not live by moral ideas alone; its existence depends upon actions in harmony with those ideas."

56. The first sentence can best be described as:

[A] compound.

[B] complex.

[C] run-on.

[D] a fragment.

[E] compound-complex.

57. The second sentence can best be described as:

[A] compound.

[B] complex.

[C] run-on.

[D] a fragment.

[E] compound-complex.

58. Warren, Robert Penn. *All The King's Men.* New York: Harcourt, Brace, 1946. Print. p415.

    The p415 sentence can best be described as:

    [A] the number of pages in the book used.

    [B] the last page the reader completed.

    [C] the citation for a portion referenced in the/a document.

    [D] the last page of dialogue in the book.

    [E] none of the choices are accurate.

59. United States. Cong. Senate. Appropriations. Schedule of Serial Set Volumes. 112 Cong., 2 sess. S. Doc. 15383A. Washington DC: U.S. Senate, 2012. Web.

    15383A can best be described as:

    [A] amendment number.

    [B] edit number.

    [C] page number.

    [D] volume number

    [E] document number.

60. Bell, A. G. (1876). *U.S. Patent No.174,465.* Washington, DC: U.S. Patent and Trademark Office.

    This is the patent citation for:

    [A] a lightbulb.

    [B] train brakes.

    [C] relativity.

    [D] telephone.

    [E] telegraph.

61. Mozart, W. A. (1970). *Die Zauberflöte* [The magic flute], K. 620 [Vocal score]. Munich, Germany: Becksche Verlagsbuchhandlung. (Original work published 1791).

    The "K. 620" is the citation for:

    [A] the 620th note in the musical score.

    [B] opus, or work number.

    [C] the number of instruments required.

    [D] the number of performers required, including voices.

    [E] none of these are correct.

62. Harris, Ann Sutherland (PhD). Seventeenth Century Art and Architecture. Lawrence King Publishing, 2005. pxv.

    The "pxv" is:

    [A] the version label.

    [B] the author's work number.

    [C] the date in Roman numeral.

    [D] the preface page number.

    [E] none of these are correct.

63. "Higher education has become a central part of the process by which high-income families can seek to assure that their children are more likely to have high incomes." Taylor, Timothy. How Higher Education Perpetuates Intergenerational Inequality. March 4, 2015. http://conversableeconomist.blogspot.com/2015/03/how-higher-education-perpetuates.html Accessed August 8, 2015.

    When prefaced with "61" in superscript before this phrase and listed on the same page, it would be referred to as a(an):

    [A] footnote.

    [B] endnote.

    [C] footer.

    [D] header.

    [E] none of these are correct.

This writer has often been asked to tutor hospitalized children with cystic fibrosis. While undergoing all the precautionary measures to see these children (i.e. scrubbing thoroughly and donning sterilized protective gear- for the child's protection), she has often wondered why their parents subject these children to the pressures of schooling and trying to catch up on what they have missed because of hospitalization, which is a normal part of cystic fibrosis patients' lives. These children undergo so many tortuous treatments a day that it seems cruel to expect them to learn as normal children do, especially with their life expectancies being as short as they are.

64. What is the author's main purpose?

    [A] To inform

    [B] To entertain

    [C] To describe

    [D] To narrate

    [E] To record

65. What is the main idea of this passage?

   [A] There is a lot of preparation involved in visiting a patient of cystic fibrosis.

   [B] Children with cystic fibrosis are incapable of living normal lives.

   [C] Certain concessions should be made for children with cystic fibrosis.

   [D] Children with cystic fibrosis die young.

   [E] The specific ways you must decontaminate yourself to visit children.

66. What is meant by the word "precautionary" in the second sentence?

   [A] Careful

   [B] Protective

   [C] Medical

   [D] Sterilizing

   [E] Reckless

67. What is the author's tone in the previous passage?

   [A] Sympathetic

   [B] Cruel

   [C] Disbelieving

   [D] Cheerful

   [E] Cautious

68. What type of organizational pattern is the author using in the selection about cystic fibrosis?

   [A] Classification

   [B] Explanation

   [C] Comparison and Contrast

   [D] Cause and Effect

   [E] Entertaining

69. How is the author so familiar with the procedures used when visiting a child with cystic fibrosis?

   [A] She has read about it.

   [B] She works in a hospital.

   [C] She is the parent of one.

   [D] She often tutors them.

   [E] She had it as a child.

   Disciplinary practices have been found to affect diverse areas of child development such as the acquisition of moral values, obedience to authority, and performance at school. Even though the dictionary has a specific definition of the word "discipline," it is still open to interpretation by people of different cultures.
   There are four types of disciplinary styles: assertion of power, withdrawal of love, reasoning, and permissiveness. Assertion of power involves the use of force to discourage unwanted behavior. Withdrawal of love involves making the love of a parent conditional on a

child's good behavior. Reasoning involves persuading the child to behave one way rather than another. Permissiveness involves allowing the child to do as he or she pleases and face the consequences of his/her actions

70. What is the meaning of the word "diverse" in the first sentence?

   [A] Many

   [B] Related to children

   [C] Disciplinary

   [D] Moral

   [E] Racially disparate

71. What organizational structure is used in the first sentence of the second paragraph?

   [A] Addition

   [B] Explanation

   [C] Definition

   [D] Simple Listing

   [E] Argumentative

72. What is the author's tone?

   [A] Disbelieving

   [B] Angry

   [C] Informative

   [D] Optimistic

   [E] None of these are correct.

73. What is the overall organizational pattern of this passage?

   [A] Generalization

   [B] Cause and Effect

   [C] Addition

   [D] Summary

   [E] Informational

One of the most difficult problems plaguing American education is the assessment of teachers. No one denies that teachers ought to be answerable for what they do, but what exactly does that mean? The Oxford American Dictionary defines accountability as: the obligation to give a reckoning or explanation for one's actions.

Does a student have to learn for teaching to have taken place? Historically, teaching has not been defined in this restrictive manner; the teacher was thought to be responsible for the quantity and quality of material covered and the way in which it was presented. However, some definitions of teaching now imply that students must learn in order for teaching to have taken place.

As a teacher who tries my best to keep current on all the latest teaching strategies, I believe that those teachers who do not bother even to pick up an educational journal every once in a while should be kept under close watch. There are many teachers out there who have been teaching for decades and refuse to change their ways even if research has proven that their methods are outdated and ineffective. There is no place in the profession of teaching for these types of individuals. It is time that the American educational system clean house, for the sake of our children

74. What is the meaning of the word "reckoning" in the third sentence?

    [A] Thought

    [B] Answer

    [C] Obligation

    [D] Explanation

    [E] Prayerful

75. What is the organizational pattern of the second paragraph?

    [A] Cause and Effect

    [B] Classification

    [C] Addition

    [D] Explanation

    [E] None of these things

76. What is the author's overall organizational pattern?

    [A] Classification

    [B] Cause and Effect

    [C] Definition

    [D] Comparison and Contrast

    [E] None of these things

77. The author's tone in the passage on the previous page is one of:

    [A] Disbelief

    [B] Excitement

    [C] Support

    [D] Concern

    [E] Empathy

78. What is meant by the word "plaguing" in the first sentence of the previous passage?

    [A] Causing problems

    [B] Causing illness

    [C] Causing anger

    [D] Causing failure

    [E] Causing unrest

(1)London was our present point of rest; we determined to remain several months in this wonderful and celebrated city. (2)Clerval desired the intercourse of the men of genius and talent who flourished at this time; but this was with me a secondary object; I was principally occupied with the means of obtaining the information necessary for the completion of my promise, and quickly availed myself of the letters of introduction that I had brought with me, addressed to the most distinguished natural philosophers.

79. The fourth word in the second sentence, "intercourse", refers to:

   [A] intimate relations between two people

   [B] interactive conversation

   [C] an in-depth artist's class

   [D] a secondary outcome after a gift is given in Victorian times

   [E] none of these options are correct

80. In the previous passage (referenced in question 79 also), what is the main theme of the selection?

   [A] Travel discussions that compare where the characters have been

   [B] Discussions about information gathering and solving an issue

   [C] Meeting gentlemen for coffee

   [D] Identifying the thought-leaders of the time

   [E] How the travelers were going to spend their time in the city.

"Oh, Madam Mina," he said, "how can I say what I owe to you? This paper is as sunshine. It opens the gate to me. I am dazed, I am dazzled, with so much light, and yet clouds roll in behind the light every time. But that you do not, cannot comprehend. Oh, but I am grateful to you, you so clever woman. Madame," he said this very solemnly, "if ever Abraham Van Helsing can do anything for your or yours, I trust you will let me know. It will be pleasure and delight if I may serve you as a friend, as a friend, but all I have ever learned, all I can ever do, shall be for you and those you love. There are darknesses in life, and there are lights. You are one of the lights. You are one of the lights. You will have a happy life and a good life, and your husband will be blessed in you."

81. The phase "This paper is as sunshine. It opens the gate to me." means

   [A] Madam Mina was holding a light in the next sentence that made it seem as bright as day.

   [B] the character speaking has been given new glasses with which to see the sunshine.

   [C] the character speaking simply has new information that is helpful to him.

   [D] that he is making a joke to Madam Mina.

   [E] none of these things.

82. Using the information only presented in the selection, he tone used by the author suggests:

   [A] Madam Mina gave Van Helsing information unwillingly.

   [B] one of the characters has been drinking a love potion.

   [C] Madam Mina wants nothing to do with Van Helsing.

   [D] that Van Helsing is making fun to Madam Mina.

   [E] Van Helsing is enamored with Madam Mina because of her helpfulness.

"Mornings, he likes to sit in his new leather chair by his new living room window, looking out across the rooftops and chimney pots, the clotheslines and telegraph lines and office towers. It's the first time Manhattan, from high above, hasn't crushed him with desire. On the contrary the view makes him feel smug. All those people down there, striving, hustling, pushing, shoving, busting to get what Willie's already got. In spades. He lights a cigarette, blows a jet of smoke against the window. Suckers."

83. The subject in this passage is

   [A] a character, and seems to be the lead in the story.

   [B] a supporting character.

   [C] has the attitude of a criminal.

   [D] female.

   [E] has been poor his whole life.

84. What kind of description is the author providing of this scene?

   [A] Backstory of the character.

   [B] A characterization of what the character is like.

   [C] A narrative, with the end of the selection giving thoughts in the first person.

   [D] The unreliable narrative about a character.

   [E] The author is using a persuasive argument.

85. What types of words are "striving, hustling, pushing, shoving, bustling"?

   [A] Adjectives

   [B] Adverbs

   [C] Nouns

   [D] Gerunds

   [E] Verbs

86. If you had to explain the phrase "crushed him" in the paragraph above and context of the paragraph, what would be the best appropriate explanation?

    [A] The city sustained him with all the opportunity available.

    [B] The city called to him to be part of its life.

    [C] The city complimented him for everything he has achieved.

    [D] The city had energized him to get what he felt he deserved.

    [E] The city smothered him with all of its offerings.

87. The author portrays the attitude of the character toward the people on the street below as:

    [A] Condescending.

    [B] Sarcastic.

    [C] Affectionate.

    [D] Tolerant.

    [E] Encouraged.

Solemnly he came forward and mounted the round gunrest. He faced about and blessed gravely thrice the tower, the surrounding country and the awaking mountains. Then, catching sight of Stephen Dedalus, he bent towards him and made rapid crosses in the air, gurgling in his throat and shaking his head. Stephen Dedalus, displeased and sleepy, leaned his arms on the top of the staircase and looked coldly at the shaking gurgling face that blessed him, equine in its length, and at the light untenured hair, grained and hued like pale oak.

88. The likely setting for this paragraph is:

    [A] a hospital.

    [B] the battlefield.

    [C] Stephen's bedroom.

    [D] beside the river.

    [E] unable to be determined.

89. The description of the main character's hair leads to the conclusion that he is:

    [A] a blonde.

    [B] a brunette.

    [C] has black hair.

    [D] has grained black and white hair.

    [E] is bald.

90. **The phrase "equine in its length" to describe the main character:**

    [A] is complementary as horses were very valuable to soldiers.

    [B] could be considered sarcastic.

    [C] reveals the way Stephen feels about the main character, which is not fond or complementary.

    [D] was a common description of the time period.

    [E] is used repeatedly in this book.

COLLEGE COMPOSITION MODULAR

PRACTICE TEST ESSAY 1

As a reminder, you have 30 minutes to compose your essay and type it on the computer.

Directions: Write an essay in which you discuss the extent to which you agree or disagree with the statement below. Support your discussion with specific reasons and examples from your reading, experience or observations.

<u>Topic:</u> *Communication is the key for success.*

Readers will assign scores based on a matrix, or scoring guide. Here is an example outline of how both student essays will be graded on a six point scale.

SCORE OF 6 - The 6 essay presents a thesis that is coherent and well-developed. The writer's ideas are detailed, intelligent, and thoroughly elaborated. The writer's use of language and structure is correct and meaningful.

SCORE OF 5 - The 5 essay presents a thesis and offers persuasive support. The writer's ideas are usually new, mature, and thoroughly developed. A command of language and a variety of structures are evident.

SCORE OF 4 - The 4 essay presents a thesis and frequently offers a plan of development, which is usually demonstrated. The writer offers sufficient details to achieve the purpose of the essay. There is capable use of language and varied sentence structure. Errors in sentence structure and usage don't interfere with the writer's main purpose.

SCORE OF 3 - The 3 essay gives a thesis and offers a plan of development, which is usually demonstrated. The writer gives support that leans toward generalized statements or a listing. Overall, the support in a 3 essay is neither adequate or coherent enough to be convincing. There are errors in sentence structure and usage that frequently interfere with the writer's ability to state the purpose.

SCORE OF 2 - The 2 essay usually states a thesis. The writer offers support that may be incomplete. Simple and disconnected sentence structure is present. Mistakes in grammar and usage often thwart the writer's ability to state the purpose.

SCORE OF 1 - The 1 essay has a thesis that is pointless or poorly articulated. Support is shallow. The language is muddled and confusing. Many mistakes in grammar and usage.

COLLEGE COMPOSITION MODULAR

PRACTICE TEST ESSAY 2

As a reminder, you have 40 minutes to read these two passages and type your essay on the computer.

Directions: Write an essay in which you incorporate the two sources of information provided below. You must use both sources and you must use appropriate citation for both sources using the author's last name, the title or by any other means that adequately identifies it. Support your discussion with specific reasons and examples from your reading, experience or observations.

Assignment: Read the following sources carefully. Then write an essay in which you develop a position on whether communities have contracts to keep peace and fellow members free from harm.

Introduction: A contract is a legal agreement between people, companies, et cetera. Miriam-Webster Dictionary.

Source 1: Hobbes, Thomas. "Leviathan." England: 1651.

Except - The final cause, end or design of men (who naturally love liberty, and dominion over others) in the introduction of that restraint upon themselves in which we see them live in Commonwealths, is the foresight of their own preservation, and of a more contented live thereby; that is to say, of getting themselves out of that miserable condition of war which is necessarily consequent, as hath been shown, to the natural passions of men when there is no visible power to keep them in awe, and tie them by fear of punishment to the performance of their covenants..."

Source 2: Golding, William. "Lord of the Flies." England: 1954.

This toy of voting was almost as pleasing as the conch. Jack started to protest but the clamor changed from the general wish for a chief to an election by acclaim of Ralph himself. None of the boys could have found good reason for this; what intelligence had been shown was traceable to Piggy while the most obvious leaders was Jack. But there was a stillness about Ralph as he sat that marked him out: there was his size, and attractive appearance; and most obscurely, yet most powerfully, there was the conch. The being that had blown that, had sat waiting for them on the platform with the delicate thing balanced on his knees, was set apart.

COLLEGE COMPOSITION MODULAR

ANSWER KEY

Question Number	Correct Answer	Your Answer	Question Number	Correct Answer	Your Answer	Question Number	Correct Answer	Your Answer
1	B		31	D		61	B	
2	C		32	C		62	D	
3	A		33	D		63	A	
4	E		34	A		64	C	
5	A		35	E		65	C	
6	B		36	A		66	B	
7	C		37	B		67	C	
8	B		38	E		68	D	
9	A		39	C		69	D	
10	C		40	D		70	A	
11	D		41	C		71	D	
12	D		42	A		72	C	
13	A		43	C		73	E	
14	D		44	A		74	D	
15	C		45	C		75	D	
16	C		46	E		76	E	
17	A		47	B		77	D	
18	D		48	E		78	A	
19	D		49	C		79	B	
20	A		50	E		80	E	
21	B		51	E		81	C	
22	E		52	C		82	E	
23	A		53	A		83	A	
24	B		54	B		84	C	
25	C		55	C		85	E	
26	A		56	B		86	E	
27	A		57	E		87	A	
28	B		58	C		88	E	
29	A		59	E		89	A	
30	A		60	D		90	C	

EXPLANATIONS

1. A <u>fearful</u> man, all in grey, <u>were</u> down by the river <u>standing</u> by the bunches of <u>rushes</u>. <u>No error</u>.

    [A] fearful

    [B] were

    [C] standing

    [D] rushes

    [E] No error

The correct answer is B.
"Were" is plural and the subject is singular; therefore, it should be was.

2. When our group of <u>friends</u> goes to Italy next year, we will be <u>seeing</u> many of the <u>countries</u> famous <u>landmarks</u>. <u>No error</u>.

    [A] friends

    [B] seeing

    [C] countries

    [D] landmarks

    [E] No error

The correct answer is C.
Countries is plural, but in this sentence, the word should be possessive, or country's.

COLLEGE COMPOSITION MODULAR

3. <u>Their</u> are no walls high enough, no <u>valleys</u> deep enough, <u>to</u> keep the warriors <u>from</u> attacking the city. <u>No error</u>.

   [A] Their

   [B] valleys

   [C] to

   [D] from

   [E] No error

The correct answer is A.
Again, the word listed - their - is possessive and here, the correct word should be the location (there).

4. <u>Whenever</u> the phone rings, the dog <u>likes</u> to run to the front door to <u>see</u> who <u>has come</u> to visit. <u>No error</u>

   [A] Whenever

   [B] likes

   [C] see

   [D] has come

   [E] No error

The correct answer is E.
as everything is right.

5. **Every one** must pass **through** Vanity Fair in order to get to the **celestial** city and receive **their** three golden eggs. **No error**

   [A] Every one

   [B] through

   [C] celestial

   [D] their

   [E] No error

The correct answer is A.
Everyone is one word, not two (as listed).

6. Suffering **has been** stronger than all other teaching, and **have** taught me to understand what **your** heart **use** to be. **No error**

   [A] has been

   [B] have

   [C] your

   [D] use

   [E] No error

The correct answer is B.
The incorrect verb tense is used - it lists "have" but should be "has".

7. The loneliest moment in <u>someone's</u> life is when they are watching <u>their</u> <u>hole</u> world fall apart, and all they can do is <u>stare</u> blankly. <u>No error</u>

[A] someone's

[B] their

[C] hole

[D] stare

[E] No error

The correct answer is C.
The appropriate spelling of "hole" in this instance is "whole".

8. I have not <u>broken</u> your heart - you have <u>broke</u> it; and in <u>breaking</u> it, you <u>have</u> broken mine. <u>No error</u>

[A] broken

[B] broke

[C] breaking

[D] have

[E] No error

The correct answer is B.
"Broke" is incorrect for the conjugation in the tense of this portion of the phrase; it should be broken, as it is two other times in the sentence.

Mr. Smith gave instructions for the painting to be hung on the wall. And then it leaped forth before his eyes: the little cottages on the river, the white clouds floating over the valley and the green of the towering mountain ranges which were seen in the distance. The painting was so vivid that it seemed almost real. Mr. Smith was now absolutely certain that the painting had been worth money.

9. From the last sentence, one can infer that:

   [A] the painting was expensive.

   [B] the painting was cheap.

   [C] Mr. Smith was considering purchasing the painting.

   [D] Mr. Smith thought the painting was too expensive and decided not to purchase it.

   [E] None of these things is true.

The correct answer is A.
Choice B is incorrect because, had the painting been cheap, chances are that Mr. Smith would no have considered his purchase. Choices C and D are ruled out by the fact that the painting had already been purchased. The author makes this clear when she says, "...the painting had been worth the money."

10. What is the main idea of this passage?

   [A] The painting that Mr. Smith purchased is expensive.

   [B] Mr. Smith purchased a painting.

   [C] Mr. Smith was pleased with the quality of the painting he had purchased.

   [D] The painting depicted cottages and valleys.

   [E] Mr. Smith was looking to buy some paintings.

The correct answer is C.
Every sentence in the paragraph alludes to this fact.

11. The author's purpose is to:

   [A] Inform

   [B] Entertain

   [C] Persuade

   [D] Narrate

   [E] Analyze

The correct answer is D.
The author is simply narrating or telling the story of Mr. Smith and his painting.

   One of the most difficult problems plaguing American education is the assessment of teachers. No one denies that teachers ought to be answerable for what they do, but what exactly does that mean? The Oxford American Dictionary defines accountability as: the obligation to give a reckoning or explanation for one's actions.

   Does a student have to learn for teaching to have taken place? Historically, teaching has not been defined in this restrictive manner; the teacher was thought to be responsible for the quantity and quality of material covered and the way in which it was presented. However, some definitions of teaching now imply that students must learn in order for teaching to have taken place.

   As a teacher who tries my best to keep current on all the latest teaching strategies, I believe that those teachers who do not bother even to pick up an educational journal every once in a while should be kept under close watch. There are many teachers out there who have been teaching for decades and refuse to change their ways even if research has proven that their methods are outdated and ineffective. There is no place in the profession of teaching for these types of individuals. It is time that the American educational system clean house, for the sake of our children.

12. What is the main idea of the passage?

[A] Teachers should not be answerable for what they do.

[B] Teachers who do not do their job should be fired.

[C] The author is a good teacher.

[D] Assessment of teachers is a serious problem in society today.

[E] Defining accountability.

The correct answer is D.
Most of the passage is dedicated to elaborating on why teacher assessment is such a problem.

13. From the passage, one can infer that:

[A] The author considers herself a good teacher.

[B] Poor teachers will be fired.

[C] Students have to learn for teaching to take place.

[D] The author will be fired.

[E] All of these are characteristics of fables

The correct answer is A.
The first sentence of the third paragraph alludes to this.

14. What is the author's purpose in writing the passage on the previous page?

   [A] To entertain

   [B] To narrate

   [C] To describe

   [D] To persuade

   [E] To make demands

The correct answer is D.
The author does some describing, but the majority of her statements seemed geared towards convincing the reader that teachers who are lazy or who do not keep current should be fired.

15. The author states that teacher assessment is a problem for:

   [A] Elementary schools

   [B] Secondary schools

   [C] American education

   [D] Families

   [E] Teachers

The correct answer is C.
This fact is directly stated in the first paragraph.

   Disciplinary practices have been found to affect diverse areas of child development such as the acquisition of moral values, obedience to authority, and performance at school. Even though the dictionary has a specific definition of the word "discipline," it is still open to interpretation by people of different cultures.
   There are four types of disciplinary styles: assertion of power, withdrawal of love, reasoning, and permissiveness. Assertion of power involves the use of force to discourage unwanted behavior. Withdrawal of love involves making the love of a parent conditional on a child's good behavior. Reasoning involves persuading the child to behave one way rather than another. Permissiveness involves allowing the child to do as he or she pleases and face the consequences of his/her actions.

COLLEGE COMPOSITION MODULAR

16. **Name the four types of disciplinary styles.**

    [A] Reasoning, power assertion, morality, and permissiveness.

    [B] Morality, reasoning, permissiveness, and withdrawal of love.

    [C] Withdrawal of love, permissiveness, power, and reasoning.

    [D] Permissiveness, morality, reasoning, and power assertion.

    [E] Explore, Inform, Entertain, Persuade.

The correct answer is C.
This is directly stated in the second paragraph.

17. **What is the main idea of the previous passage?**

    [A] Different people have different ideas of what discipline is.

    [B] Permissiveness is the most widely used disciplinary style.

    [C] Most people agree on their definition of discipline.

    [D] There are four disciplinary styles.

    [E] Child development needs to focus on obedience to authority.

The correct answer is A.
Choice C is not true, the opposite is stated in the passage. Choice B could be true, but we have no evidence of this. Choice D is just one of the many facts listed in the passage.

18. **What is the author's purpose in writing this?**

    [A] To describe

    [B] To narrate

    [C] To entertain

    [D] To inform

    [E] To argue

The correct answer is D.
The author is providing the reader with information about disciplinary practices.

COLLEGE COMPOSITION MODULAR

19. **From reading this passage, we can conclude that:**

    [A] The author is a teacher.

    [B] The author has many children.

    [C] The author has written a book about discipline.

    [D] The author has done a lot of research on discipline.

    [E] The author has at least two siblings.

The correct answer is D.
Given all the facts mentioned in the passage, this is the only inference one can make.

20. **What does the technique of reasoning involve?**

    [A] Persuading the child to behave in a certain way.

    [B] Allowing the child to do as he/she pleases.

    [C] Using force to discourage unwanted behavior.

    [D] Making love conditional on good behavior.

    [E] Distracting the child in order to get them to behave appropriately.

The correct answer is A.
This fact is directly stated in the second paragraph.

Each underlined portion of sentences 21-23 contains one or more errors in grammar, usage, mechanics, or sentence structure. Circle the choice that best corrects the error without changing the meaning of the original sentence. Choice E may repeat the underlined portion. Select the identical phrase if you find no error.

21. **Walt Whitman was famous for <u>his composition, *Leaves of Grass*, serving as a nurse during the Civil War, and a devoted son</u>.**

    [A] Leaves of Grass, his service as a nurse during the Civil War, and a devoted son.

    [B] composing Leaves of Grass, serving as a nurse during the Civil War, and being a devoted son.

    [C] his composition, Leaves of Grass, his nursing during the Civil War, and his devotion as a son.

    [D] serving as a nurse during the civil war, being a devoted son and Leaves of Grass.

    [E] his composition, Leaves of Grass, serving as a nurse during the Civil War, and a devoted son.

The correct answer is B.
To be parallel, the sentence needs three gerunds. The other sentences use both gerunds and nouns, which is a lack of parallelism.

22. **There were <u>fewer pieces</u> of evidence presented during the second trial.**

    [A] fewer peaces

    [B] less peaces

    [C] less pieces

    [D] not as many peaces

    [E] fewer pieces

The correct answer is E.
"Less" is impossible in the plural, and "peace" is the opposite of war, not a "piece" of evidence.

COLLEGE COMPOSITION MODULAR

23. Wally groaned, "Why do I have to do an oral interpretation of "The Raven."

[A] groaned "Why ... of 'The Raven'?"

[B] groaned "Why ... of "The Raven"?

[C] groaned "Why ... of "The Raven?"

[D] groaned, "Why ... of "The Raven."

[E] groaned, "Why... of *The Raven*?"

The correct answer is A.
The question mark in a quotation that is an interrogation should be within the quotation marks. Also, when quoting a title that is styled in quotation marks (like the title of a poem or short story) within another quotation, one should use single quotation marks ('...') for the title of this work, and they should close before the final quotation mark.

Microbiology is the study of tiny organisms that can only be seen through a magnifying glass or microscope. Scientists have used microbiology to help prevent and cure certain diseases. It has also been important in the development of new and better foods.

24. What is the main idea of this passage?

[A] Microbiology has been used to prevent and cure certain diseases.

[B] Through microbiology, scientists have made discoveries that have helped many people.

[C] Microbiology is the study of tiny organisms.

[D] It is necessary to have a magnifying glass or microscope when engaged in a microbiological study.

[E] none of the above.

The correct answer is B.
Two of the sentences in the paragraph support that this is the main idea.

Many people insist on wearing "real" fur coats even though artificial furs have been available for over 30 years. It is cruel to torture animals just to be fashionable. Save an animal by wearing artificial fur coats instead of "real" ones.

25. The author's purpose is to

    [A] Desccribe

    [B] Inform

    [C] Persuade

    [D] Narrate

    [E] Summarize

The correct answer is C.
By mentioning that artificial furs are available and that it is cruel to torture animals, the author is attempting to convince the readers to abandon "real" furs and wear artificial ones instead.

Plants are very versatile living organisms. They are constantly adapting to survive in their environments. Some plants have grown spines to protect themselves from herbivores. Plants that grow in cold regions grow close to the ground to avoid harsh winds.

26. What type of organizational pattern is the author using?

    [A] Cause and Effect

    [B] Generalization

    [C] Comparison and Contrast

    [D] Simple Listing

    [E] Analogy

The correct answer is A.
The author lists some ways in which plants have changed and the reasons why.

Rembrandt and Van Gogh were two Dutch painters. Both were from wealthy families. Both showed incredible talent at a young age. Van Gogh did not begin to paint seriously until he was twenty-seven. Rembrandt, on the other hand, had already completed many paintings by that age.

27. Which organizational pattern does the author use?

    [A] Comparison and Contrast

    [B] Simple Listing

    [C] Cause and Effect

    [D] Definition

    [E] Description

The correct answer is A.
Since the author is demonstrating how Rembrandt and Van Gogh were alike and how they were different, the correct answer is (A).

Charles Lindbergh had no intention of becoming a pilot. He was enrolled in the University of Wisconsin until a flying lesson changed the entire course of his life. He began his career as a pilot by performing daredevil stunts at fairs

28. The author wrote this paragraph primarily to:

    [A] describe

    [B] inform

    [C] entertain

    [D] narrate

    [E] analyze

The correct answer is B.
Since the author is simply telling us or informing us about the life of Charles Lindbergh, the correct answer here is (B).

29. Addressing someone absent or something inhuman as though present and able to respond describes a figure of speech known as:

[A] personification

[B] synecdoche

[C] metonymy

[D] apostrophe

[E] rhetorical strategy

The correct answer is A.
as it is the definition of personification.

(1) It was a cold and windy night. (2) Everyone was close around the fire in order to keep warm. (3) It was lonely for the little boy, who waited for his mother to bring him a marshmallow to toast on a stick. (4) His sister died just weeks ago and he really missed her.

30. In sentence (2), a better way to phrase "was close" could be:

[A] huddled

[B] gather

[C] stood

[D] left from

[E] none of these options are better

The correct answer is A.
Huddle means to get close, and at the end of that sentence, it describes that they were around the fire to keep warm. Thus, huddle is a better choice than B or C; D is the opposite of the activity being described.

31. In sentence (4), the author is describing what emotion?

[A] hunger

[B] happiness

[C] coldness

[D] sadness

[E] anger

The correct answer is D.
The end of the sentence talks about the subject really missing his sister, and there is no words that would describe anger at her being gone. If you did not read the sentence, you may try to go off of the prior question and guess coldness, but that would be wrong. Also, happiness is the opposite of what the author is conveying and is not a correct option.

> As she mused the pitiful vision of her mother's life laid its spell on the very quick of her being—that life of commonplace sacrifices closing in final craziness. She trembled as she heard again her mother's voice saying constantly with foolish insistence: Derevaun Seraun! Derevaun Seraun!
> ** [Derevaun Seraun means "The end of pleasure is pain!" (Gaelic)]

32. The following passage is written from which point of view?

[A] First person, narrator

[B] Second person, direct address

[C] Third person, omniscient

[D] First person, omniscient

[E] First person, direct address

The correct answer is C.
All of the options can be eliminated by seeing that the author uses the pronoun "she" which is third person. There is only one third person selection.

33. **To understand the origins of a word, one must study the:**

    [A] synonyms

    [B] inflections

    [C] phonetics

    [D] etymology

    [E] epidemiology

The correct answer is D.
As the definition of etymology is the study of the origins of words.

34. **Which is the best definition for syntax?**

    [A] The specific order of word choices by an author to create a particular mood or feeling in the reader

    [B] Writing that explains something thoroughly

    [C] The background or exposition for a short story or drama

    [D] Word choices that help teach a truth or moral

    [E] Proper elocution

The correct answer is A.
The definition of syntax is the specific order and particular word choices of an author to convey a mood or feeling to a reader.

COLLEGE COMPOSITION MODULAR

35. Which is the least true statement concerning an author's literary tone?

   [A] Tone is partly revealed through the selection of details.

   [B] Tone is the expression of the author's attitude toward his or her subject.

   [C] Tone can be expressed in a variety of ways by an author.

   [D] Tone in literature corresponds to the tone of voice a speaker uses.

   [E] Tone in literature is usually satiric or angry.

The correct answer is E.
As all of the options A through D are relevant to the definition of an author's tone, E - a very lopsided and opinionated option - is the correct answer.

36. Regarding the study of poetry, which elements are least applicable to all types of poetry?

   [A] Setting and audience

   [B] Theme and tone

   [C] Pattern and diction

   [D] Diction and rhyme scheme

   [E] Words and symbols

The correct answer is A.
Certain poems are very specific in their symbols, rhyme scheme, diction, pattern and theme. The best answer for which option is not as important to poetry is A.

There is no frigate like a book
To take us lands away,
Nor any coursers like a page
Of prancing poetry;
This traverse may the poorest take
Without oppress of toll;
How frugal is the chariot
That bears the human soul!

37. How many types of transport types does the author incorporate?

    [A] two

    [B] three

    [C] four

    [D] five

    [E] none

The correct answer is B
There are three modes of transport in the poem. This is further confirmed in the next question.

38. **If the words 'frigate, coursers, and chariot' were replaced with synonyms, what would the best choice of the following options include?**

   [A] Train, car, carriage

   [B] Train, horse, carriage

   [C] Ship, car, carriage

   [D] Ship, car, train

   [E] Ship, horse, carriage

The correct answer is E.
This is an analysis question to see if you understand synonyms and is important in the composition exam. Alternative words for frigate, coursers and chariot are ship, horse and carriage.

39. **What is a good paraphrase of "To take us lands away" that Ms. Dickinson writes in this poem?**

   [A] War makes it unsafe to travel, so we can just read about places.

   [B] Poems will drive us to save our souls.

   [C] Books can engage us to see new things

   [D] Authors can show us how to go on vacation.

   [E] It shows poems are short and fun.

The correct answer is C.
Books, and poems, can virtually take us anywhere that we can imagine.

Tyger! Tyger! burning bright
In the forests of the night,
What immortal hand or eye
Could frame thy fearful symmetry? (line 4)

In what distant deeps or skies
Burnt the fire of thine eyes?
On what wings dare he aspire?
What the hand dare seize the flame? (line 8)

And what shoulder, & what art,
Could twist the sinews of they heart?
And when thy heart began to beat,
What dread hand? & what dread feet? (line 12)

40. Sinews, in the third stanza, can be best compared to:

   [A] thread.

   [B] a cage.

   [C] rope.

   [D] heart strings or emotions.

   [E] burnt fire, from the second stanza.

The correct answer is D.
Sinews, while it is possible that anything from A through D could be correct, the only appropriate option is heart strings. Option E is simply misleading.

41. Another phrase for "deeps or skies" that would fit in this poem could be:

[A] caves or planes.

[B] trees or forests.

[C] seas or air.

[D] waves or wind.

[E] oceans or lakes.

The correct answer is C.
Again, this is about comprehension of the composition and your ability to identify appropriate synonyms in context of the selection. In the other pairs, one word may be accurate but the other option is not appropriate.

42. In line 7 of this poem, what word below most nearly means "aspire"?

[A] Soar.

[B] Plunge.

[C] Scheme.

[D] Travel.

[E] Admire.

The correct answer is A.
This is the best choice and the other options are not appropriate synonyms.

> These are morning matters, pictures you dream as the final wave heaves you up on the sand in the bright light and drying air. You remember pressure, and a curved sleep you rested against, soft, like a scallop in its shell. But the air hardens your skin; you stand; you leave the lighted shore to explore some dim headland, and soon you're lost in the leafy interior, intent, remembering nothing.
>
> I still think of that old tomcat, mornings, when I wake. Things are tamer now; I sleep with the window shut. The cats and our rites are gone and my life is changed, but the memory remains of something powerful playing over me. I wake expectant, hoping to see a new thing. If I'm lucky I might be jogged awake by a strange bird call. I dress in a hurry, imagining the yard flapping with auks, or flamingos. This morning it was a wood duck, down at the creek. It flew away.

43. The phrase, "like a scallop in its shell" is an example of:

[A] an irony.

[B] a simile.

[C] a metaphor.

[D] personification.

[E] euphemism.

The correct answer is C.
This is a definition type of question, and it is the only possible answer.

44. The phrase "the air hardens your skin" within the context of the passage most likely refers to what?

[A] The morning air woke the character up from dreaming.

[B] The scallop shell bed the character sleeps in has opened.

[C] The air dries out the character's skin.

[D] The coldness of the room turns off the brain of the character.

[E] The air turns the character's skin cold when the cat leaves the bed.

The correct answer is A.
The character describes waking up in the morning, and it is the closest rephrasing of the author's words.

One of the most difficult problems plaguing American education is the assessment of teachers. No one denies that teachers ought to be answerable for what they do, but what exactly does that mean? The Oxford American Dictionary defines accountability as: the obligation to give a reckoning or explanation for one's actions.

Does a student have to learn for teaching to have taken place? Historically, teaching has not been defined in this restrictive manner; the teacher was thought to be responsible for the quantity and quality of material covered and the way in which it was presented. However, some definitions of teaching now imply that students must learn in order for teaching to have taken place.

As a teacher who tries my best to keep current on all the latest teaching strategies, I believe that those teachers who do not bother even to pick up an educational journal every once in a while should be kept under close watch. There are many teachers out there who have been teaching for decades and refuse to change their ways even if research has proven that their methods are outdated and ineffective. There is no place in the profession of teaching for these types of individuals. It is time that the American educational system clean house, for the sake of our children

45. Where does the author get her definition of "accountability?"

[A] Webster's Dictionary

[B] Encyclopedia Brittanica

[C] Oxford Dictionary

[D] World Book Encyclopedia

[E] Wikipedia

The correct answer is C.
It is stated in the first paragraph.

46. In the second paragraph, the second sentence can best be described as:

[A] compound.

[B] complex.

[C] run-on.

[D] a fragment.

[E] compound-complex.

The correct answer is E.

A compound-complex sentence has two independent sentences are conjoined with the semi-colon.

47. Taite, Richard. "Five Things to Know About Recovery from Alcohol." *Psychology Today*. Web. (https://www.psychologytoday.com/blog/ending-addiction-good/201510/five-things-know-about-recovery-alcohol-or-drugs) October 16, 2015.

    In the citation, 16 October 2015 provides what information?

    [A] Date printed

    [B] Date accessed

    [C] Date placed on the Internet

    [D] Date the last person accessed it

    [E] None of these are correct

The correct answer is B.
The date it was accessed on the Internet.

48. Nelson, MD., Lewis S et al. Addressing the Opioid Epidemic. *JAMA*. 13 October 2015; 314(14): 1453-1454.

    The (14) refers to:

    [A] the fourteenth article in the magazine.

    [B] the fourteenth article published by this author.

    [C] there are fourteen articles on opioids in this issue.

    [D] there are fourteen authors.

    [E] This is the fourteenth issue in the series, in volume 314.

The correct answer is E
The citation for the correct volume.

49. In the *JAMA* citation previously, 1454-1454 refers to what?

[A] The number of issues this has magazine has published.

[B] How many articles have discussed opioids in the magazine's history

[C] Page numbers for this citation.

[D] Ongoing page numbers for the table of contents in this magazine.

[E] Tagnemics

The correct answer is C.
As it lists the correct page numbers for this article in the JAMA periodical.

50. The word 'print' at the end of a ci-tation is a reference for:

[A] the article is from a newspaper.

[B] the article is from a book.

[C] the article is from a periodical.

[D] the article was not accessed online.

[E] none of these selections are accurate.

The correct answer is E.
As A through D are all possibly accurate, option E is correct because you need more information to choose which print item is correct.

51. Ciottone, Gregory et al. *Disaster Medicine, Second Edition*. Elsevier, digital. September 24, 2015. ISBN-13: 978-0323286657

    The "et al" refers to:

    [A] no hard cover copy is available.

    [B] the content is digital only.

    [C] this has been published in the United States.

    [D] that Ciottone is the editor.

    [E] more than one author should be listed.

The correct answer is E.
That more than one author should be listed.

52. Serra, Luigi. *Domencio Zampieri, detto Il Domenichino*. E. Calzone, ed. 1909. Princeton University.

    Who is the editor?

    [A] Serra Luigi

    [B] Luigi Serra

    [C] E. Calzone

    [D] Domenico Zampieri

    [E] Domenichino

The correct answer is C.
As Calzone is the editor. Luigi Serra is the author, and D and E are the names and alias of the artist about whom Serra writes. Regardless of language, the citation formats are the same.

53. Cattong, Bruce. "Grant and Lee: A Study in Contrasts." *The Bedford Reader.* 9th ed. Ed. X. J. Kennedy et al. Boston: Bedford/St. Martin's, 2006. 258-61. Print. This is an ex-ample of what kind of citation for-mat?

   [A] MLA

   [B] APA

   [C] Chicago

   [D] Turabian

   [E] None of these

The correct answer is A.
As this is MLA citation format.

54. Aloise-Young, P. A. (1993). The development of self-presentation: Self-promotion in 6- to 10- year-old children. *Social Cognition, II*, 201-222. This is an example of what kind of citation?

   [A] MLA

   [B] APA

   [C] Chicago

   [D] Turabian

   [E] None of these

The correct answer is B.
As this is APA citation format.

55. Smith, John Maynard. "The Origin of Altruism." *Nature* 393 (1998): 639-40. This is an example of which kind of citation?

   [A] MLA

   [B] APA

   [C] Chicago

   [D] Turabian

   [E] None of these

The correct answer is C
as this is Chicago citation format.

"(1)These good folk, who have only just begun to think and act for themselves, are slow as yet to grasp the changed conditions which should attach them to these theories. (2)They have only reached those ideas which conduce to economy and to physical welfare; in the future, if someone else carries on this work of mine, they will come to understand the principles that serve to uphold and preserve public order and justice. (3)As a matter of fact, it is not sufficient to be an honest man, you must appear to be honest in the eyes of others. (4)Society does not live by moral ideas alone; its existence depends upon actions in harmony with those ideas."

56. The first sentence can best be described as:

   [A] compound.

   [B] complex.

   [C] run-on.

   [D] a fragment.

   [E] compound-complex.

The correct answer is B.
The writer uses expressions such as "protective gear" and "child's protection" to emphasize this.

COLLEGE COMPOSITION MODULAR

57. The second sentence can best be described as:

[A] compound.

[B] complex.

[C] run-on.

[D] a fragment.

[E] compound-complex.

The correct answer is E.
There is a semi-colon and two independent phrases with dependent clauses - this describes compound-complex.

58. Warren, Robert Penn. *All The King's Men.* **New York: Harcourt, Brace, 1946. Print. p415.**

The p415 sentence can best be described as:

[A] the number of pages in the book used.

[B] the last page the reader completed.

[C] the citation for a portion referenced in the document.

[D] the last page of dialogue in the book.

[E] none of the choices are accurate.

The correct answer is C.
The page number reference shows where the citation is located in the book.

59. United States. Cong. Senate. Appropriations. Schedule of Serial Set Volumes. 112 Cong., 2 sess. S. Doc. 15383A. Washington DC: U.S. Senate, 2012. Web.

    15383A can best be described as:

    [A] amendment number.

    [B] edit number.

    [C] page number.

    [D] volume number

    [E] document number.

The correct answer is E.
Congressional documents are numbered and in this citation, the abbreviation prior to the number explains this is a document number.

60. Bell, A. G. (1876). *U.S. Patent No. 174,465*. Washington, DC: U.S. Patent and Trademark Office.

    This is the patent citation for:

    [A] a lightbulb.

    [B] train brakes.

    [C] relativity.

    [D] telephone.

    [E] telegraph.

The correct answer is D.
As this is a patent, the name listed is the patent holder, so outside information again needs be used. Alexander Graham Bell invented the telephone.

61. Mozart, W. A. (1970). *Die Zauberflöte* [The magic flute], K. 620 [Vocal score]. Munich, Germany: Becksche Verlagsbuchhandlung. (Original work published 1791).

    The "K. 620" is the citation for:

    [A] the 620th note in the musical score.

    [B] opus, or work number.

    [C] the number of instruments required.

    [D] the number of performers required, including voices.

    [E] none of these are correct.

The correct answer is B.
When citing music, "K." is the abbreviation during the Classical era for the German word, Kochel-Verzeichnis, and is the "opus" (latin for "work" and followed by a number).

62. Harris, Ann Sutherland (PhD). Seventeenth Century Art and Architecture. Lawrence King Publishing, 2005. pxv.   The "pxv" is:

    [A] the version label.

    [B] the author's work number.

    [C] the date in Roman numeral.

    [D] the preface page number.

    [E] none of these are correct.

The correct answer is D.
in reference to preface pages, which are denoted with small Roman numerals.

63. "Higher education has become a central part of the process by which high-income families can seek to assure that their children are more likely to have high incomes." Taylor, Timothy. How Higher Education Perpetuates Intergenerational Inequality. March 4, 2015. http://conversableeconomist.blogspot.com/2015/03/how-higher-education-perpetuates.html Accessed August 8, 2015.

    When prefaced with "61" in superscript before this phrase and listed on the same page, it would be referred to as a(an):

    [A] footnote.

    [B] endnote.

    [C] footer.

    [D] header.

    [E] none of these are correct.

The correct answer is A.

This writer has often been asked to tutor hospitalized children with cystic fibrosis. While undergoing all the precautionary measures to see these children (i.e. scrubbing thoroughly and donning sterilized protective gear- for the child's protection), she has often wondered why their parents subject these children to the pressures of schooling and trying to catch up on what they have missed because of hospitalization, which is a normal part of cystic fibrosis patients' lives. These children undergo so many tortuous treatments a day that it seems cruel to expect them to learn as normal children do, especially with their life expectancies being as short as they are.

64. What is the author's main purpose?

   [A] To inform

   [B] To entertain

   [C] To describe

   [D] To narrate

   [E] To record

The correct answer is C.
The author states that she wonders "why parents subject these children to the pressures of schooling" and that "it seems cruel to expect them to learn as normal children do." In making these statements she appears to be expressing the belief that these children should not have to do what "normal" children do. They have enough to deal with – their illness itself.

65. What is the main idea of this passage?

   [A] There is a lot of preparation involved in visiting a patient of cystic fibrosis.

   [B] Children with cystic fibrosis are incapable of living normal lives.

   [C] Certain concessions should be made for children with cystic fibrosis.

   [D] Children with cystic fibrosis die young.

   [E] The specific ways you must decontaminate yourself to visit children.

The correct answer is C.
The author is simply describing her experience in working with children with cystic fibrosis.

COLLEGE COMPOSITION MODULAR

66. What is meant by the word "precautionary" in the second sentence?

    [A] Careful

    [B] Protective

    [C] Medical

    [D] Sterilizing

    [E] Reckless

The correct answer is B.

67. What is the author's tone in the previous passage?

    [A] Sympathetic

    [B] Cruel

    [C] Disbelieving

    [D] Cheerful

    [E] Cautious

The correct answer is C.
The author appears to simply be stating the facts.

68. What type of organizational pattern is the author using in the selection about cystic fibrosis?

    [A] Classification

    [B] Explanation

    [C] Comparison and Contrast

    [D] Cause and Effect

    [E] Entertaining

The correct answer is D.
The author has taken a subject and shown how one disease affects the childrens' lives in a variety of ways.

69. How is the author so familiar with the procedures used when visiting a child with cystic fibrosis?

   [A] She has read about it.

   [B] She works in a hospital.

   [C] She is the parent of one.

   [D] She often tutors them.

   [E] She had it as a child.

The correct answer is D.
The author states in the selection that she tutors children with cystic fibrosis.

   Disciplinary practices have been found to affect diverse areas of child development such as the acquisition of moral values, obedience to authority, and performance at school. Even though the dictionary has a specific definition of the word "discipline," it is still open to interpretation by people of different cultures.
   There are four types of disciplinary styles: assertion of power, withdrawal of love, reasoning, and permissiveness. Assertion of power involves the use of force to discourage unwanted behavior. Withdrawal of love involves making the love of a parent conditional on a child's good behavior. Reasoning involves persuading the child to behave one way rather than another. Permissiveness involves allowing the child to do as he or she pleases and face the consequences of his/her actions

70. What is the meaning of the word "diverse" in the first sentence?

   [A] Many

   [B] Related to children

   [C] Disciplinary

   [D] Moral

   [E] Racially disparate

The correct answer is A.
As it affects many areas of child development, like the ones mentioned at the end of the sentence.

71. **What organizational structure is used in the first sentence of the second paragraph?**

   [A] Addition

   [B] Explanation

   [C] Definition

   [D] Simple Listing

   [E] Argumentative

The correct answer is D.
Given the options, the correct answer is D - simple listing.

72. **What is the author's tone?**

   [A] Disbelieving

   [B] Angry

   [C] Informative

   [D] Optimistic

   [E] None of these are correct.

The correct answer is C.
The piece is informative about the topic. The other options are emotional rather than descriptive about style.

73. **What is the overall organizational pattern of this passage?**

   [A] Generalization

   [B] Cause and Effect

   [C] Addition

   [D] Summary

   [E] Informational

The correct answer is E.
As in the previous question, the correct answer is informational, answer E.

COLLEGE COMPOSITION MODULAR

One of the most difficult problems plaguing American education is the assessment of teachers. No one denies that teachers ought to be answerable for what they do, but what exactly does that mean? The Oxford American Dictionary defines accountability as: the obligation to give a reckoning or explanation for one's actions.

Does a student have to learn for teaching to have taken place? Historically, teaching has not been defined in this restrictive manner; the teacher was thought to be responsible for the quantity and quality of material covered and the way in which it was presented. However, some definitions of teaching now imply that students must learn in order for teaching to have taken place.

As a teacher who tries my best to keep current on all the latest teaching strategies, I believe that those teachers who do not bother even to pick up an educational journal every once in a while should be kept under close watch. There are many teachers out there who have been teaching for decades and refuse to change their ways even if research has proven that their methods are outdated and ineffective. There is no place in the profession of teaching for these types of individuals. It is time that the American educational system clean house, for the sake of our children

74. What is the meaning of the word "reckoning" in the third sentence?

   [A] Thought

   [B] Answer

   [C] Obligation

   [D] Explanation

   [E] Prayerful

The correct answer is D.
As given in the definition - right after the word "reckoning".

COLLEGE COMPOSITION MODULAR

75. What is the organizational pattern of the second paragraph?

[A] Cause and Effect

[B] Classification

[C] Addition

[D] Explanation

[E] None of these things

The correct answer is D.
As an explanation is the organizational pattern for that paragraph.

76. What is the author's overall organizational pattern?

[A] Classification

[B] Cause and Effect

[C] Definition

[D] Comparison and Contrast

[E] None of these things

The correct answer is E.
For the overall organizational pattern is not one of the options listed.

77. The author's tone in the passage on the previous page is one of:

[A] Disbelief

[B] Excitement

[C] Support

[D] Concern

[E] Empathy

The correct answer is D.
The author's tone is concern, or D.

78. What is meant by the word "plagu- ing" in the first sentence of the previous passage?

[A] Causing problems

[B] Causing illness

[C] Causing anger

[D] Causing failure

[E] Causing unrest

The correct answer is A.
Another way of saying causing problems.

(1)London was our present point of rest; we determined to remain several months in this wonderful and celebrated city. (2)Clerval desired the intercourse of the men of genius and talent who flourished at this time; but this was with me a secondary object; I was principally occupied with the means of obtaining the information necessary for the completion of my promise, and quickly availed myself of the letters of introduction that I had brought with me, addressed to the most distinguished natural philosophers.

79. The fourth word in the second sentence, "intercourse", refers to:

[A] intimate relations between two people

[B] interactive conversation

[C] an in-depth artist's class

[D] a secondary outcome after a gift is given in Victorian times

[E] none of these options are correct

The correct answer is B.
An interactive conversation. While the other answers may indeed be possible definitions, context is important to select the correct answer.

80. **In the previous passage (referenced in question 79 also), what is the main theme of the selection?**

   [A] Travel discussions that compare where the characters have been

   [B] Discussions about information gathering and solving an issue

   [C] Meeting gentlemen for coffee

   [D] Identifying the thought-leaders of the time

   [E] How the travelers were going to spend their time in the city.

The correct answer is E.
While B is a possible answer, the most correct and appropriate answer is E, how they are going to spend time in the city, using their time wisely.

Read the following paragraph and answer the two questions that follow.

> "Oh, Madam Mina," he said, "how can I say what I owe to you? This paper is as sunshine. It opens the gate to me. I am dazed, I am dazzled, with so much light, and yet clouds roll in behind the light every time. But that you do not, cannot comprehend. Oh, but I am grateful to you, you so clever woman. Madame," he said this very solemnly, "if ever Abraham Van Helsing can do anything for your or yours, I trust you will let me know. It will be pleasure and delight if I may serve you as a friend, as a friend, but all I have ever learned, all I can ever do, shall be for you and those you love. There are darknesses in life, and there are lights. You are one of the lights. You are one of the lights. You will have a happy life and a good life, and your husband will be blessed in you."

81. **The phase "This paper is as sunshine. It opens the gate to me." means**

   [A] Madam Mina was holding a light in the next sentence that made it seem as bright as day.

   [B] the character speaking has been given new glasses with which to see the sunshine.

   [C] the character speaking simply has new information that is helpful to him.

   [D] that he is making a joke to Madam Mina.

   [E] none of these things.

The correct answer is C.
As the new information was helpful to him.

82. Using the information only presented in the selection, he tone used by the author suggests:

   [A] Madam Mina gave Van Helsing information unwillingly.

   [B] one of the characters has been drinking a love potion.

   [C] Madam Mina wants nothing to do with Van Helsing.

   [D] that Van Helsing is making fun to Madam Mina.

   [E] Van Helsing is enamored with Madam Mina because of her helpfulness.

The correct answer is E
as Van Helsing effuses complements after Madam is helpful to him.

> "Mornings, he likes to sit in his new leather chair by his new living room window, looking out across the rooftops and chimney pots, the clotheslines and telegraph lines and office towers. It's the first time Manhattan, from high above, hasn't crushed him with desire. On the contrary the view makes him feel smug. All those people down there, striving, hustling, pushing, shoving, busting to get what Willie's already got. In spades. He lights a cigarette, blows a jet of smoke against the window. Suckers."

83. The subject in this passage is

   [A] a character, and seems to be the lead in the story.

   [B] a supporting character.

   [C] has the attitude of a criminal.

   [D] female.

   [E] has been poor his whole life.

The correct answer is A.
The other options are not substantiated by the items in the passage, so A is the best choice

84. What kind of description is the author providing of this scene?

[A] Backstory of the character.

[B] A characterization of what the character is like.

[C] A narrative, with the end of the selection giving thoughts in the first person.

[D] The unreliable narrative about a character.

[E] The author is using a persuasive argument.

The correct answer is C
which is provides the definition of a narrative.
Backstory describes the past and he is speaking in the present. There are no personal descriptions and there is no topic that the character is trying to persuade the reader to adopt. And lastly, the leap of assuming the character is unreliable is not supported by the passage.

85. What types of words are "striving, hustling, pushing, shoving, bustling"?

[A] Adjectives

[B] Adverbs

[C] Nouns

[D] Gerunds

[E] Verbs

The correct answer is E.
This is definition and the action words are all verbs.

86. **If you had to explain the phrase "crushed him" in the paragraph above and context of the paragraph, what would be the best appropriate explanation?**

   [A] The city sustained him with all the opportunity available.

   [B] The city called to him to be part of its life.

   [C] The city complimented him for everything he has achieved.

   [D] The city had energized him to get what he felt he deserved.

   [E] The city smothered him with all of its offerings.

The correct answer is E.
As the city was so attractive to him with options and in this selection, the character describes how the city used to be oppressive to him with its options.

87. **The author portrays the attitude of the character toward the people on the street below as:**

   [A] Condescending.

   [B] Sarcastic.

   [C] Affectionate.

   [D] Tolerant.

   [E] Encouraged.

The correct answer is A.
C, D and E are too "positive" and B is not applicable.

Solemnly he came forward and mounted the round gunrest. He faced about and blessed gravely thrice the tower, the surrounding country and the awaking mountains. Then, catching sight of Stephen Dedalus, he bent towards him and made rapid crosses in the air, gurgling in his throat and shaking his head. Stephen Dedalus, displeased and sleepy, leaned his arms on the top of the staircase and looked coldly at the shaking gurgling face that blessed him, equine in its length, and at the light untenured hair, grained and hued like pale oak.

88. The likely setting for this paragraph is:

   [A] a hospital.

   [B] the battlefield.

   [C] Stephen's bedroom.

   [D] beside the river.

   [E] unable to be determined.

The correct answer is E.
While it may seem like a battlefield, the characters on on a stairwell (and there would likely not be stairs on a field). There is no indication that they are in a bedroom or a hospital, so these answers are blatantly wrong

89. The description of the main character's hair leads to the conclusion that he is:

   [A] a blonde.

   [B] a brunette.

   [C] has black hair.

   [D] has grained black and white hair.

   [E] is bald.

The correct answer is A.
Blonde, as the last lines describe his hair as the color of pale oak. Thus, brunette as well as black or black and white are wrong. Bald could be construed from "hued", but hue means color and other indicators also point to blonde.

COLLEGE COMPOSITION MODULAR

90. The phrase "equine in its length" to describe the main character:

[A] is complementary as horses were very valuable to soldiers.

[B] could be considered sarcastic.

[C] reveals the way Stephen feels about the main character, which is not fond or complementary.

[D] was a common description of the time period.

[E] is used repeatedly in this book.

The correct answer is C.
It is an insult. While A is true that horses were valuable, the correlation to a person's looks was not meant to be flattering. Sarcasm is not applicable in this example, and we cannot determine if it was either a common description of the time period or used elsewhere in the book.

ENGLISH LITERATURE

Description of the Examination
The English Literature examination covers material from the past 2,500 years. The different critical abilities and literary terms identified in a semester-long literature course are covered in this examination.

College Literature courses go beyond a general understanding of English to incorporate analytical terms as well as the ability to interpret and understand multiple genres of writing. The exam covers topics such as the identification of poetic devices and authors, appropriate application of literary devices, and the terms to describe effects in passages.

The examination contains approximately 95 questions to be answered in 90 minutes. Any time candidates spend on tutorials and providing personal information is in addition to the actual testing time.

This practice examination is intended to help the student practice at the appropriate level of difficulty to do well on the CLEP English Literature exam. These questions do not actually appear on the CLEP English Literature exam.

There is also an optional essay component of this exam; that will not be outlined in this study guide as each school decides if they will accept this portion and they grade it independently.

Knowledge and Skills Required
The subject matter of the English Literature examination is drawn from the following topics. The percentages next to the main topics indicate the approximate percentage of exam questions on that topic.

35%–40%	**Knowledge**
	• pertaining to various literary devices and content knowledge, requiring a strong understanding of English Language Arts.
50%-65%	**Ability**
	• to identify mood, context, excerpt origin, style, and understand examples of literary criticism

On the next page, the sample test begins. There are 90 questions that you must answer in less than 90 minutes. Remember, your goals for this test are those questions you answer accurately; it is not based on how many are incorrect. Take your time, and good luck.

ENGLISH LITERATURE

DIRECTIONS: Read each item and select the best response.

1. An example of Restoration writing is:

    [A] *The New Atlantis*

    [B] *Hamlet*

    [C] *Leviathan*

    [D] *The Principia*

    [E] *Gulliver's Travels*

2. The following passage is written from which point of view?

    As she mused the pitiful vision of her mother's life laid its spell on the very quick of her being—that life of commonplace sacrifices closing in final craziness. She trembled as she heard again her mother's voice saying constantly with foolish insistence: Derevaun Seraun! Derevaun Seraun!*
        * ["The end of pleasure is pain!" (Gaelic)]

    [A] First person, narrator

    [B] Second person, direct address

    [C] Third person, omniscient

    [D] First person, omniscient

    [E] First person, direct address

3. The device of personification is used in which example below?

    [A] "Beg me no beggary by soul or parents, whining dog!"

    [B] "We few, we happy few, we band of brothers."

    [C] "O wind thy horn, thou proud fellow."

    [D] "And that one talent which is death to hide."

    [E] "Happiness sped through the halls cajoling as it went."

4. Which of the following is not one of the four forms of discourse?

    [A] Exposition

    [B] Description

    [C] Rhetoric

    [D] Persuasion

    [E] Narration

ENGLISH LITERATURE

5. "Every one must pass through Vanity Fair to get to the celestial city" is an allusion to a:

   [A] Chinese folk tale

   [B] Norse saga

   [C] British allegory

   [D] German fairy tale

   [E] French drama

6. To understand the origins of a word, one must study the:

   [A] synonyms

   [B] inflections

   [C] phonetics

   [D] etymology

   [E] epidemiology

   And more to lulle him in his slumber soft,
   A trickling streame from high rock tumbling downe,
   And ever-drizzling raine upon the loft.
   Mixt with a murmuring winde, much like the sowne
   Of swarming bees, did cast him in a swowne
   No other noyse, nor peoples troublous cryes.
   As still are wont t'annoy the walle'd towne,
   Might there be heard: but careless Quiet lyes,
   Wrapt in eternall silence farre from enemyes.

7. Which term best describes the form of the poetic excerpt?

   [A] Ballad

   [B] Elegy

   [C] Octava rima

   [D] Spenserian stanza

   [E] Eulogy

   My galley charg'ed with forgetfulness
   Through sharp seas, in winter night doth pass
   'Tween rock and rock; and eke mine enemy, alas,
   That is my lord steereth with cruelness.
   And every oar a thought in readiness,
   As though that death were light in such a case.
   An endless wind doth tear the sail apace
   Or forc'ed sighs and trusty fearfulness.
   A rain of tears, a cloud of dark disdain,
   Hath done the wearied cords great hindrance,
   Wreathed with error and eke with ignorance.
   The stars be hid that led me to this pain
   Drowned is reason that should me consort,
   And I remain despairing of the poet.

ENGLISH LITERATURE

8. **Which term accurately names the form of the sonnet?**

    [A] Petrarchan or Italian sonnet

    [B] Shakespearean or Elizabethan sonnet

    [C] Romantic sonnet

    [D] Spenserian sonnet

    [E] Dante's sonnet

9. **Arthur Miller wrote *The Crucible* as a parallel to what twentieth-century event?**

    [A] Sen. McCarthy's House Un-American Activities Committee hearings

    [B] The Cold War

    [C] The fall of the Berlin Wall

    [D] The Persian Gulf War

    [E] The Great Depression

10. **Which of the following is not a characteristic of a fable?**

    [A] Animals that feel and talk like humans

    [B] Happy solutions to human dilemmas

    [C] Teaches a moral or standard for behavior

    [D] Illustrates specific people or groups without directly naming them

    [E] All of these are characteristics of fables

11. **Which of the following was not written by Jonathan Swift?**

    [A] *A Voyage to Lilliput*

    [B] *A Modest Proposal*

    [C] *Samson Agonistes*

    [D] *A Tale of a Tub*

    [E] *Drapier's Letters*

12. **Which is the best definition for diction?**

   [A] The specific word choices of an author to create a particular mood or feeling in the reader

   [B] Writing that explains something thoroughly

   [C] The background or exposition for a short story or drama

   [D] Word choices that help teach a truth or moral

   [E] Proper elocution

13. **Which is an untrue statement about literary themes?**

   [A] The theme is the central idea in a literary work.

   [B] A theme can be a thematic concept.

   [C] All parts of the work (plot, setting, mood) should contribute to the theme in some way.

   [D] By analyzing the various elements of the work, the reader should be able to arrive at an indirectly stated theme.

   [E] The theme is always stated directly somewhere in the text.

14. **Which is the least true statement concerning an author's literary tone?**

   [A] Tone is partly revealed through the selection of details.

   [B] Tone is the expression of the author's attitude toward his or her subject.

   [C] Tone in literature is usually satiric or angry.

   [D] Tone in literature corresponds to the tone of voice a speaker uses.

   [E] Tone can be expressed in a variety of ways by an author.

15. **Regarding the study of poetry, which elements are least applicable to all types of poetry?**

   [A] Setting and audience

   [B] Theme and tone

   [C] Pattern and diction

   [D] Diction and rhyme scheme

   [E] Words and symbols

ENGLISH LITERATURE

16. Which of the following definitions best describes a parable?

   [A] A short, entertaining account of some happening, usually using talking animals as characters

   [B] A slow, sad song, poem or prose work expressing lamentation

   [C] An extended narrative work expressing universal truths concerning domestic life

   [D] A short, simple story of an occurrence of a familiar kind, from which a moral or religious lesson may be drawn

   [E] A long, involved story that reveals hidden lessons after much discussion and deliberation.

17. Which of the following is the best description of existentialism?

   [A] The philosophical doctrine that matter is the only reality and that everything in the world (including thought, will, and feeling) is rightly explained exclusively in terms of matter

   [B] A philosophy that views things as they should be or as one would wish them to be

   [C] A philosophical and literary movement, variously religious and atheistic, stemming from Kierkegaard and represented by Sartre

   [D] The belief that all events are determined by fate and are hence inevitable

   [E] The fear of losing one's identity, suspicion of activities and aggressions of others.

ENGLISH LITERATURE

18. **Which of the following is the best definition of imagism?**

   [A] A doctrine teaching that comfort is the only goal of value in life

   [B] The rejection of all religious and moral principles, often in the belief that life is meaningless and just represented by images

   [C] The belief that people are motivated entirely by self-centeredness

   [D] The doctrine that the human mind cannot know whether there is a God, an ultimate cause, or anything beyond material phenomena

   [E] A movement in modern poetry (c. 1910–1918) characterized by precise, concrete images, free verse, and suggestion rather than complete statement

19. **Which choice below best defines naturalism?**

   [A] A belief that the writer or artist should apply scientific objectivity in his or her observation and treatment of life without imposing values or judgments

   [B] The doctrine that teaches that the existing world is the best to be hoped for

   [C] The doctrine teaching that God is not a personality, but that all laws, forces, and manifestations of the universe are God-related

   [D] A philosophical doctrine professing that the truth of all knowledge must constantly be reexamined

   [E] A belief that enhancing a character's surroundings with the environment will improve the reader's understanding

ENGLISH LITERATURE

20. The tendency to emphasize and value the qualities and peculiarities of life in a particular geographic area exemplifies:

    [A] pragmatism

    [B] regionalism

    [C] pantheism

    [D] abstract expressionism

    [E] utilitarianism

21. The arrangement of words in sentences best describes:

    [A] style

    [B] discourse

    [C] thesis

    [D] syntax

    [E] none of the above

22. The substitution of "went to his rest" for "died" is an example of:

    [A] bowdlerism

    [B] jargon

    [C] euphemism

    [D] malapropism

    [E] simile

23. Explanatory or informative discourse is:

    [A] exposition

    [B] narration

    [C] persuasion

    [D] description

    [E] discussion

24. A conversation between two or more people is called a:

    [A] parody

    [B] dialogue

    [C] monologue

    [D] analogy

    [E] diatribe

25. "Clean as a whistle" and "easy as falling off a log" are examples of:

    [A] semantics

    [B] parody

    [C] clichés

    [D] irony

    [E] satire

ENGLISH LITERATURE

26. Addressing someone absent or something inhuman as though present and able to respond describes a figure of speech known as:

    [A] personification

    [B] synecdoche

    [C] metonymy

    [D] apostrophe

    [E] rhetorical strategy

27. Slang or jargon expressions associated with a particular ethnic, age, socioeconomic, or professional group reflect:

    [A] aphorisms

    [B] allusions

    [C] idioms

    [D] euphemisms

    [E] stereotypes

Question 28

The characters of the novel also show how deeply it has been meditated; for, though none of them may excite the personal interest which clings to Sam Weller or little Dombey, they are better fitted to each other and the story in which they appear than is usual with Dickens. They all combine to produce the unity of impression which the work leaves on the mind. Individually they will rank among the most original of the author's creations.
- *The Atlantic Monthly*, 1861

28. In line 1, the critic refers to a particular novel by Charles Dickens. Which one?

    [A] *Great Expectations*

    [B] *The Old Curiosity Shop*

    [C] *David Copperfield*

    [D] *A Christmas Carol*

    [E] *Oliver Twist*

ENGLISH LITERATURE

29. Which event triggered the beginning of Modern English?

   [A] Conquest of England by the Normans in 1066

   [B] Introduction of the printing press to the British Isles

   [C] Publication of Samuel Johnson's lexicon

   [D] The American Revolution

   [E] Creation of the British East India Company

30. Which of the following is not true about the English language?

   [A] English is the easiest language to learn.

   [B] English is the least inflected language.

   [C] English has the most extensive vocabulary of any language.

   [D] English originated as a Germanic tongue.

   [E] A new word is added to the English Dictionary every two hours.

31. Match each of the following poets to the poem that he or she wrote.
      I.   Maya Angelou
      II. e. e. cummings
      III. Andrew Marvell
      IV. Sylvia Plath

   "To His Coy Mistress" _____

   "[in Just-]" _____

   "Phenomenal Woman" _____

   "Lady Lazarus" _____

32. Children's literature became established as a distinct genre in the:

   [A] sixteenth century

   [B] seventeenth century

   [C] eighteenth century

   [D] nineteenth century

   [E] twentieth century

ENGLISH LITERATURE

33. **What is the main form of discourse in this passage?**

    "It would have been hard to find a passer-by more wretched in appearance. He was a man of middle height, stout and hardy, in the strength of maturity; he might have been forty-six or seven. A slouched leather cap hid half his face, bronzed by the sun and wind, and dripping with sweat."

    [A] Description

    [B] Narration

    [C] Exposition

    [D] Persuasion

    [E] Foreshadowing

34. **Oral debate is most closely associated with which form of literary discourse?**

    [A] Description

    [B] Exposition

    [C] Narration

    [D] Persuasion

    [E] Poetic

35. **Which of the following works is a satire?**

    [A] Boris Pasternak's Dr. Zhivago

    [B] Albert Camus's The Stranger

    [C] Henry David Thoreau's "On the Duty of Civil Disobedience"

    [D] Benjamin Franklin's "Rules by Which a Great Empire May Be Reduced to a Small One"

    [E] C. S. Lewis' Prince Caspian

36. **Charles Dickens, Robert Browning, and Robert Louis Stevenson were:**

    [A] Classicists

    [B] Medievalists

    [C] Elizabethans

    [D] Absurdists

    [E] Victorians

ENGLISH LITERATURE

37. Which of the following is a characteristic of blank verse?

[A] Meter in iambic pentameter

[B] Clearly specified rhyme scheme

[C] Lack of figurative language

[D] Unspecified rhythm

[E] Presence of rhyming couplets

38. Which of the following is the correct chronological order of authors?

[A] Defoe, Descartes, Dumas

[B] Descartes, Dumas, Defoe

[C] Dumas, Defoe, Descartes

[D] Defoe, Descartes, Dumas

[E] Descartes, Defoe, Dumas

39. Her mother was jailed in Newgate Prison, given a reprieve and sent to America. Living with a foster mother, she grows up to be employed in a household where both brothers claim to love her, and she marries the younger brother. After the death of one of her children, she learns that her mother in law is really her biological mother - so her husband is her half-brother. What novel is described by this plot summary?

[A] *Pride and Prejudice*

[B] *Moll Flanders*

[C] *Wuthering Heights*

[D] *Novum Organum*

[E] *Sons and Lovers*

40. A passage about death and idyllic rural life is called a:

[A] ballad

[B] sonnet

[C] pastoral elegy

[D] metafiction

[E] lyric

41. The correct order of the following authors by birth is:

[A] Alexander Pope, Samuel Johnson, William Shakespeare, John Donne, William Thackeray

[B] William Shakespeare, John Donne, Samuel Johnson, Alexander Pope, William Thackeray

[C] John Donne, William Shakespeare, Alexander Pope, Samuel Johnson, William Thackeray

[D] William Shakespeare, John Donne, Alexander Pope, Samuel Johnson, William Thackeray

[E] John Donne, William Shakespeare, Samuel Johnson, Alexander Pope, William Thackeray

A mote it is to trouble the mind's eye.
In the most high and palmy state of Rome,
A little ere the mightiest Julius fell,
The graves stood tenantless and the sheeted dead
Did squeak and gibber in the Roman streets:
As stars with trains of fire and dews of blood,
Disasters in the sun; and the moist star
Upon whose influence Neptune's empire stands
Was sick almost to doomsday with eclipse:
And even the like precurse of fierce events,
As harbingers preceding still the fates
And prologue to the omen coming on,
Have heaven and earth together demonstrated
Unto our climatures and countrymen. o
But soft, behold! lo, where it comes again!

42. Who speaks these lines?

[A] Horatio

[B] Romeo

[C] Hamlet

[D] Othello

[E] Macbeth

43. A collection of twenty stories inspired by the Hundred Years War was written by:

[A] Walter Scott

[B] John Milton

[C] John Donne

[D] William Wordsworth

[E] Geoffrey Chaucer

These good folk, who have only just begun to think and act for themselves, are slow as yet to grasp the changed conditions which should attach them to these theories. They have only reached those ideas which

ENGLISH LITERATURE

conduce to economy and to physical welfare; in the future, if someone else carries on this work of mine, they will come to understand the principles that serve to uphold and preserve public order and justice. As a matter of fact, it is not sufficient to be an honest man, you must appear to be honest in the eyes of others. Society does not live by moral ideas alone; its existence depends upon actions in harmony with those ideas.

44. The passage describes:

    [A] A judge's verdict

    [B] A tax collector's dilemma

    [C] The community view of a doctor

    [D] A king's sovereign rights

    [E] None of these are correct.

Questions 45-47

London was our present point of rest; we determined to remain several months in this wonderful and celebrated city. Clerval desired the intercourse *(Line 4)* of the men of genius and talent who flourished at this time; but this was with me a secondary object; I was principally occupied with the means of obtaining the information necessary for the completion of my promise, and quickly availed myself of the letters of introduction that I had brought with me, addressed to the most distinguished natural philosophers.

45. This is a passage written by:

    [A] Mary Shelley

    [B] Charles Dickens

    [C] Jane Austen

    [D] Percy Shelley

    [E] Willa Cather

46. What is the main theme of the selection?

    [A] Travel discussions that compare where the characters have been

    [B] Discussions about information gathering and solving an issue

    [C] Meeting gentlemen for coffee

    [D] Identifying the thought-leaders of the time

    [E] How the traveler were going to select the next city they visit

47. In line 4 of the selection, intercourse means:

    [A] crossroads

    [B] relationship

    [C] discussion

    [D] meeting place

    [E] sexual relations

ENGLISH LITERATURE

48. **An example of a metaphysical poet would be:**

    [A] Christopher Marlowe

    [B] George Peele

    [C] William Shakespeare

    [D] John Donne

    [E] George Cascoigne

49. **An example of a cavalier poet would be:**

    [A] Richard Lovelace

    [B] Mary Sidney Hebert

    [C] Lancelot Andrewes

    [D] John Milton

    [E] Hugh Latimer

50. **An example of a Jacobean poet would be:**

    [A] John Bale

    [B] Margaret Cavendish

    [C] John Skelton

    [D] John Heywood

    [E] Nicolas Udall

51. **Charles Darwin did not write which of the following?**

    [A] *The Voyage of the Beagle*

    [B] *The Origin of the Species*

    [C] *The Descent of Man*

    [D] *Bureaucracy*

    [E] He only wrote two of these.

52. **Which of the following was not actually written by Lewis Carroll?**

    [A] *Alice's Adventures in Wonderland*

    [B] *Through the Looking Glass*

    [C] *The Hunting of the Snark*

    [D] *Sylvie and Bruno*

    [E] *After Wonderland*

53. **Which of the following is not a mode of English literature?**

    [A] epistolary

    [B] picaresque

    [C] novella

    [D] melodramatic

    [E] chivalric

ENGLISH LITERATURE

Questions 54-56

"Oh, Madam Mina," he said, "how can I say what I owe to you? This paper is as sunshine. It opens the gate to me. I am dazed, I am dazzled, with so much light, and yet clouds roll in behind the light every time. But that you do not, cannot comprehend. Oh, but I am grateful to you, you so clever woman. Madame,ds roll in behind the light every time. ed at this Helsing can do anything for your or yours, I trust you will let me know. It will be pleasure and delight if I may serve you as a friend, as a friend, but all I have ever learned, all I can ever do, shall be for you and those you love. There are darknesses in life, and there are lights. You are one of the lights. You are one of the lights. You will have a happy life and a good life, and your husband will be blessed in you."

54. What type of novel is this?

   [A] Gothic

   [B] Renaissance

   [C] Jacobean

   [D] Medieval

   [E] Restoration

55. Who is the author?

   [A] Washington Irving

   [B] Margaret Fuller

   [C] Bram Stoker

   [D] Horace Greeley

   [E] Arthur Conan Doyle

56. The phrase, "This paper is as sunshine. It opens the gate to me," means

   [A] Madam Mina was holding a light in the next sentence that made it seem as bright as day.

   [B] The character speaking has been given new glasses with which to see the sunshine.

   [C] The character speaking has new information that is helpful to him.

   [D] He is making a joke to Madam Mina.

   [E] None of the above.

Questions 57-61

Strong man though he was, there is no doubt that he had behaved rather foolishly over the medicine. If he had a weakness, it was for thinking that all his life he had taken medicine boldly, and so now, when Michael dodged the spoon in Nana's mouth, he had said reprovingly, "Be a man, Michael."

ENGLISH LITERATURE

57. The passage is excerpted from:

[A] Little Women

[B] The Adventures of Peter Pan

[C] Tess of the D'Urbervilles

[D] The Faerie Queene

[E] Oliver Twist

58. Is this the first time the main character was used by this author?

[A] Yes, there are no other references.

[B] No, the author used him as a cameo in *The Little White Bird*.

[C] No, the author used him in a magazine series.

[D] No, the author wrote several books before this one using him.

[E] No, the author used him in an advertisement first

59. Who is talking to Michael in the passage?

[A] Mrs. Darling

[B] Wendy

[C] Peter

[D] Mr. Darling

[E] John

60. In what chapter does the star of the story make his first appearance through reference and explanation?

[A] Chapter 1

[B] Chapter 2

[C] Chapter 3

[D] Chapter 4

[E] Chapter 5

61. The author of this novel is:

[A] J. M. Barrie

[B] Louisa May Alcott

[C] E. Nesbit

[D] Lucy Montgomery

[E] Mary Ann Evans

ENGLISH LITERATURE

62. **Robert Louis Stevenson's most famous novel is:**

    [A] *Great Expectations*

    [B] *Treasure Island*

    [C] *Atonement*

    [D] *Pilgrim's Progress*

    [E] *Howard's End*

    How sweet is the Shepherd's sweet lot!
    From the morn to the evening he strays;
    He shall follow his sheep all the day,
    And his tongue shall be filled with praise.

    For he hears the lamb's innocent call,
    And he hears the ewe's tender reply;
    He is watchful while they are in peace,
    For they know when their Shepherd is nigh.

63. **The tone of the poem is:**

    [A] peaceful.

    [B] argumentative.

    [C] mocking.

    [D] eclectic.

    [E] suspicious.

64. **All of the following were written in the nineteenth century EXCEPT:**

    [A] Picture of Dorian Gray

    [B] Agnes Grey

    [C] Pickwick Papers

    [D] David Copperfield

    [E] Lord Jim

65. **The following authors all published in the 1800s EXCEPT:**

    [A] Jonathan Swift

    [B] James Joyce

    [C] Virginia Woolf

    [D] Elizabeth Barrett Browning

    [E] Lewis Carroll

66. **The following characteristics are true of post-colonial movement EXCEPT:**

    [A] engagement with colonialism's power structures.

    [B] the destabilization of ideas of homeland.

    [C] a mother country's continued influence in the arts.

    [D] the presentation of concepts critical of non-western cultures.

    [E] the destabilization of ideas of the West

ENGLISH LITERATURE

67. Abstract imagery is:

[A] the reaction to the Symbolist movement.

[B] a type of catachresis known as a mixed metaphor.

[C] language that cannot be perceived with the five senses.

[D] updating older language to reflect the abstract movement.

[E] the creation of a sense of removed experience from an event.

68. Alliteration is:

[A] addition of an extra unstressed syllable.

[B] transcription from a speaker.

[C] presentation of two alternatives in parallel structure.

[D] close proximity of repeated consonant sounds.

[E] insertion of an unnecessary vowel sound.

69. Who wrote *Paradise Lost*?

[A] John Ford

[B] John Milton

[C] John Webster

[D] John Fletcher

[E] John Donne

70. Which famous author and friends dressed up in costumes in order to convince the Royal Navy they were Abyssinian Princes?

[A] Virginia Woolf

[B] Emily Bronte

[C] Charlotte Bronte

[D] Mary Shelley

[E] None of these authors did this.

71. The earliest use of "wicked" to mean "cool" was included in a novel by which of the following authors?

[A] D. H. Lawrence

[B] Hugh Lofting

[C] F. Scott Fitzgerald

[D] Jonathan Swift

[E] T. S. Eliot

72. Ben Jonson is known for:

[A] sonnets

[B] satirical plays

[C] medieval essays

[D] pastoral prose

[E] Elizabethan tragedy

ENGLISH LITERATURE

73. Although he was a judge and legal administrator by avocation, he collected stories as a child in the Scottish highlands and began his writing career by translating German documents. This best describes:

    [A] G. Bernard Shaw

    [B] C. S. Lewis

    [C] John Banim

    [D] Robert Burns

    [E] Walter Scott

74. Critics reviewed this novel and disliked "its dystopian satire of totalitarian regimes, nationalism, the class system, bureaucracy, and world leaders' power struggles," while others panned it as a "nihilistic prophesy on the downfall of humankind." Which novel does this describe?

    [A] *Animal House*

    [B] *1984*

    [C] *South of Broad*

    [D] *The Waste Land*

    [E] *Culture and Anarchy*

While the present century was in its teens and on one sunshiny morning in June, there drove up to the great iron gate of Miss Pinkertonreat iron g its teens and on oneChiswick Mall, a large family coach, with two fat horses in blazing harness, driven by a fat coachman in a three-cornered hat and wig, at the rate of four miles an hour.

75. This is the opening line of:

    [A] *Vanity Fair*

    [B] *The Great Gatsby*

    [C] *To Kill a Mockingbird*

    [D] *Hermann and Dorothea*

    [E] *Fair Maid of the West*

76. The author of the passage is:

    [A] John Fisher

    [B] Thomas Malory

    [C] Christopher Smart

    [D] William Makepeace Thackeray

    [E] Robert Greene

77. *Beowulf* is set in what region of the world?

    [A] British Isles

    [B] Scandinavia

    [C] Prussia

    [D] Russia

    [E] Gaul

ENGLISH LITERATURE

78. What is the primary focus of *Beowulf*?

    [A] The Crusaders trying to return from the Middle East to Europe

    [B] America's wealth, power, and influence over Russia

    [C] Good over evil, with the king's funeral finishing the story

    [D] The expansion of Russia towards the west and southward toward the Mediterranean Sea

    [E] Examples of how the sun never sets over the British Isles

79. Which of the following is not one of the Canterbury Tales?

    [A] "The Cook's Tale"

    [B] "The Wife of Bath's Tale"

    [C] "Sir Thopas' Tale"

    [D] "The Manciple's Tale"

    [E] "Sir Eduoard's Tale"

Question 80-82

> To be or not to be— that is the question
> Whether 'tis nobler in the mind to suffer
> The slings and arrows of outrageous fortune
> Or to take arms against a sea of troubles
> And by opposing end them. To die, to sleep —
> No more — and by a sleep to say we end
> The heartache, and the thousand natural shocks
> That flesh is heir to. 'Tis a consummation
> Devoutly to be wished. To die, to sleep—
> To sleep—perchance to dream…

80. This is an example of a:

    [A] monologue

    [B] soliloquy

    [C] appeal

    [D] benediction

    [E] none of the above

81. The character that speaks these lines is:

    [A] Romeo

    [B] Mercutio

    [C] Ceasar

    [D] Hamlet

    [E] Macbeth

ENGLISH LITERATURE

82. The tone of this selection is:

    [A] despairing

    [B] joyful

    [C] longing

    [D] remorseful

    [E] self-promotion

Question 83

Nobody wanted your dance,
Nobody wanted your strange
    glitter, your floundering
Drowning life and your effort to
    save yourself,
Treading water, dancing the
    dark turmoil,
Looking for something to give.

83. This passage's tone is created by using one of the following means:

    [A] allegories

    [B] euphemisms

    [C] alliteration

    [D] irony

    [E] metaphors

84. Walter Scott wrote all of the following EXCEPT:

    [A] *Rob Roy*

    [B] *Ivanhoe*

    [C] *Waverly*

    [D] *The Talisman*

    [E] *Kidnapped*

85. H. G. Wells wrote all of the following EXCEPT:

    [A] *The Dream*

    [B] *War of the Worlds*

    [C] *Time Machine*

    [D] *Vivian Grey*

    [E] *Meanwhile*

86. The correct order of Jane Austin's novels by publication is:

    [A] Emma, Sense & Sensibility, Pride & Prejudice, Persuasion

    [B] Emma, Persuasion, Sense & Sensibility, Pride & Prejudice

    [C] Persuasion, Sense & Sensibility, Pride & Prejudice, Emma

    [D] Sense & Sensibility, Pride & Prejudice, Emma, Persuasion

    [E] Pride & Prejudice, Sense & Sensibility, Emma, Persuasion

ENGLISH LITERATURE

Question 87

All the world's a stage
And all the men and women
    merely players;
They have their exits and their
    entrances,
And one man in his time plays
    many parts,
His acts being seven ages.

87. This is a passage from:

   [A] *The Tempest*

   [B] *As You Like It*

   [C] *Much Ado About Nothing*

   [D] *Twelfth Night*

   [E] *King Lear*

88. The politician John Elwes, who had inherited a fortune but was reluctant to spend a penny - even living in empty apartments - is thought to have served as partial inspiration for which literary work?

   [A] A Christmas Carol

   [B] Tale of Two Cities

   [C] Pickwick Papers

   [D] Mystery of Edwin Drood

   [E] The Battle of Life

89. Events taking place on a single day, following three major characters through Dublin, describes what 20th century novel?

   [A] *A Handful of Dust*

   [B] *The Third Man*

   [C] *Dubliners*

   [D] *Ulysses*

   [E] *The Heart of the Matter*

90. In literature, evoking feelings of pity or compassion is creating:

   [A] colloquy

   [B] irony

   [C] pathos

   [D] paradox

   [E] emphatic response.

ENGLISH LITERATURE

ANSWER KEY

Question Number	Correct Answer	Your Answer
1	D	
2	C	
3	E	
4	C	
5	C	
6	D	
7	D	
8	A	
9	A	
10	B	
11	C	
12	A	
13	E	
14	C	
15	A	
16	D	
17	C	
18	E	
19	A	
20	B	
21	D	
22	B	
23	A	
24	B	
25	C	
26	D	
27	E	
28	A	
29	B	
30	A	

Question Number	Correct Answer	Your Answer
31	III., II., I., IV	
32	B	
33	A	
34	D	
35	D	
36	E	
37	A	
38	E	
39	B	
40	C	
41	D	
42	A	
43	E	
44	C	
45	A	
46	B	
47	C	
48	D	
49	A	
50	B	
51	D	
52	E	
53	C	
54	A	
55	C	
56	C	
57	B	
58	B	
59	D	
60	A	

Question Number	Correct Answer	Your Answer
61	A	
62	B	
63	A	
64	E	
65	A	
66	B	
67	C	
68	D	
69	B	
70	A	
71	C	
72	B	
73	E	
74	B	
75	A	
76	D	
77	B	
78	C	
79	E	
80	B	
81	D	
82	A	
83	B	
84	E	
85	D	
86	D	
87	B	
88	A	
89	D	
90	C	

ENGLISH LITERATURE

EXPLANATIONS

1. **An example of Restoration writing is:**

    [A] *The New Atlantis*

    [B] *Hamlet*

    [C] *Leviathan*

    [D] *The Principia*

    [E] *Gulliver's Travels*

The correct answer is D.
The Restoration is the period from 1660 through the mid-1680s; it is the timing of Charles II being placed on the throne and reestablishing the traditional monarchy (ending around his death in 1665). *The Principia*, Sir Isaac Newton's mathematical discourse published in 1687, is the best answer. *The New Atlantis* (A), an incomplete utopian novel by Sir Francis Bacon, was published in 1626. *Hamlet* (B) was Shakespeare's master work of 1603. *Leviathan* (C), a seminal work of political philosophy written by Thomas Hobbes, was published in 1651. *Gulliver's Travels* (E) was written by Jonathan Swift 100 years after this literary era.

ENGLISH LITERATURE

2. The following passage is written from which point of view?

   As she mused the pitiful vision of her mother's life laid its spell on the very quick of her being—that life of commonplace sacrifices closing in final craziness. She trembled as she heard again her mother's voice saying constantly with foolish insistence: Derevaun Seraun! Derevaun Seraun!*

   * ["The end of pleasure is pain!" (Gaelic)]

   [A] First person, narrator

   [B] Second person, direct address

   [C] Third person, omniscient

   [D] First person, omniscient

   [E] First person, direct address

The correct answer is C.
With the absence of any first person or second person pronouns (e.g. "I" and "you"), and the use of the pronoun "she," it is clearly in the third person. Answers A, D and E are all variations on the first person point of view. Answer B would require that the passage be addressed to a "you."

3. The device of personification is used in which example below?

   [A] "Beg me no beggary by soul or parents, whining dog!"

   [B] "We few, we happy few, we band of brothers."

   [C] "O wind thy horn, thou proud fellow."

   [D] "And that one talent which is death to hide."

   [E] "Happiness sped through the halls cajoling as it went."

The correct answer is E.
Happiness is a human emotion and concept, being described as a person. Answers A and D are examples of metaphorical language, but not specifically personification. Answers B and C are examples of poetic language, not necessarily figurative.

ENGLISH LITERATURE

4. Which of the following is not one of the four forms of discourse?

[A] Exposition

[B] Description

[C] Rhetoric

[D] Persuasion

[E] Narration

The correct answer is C.
Rhetoric is an umbrella term for techniques of expressive and effective speech. Rhetorical figures are ornaments of speech such as anaphora, antithesis, and metaphor. The other four choices are specific forms of discourse. Exposition (A) delivers information. Description (B) renders characters and settings more vividly through the employment of specific details. Persuasion (D) is the argumentative mode of discourse. Narration (E) is storytelling.

5. "Every one must pass through Vanity Fair to get to the celestial city" is an allusion to a:

[A] Chinese folk tale

[B] Norse saga

[C] British allegory

[D] German fairy tale

[E] French drama

The correct answer is C.
This is a reference to John Bunyan's *Pilgrim's Progress from This World to That Which Is To Come* (Part 1, 1678; Part II, 1684), in which the hero, Christian, flees the City of Destruction and must undergo different trials and tests to get to the Celestial City.

ENGLISH LITERATURE

6. To understand the origins of a word, one must study the:

[A] synonyms

[B] inflections

[C] phonetics

[D] etymology

[E] epidemiology

The correct answer is D.
Etymology is the study of word origins. Synonyms (A) are the equivalents in meaning to other words can substitute for them in certain contexts. Inflections (B) are the modifications of words according to their grammatical functions, usually by employing variant word endings to indicate such qualities as tense, gender, case, and number. Phonetics (C) is the science devoted to the physical analysis of the sounds of human speech, whereas epidemiology (E) is the study of human disease outbreak and transmission.

ENGLISH LITERATURE

And more to lulle him in his slumber soft,
A trickling streame from high rock tumbling downe,
And ever-drizzling raine upon the loft.
Mixt with a murmuring winde, much like the sowne
Of swarming bees, did cast him in a swowne
No other noyse, nor peoples troublous cryes.
As still are wont t'annoy the walle'd towne,
Might there be heard: but careless Quiet lyes,
Wrapt in eternall silence farre from enemyes.

7. Which term best describes the form of the poetic excerpt?

   [A] Ballad

   [B] Elegy

   [C] Octava rima

   [D] Spenserian stanza

   [E] Eulogy

The correct answer is D.
A Spenserian stanza has nine lines, with a concluding single line. A ballad (A) is a rhymed poem about love. An elegy (B) originated as a Greek poem about death. Octava rima (C) is a specific eight line rhythmic schedule. A eulogy (E) is a statement given at a funeral.

ENGLISH LITERATURE

My galley charg'ed with forgetfulness
Through sharp seas, in winter night doth pass
'Tween rock and rock; and eke mine enemy, alas,
That is my lord steereth with cruelness.
And every oar a thought in readiness,
As though that death were light in such a case.
An endless wind doth tear the sail apace
Or forc'ed sighs and trusty fearfulness.
A rain of tears, a cloud of dark disdain,
Hath done the wearied cords great hindrance,
Wreathed with error and eke with ignorance.
The stars be hid that led me to this pain
Drowned is reason that should me consort,
And I remain despairing of the poet.

8. Which term accurately names the form of the sonnet?

   [A] Petrarchan or Italian sonnet

   [B] Shakespearean or Elizabethan sonnet

   [C] Romantic sonnet

   [D] Spenserian sonnet

   [E] Dante's sonnet

The correct answer is A.
The best choice, though perhaps students may have considered the romantic sonnet, is the Petrarchan sonnet (Italian sonnet), named after the Italian poet Petrarch (1304-74), where the sonnet is divided into an octave rhyming abba abba and sestet normally rhyming cde cde,. A Shakespearean sonnet (B) carries a pattern over the twelve lines of abab cdcd efef and completes with a couplet of gg. A romantic sonnet (C) could be either Shakespearean or Petrarchan in nature, but generally does not follow a set pattern. Spenserian sonnets (D) use iambic pentameter of abab bcbc cdcd ee; this sample does not follow any of these. Dante's sonnets (E) use styles of prose and verse.

ENGLISH LITERATURE

9. Arthur Miller wrote *The Crucible* as a parallel to what twentieth-century event?

[A] Sen. McCarthy's House Un- American Activities Committee hearings

[B] The Cold War

[C] The fall of the Berlin Wall

[D] The Persian Gulf War

[E] The Great Depression

The correct answer is A.
The Salem witch hunts of the 17th century gave Miller a near-parallel storyline to the McCarthy communist list process, thus A is the correct answer. The Cold War (B) and the Persian Gulf War (D) do not align with the story in *The Crucible* as neatly as the Communism lists. Likewise, the Great Depression (E) was an economic crisis, not a conflict of religion and society, and the fall of the Berlin Wall (1990-1992), while an event of enormous consequence in the course of the Cold War, is without any symbolic associations reflected in *The Crucible*.

10. Which of the following is not a characteristic of a fable?

[A] Animals that feel and talk like humans

[B] Happy solutions to human dilemmas

[C] Teaches a moral or standard for behavior

[D] Illustrates specific people or groups without directly naming them

[E] All of these are characteristics of fables

The correct answer is B.
Fables do not present a happy solution to a human dilemma (so E is wrong and B is correct). A fable is a short tale with animals, humans, gods, or even inanimate objects as characters. Fables often conclude with a moral, delivered in the form of an epigram (a short, witty, and ingenious statement in verse). Fables are among the oldest forms of writing in human history: They appear in Egyptian papyri from 1500 BCE. The most famous fables are those of Aesop, a Greek slave living in about 600 BCE. In India, the Panchatantra appeared in the third century BCE. The most famous modern fables are those of seventeenth-century French poet Jean de La Fontaine.

ENGLISH LITERATURE

11. Which of the following was not written by Jonathan Swift?

    [A] *A Voyage to Lilliput*

    [B] *A Modest Proposal*

    [C] *Samson Agonistes*

    [D] *A Tale of a Tub*

    [E] *Drapier's Letters*

The correct answer is C.
Samson Agonistes is a poem by John Milton. It was published in 1671, in the same volume as *Paradise Regained*. *A Voyage to Lilliput* is the first part of Swift's lengthy satire, commonly known as *Gulliver's Travels*. The *Drapier's Letters* were political pamphlets, indirectly criticizing British rule over Ireland, released under a pseudonym. Answers B and D are satires.

12. Which is the best definition for diction?

    [A] The specific word choices of an author to create a particular mood or feeling in the reader

    [B] Writing that explains something thoroughly

    [C] The background or exposition for a short story or drama

    [D] Word choices that help teach a truth or moral

    [E] Proper elocution

The correct answer is A.
Diction refers to an author's choice of words, expressions, and style to convey his or her meaning. While elocution (E) is also appropriate for close consideration, it deals with the particular speech and pronunciation of the words, not the selection of the words and expressions, so it is not the best selection.

ENGLISH LITERATURE

13. Which is an untrue statement about literary themes?

[A] The theme is the central idea in a literary work.

[B] A theme can be a thematic concept.

[C] All parts of the work (plot, setting, mood) should contribute to the theme in some way.

[D] By analyzing the various elements of the work, the reader should be able to arrive at an indirectly stated theme.

[E] The theme is always stated directly somewhere in the text.

The correct answer is E.
The theme may be stated directly, but it can also be implicit in various aspects of the work, such as the interactions among characters, symbolism, or description.

14. Which is the least true statement concerning an author's literary tone?

[A] Tone is partly revealed through the selection of details.

[B] Tone is the expression of the author's attitude toward his or her subject.

[C] Tone in literature is usually satiric or angry.

[D] Tone in literature corresponds to the tone of voice a speaker uses.

[E] Tone can be expressed in a variety of ways by an author.

The correct answer is C.
Tone in literature conveys a mood and can be as varied as the tone of voice of a speaker (see D), for example, sad, nostalgic, whimsical, angry, formal, intimate, satirical, or sentimental. The answer C is too limited, and is the correct answer for this question.

ENGLISH LITERATURE

15. Regarding the study of poetry, which elements are least applicable to all types of poetry?

[A] Setting and audience

[B] Theme and tone

[C] Pattern and diction

[D] Diction and rhyme scheme

[E] Words and symbols

The correct answer is A.
Setting and audience are important elements of narrative, and while some poetry is narrative in nature, there are many poems in which the setting and audience are unimportant.

16. Which of the following definitions best describes a parable?

[A] A short, entertaining account of some happening, usually using talking animals as characters

[B] A slow, sad song, poem or prose work expressing lamentation

[C] An extended narrative work expressing universal truths concerning domestic life

[D] A short, simple story of an occurrence of a familiar kind, from which a moral or religious lesson may be drawn

[E] A long, involved story that reveals hidden lessons after much discussion and deliberation.

The correct answer is D.
A parable is usually brief and should be interpreted as an allegory teaching a moral lesson. Jesus's parables are the model of the genre, but modern, secular examples exist, such as Wilfred Owen's *The Parable of The Old Man and The Young* (1920), or John Steinbeck's prose work *The Pearl* (1948).

ENGLISH LITERATURE

17. Which of the following is the best description of existentialism?

[A] The philosophical doctrine that matter is the only reality and that everything in the world (including thought, will, and feeling) is rightly explained exclusively in terms of matter

[B] A philosophy that views things as they should be or as one would wish them to be

[C] A philosophical and literary movement, variously religious and atheistic, stemming from Kierkegaard and represented by Sartre

[D] The belief that all events are determined by fate and are hence inevitable

[E] The fear of losing one's identity, suspicion of activities and aggressions of others.

The correct answer is C.
Even though there are other very important thinkers in the movement known as Existentialism, such as Albert Camus and Maurice Merleau-Ponty, Soren Kierkegaard and Jean-Paul Sartre remain the main figure in this movement.

18. Which of the following is the best definition of imagism?

[A] A doctrine teaching that comfort is the only goal of value in life

[B] The rejection of all religious and moral principles, often in the belief that life is meaningless and just represented by images

[C] The belief that people are motivated entirely by self-centeredness

[D] The doctrine that the human mind cannot know whether there is a God, an ultimate cause, or anything beyond material phenomena

[E] A movement in modern poetry (c. 1910–1918) characterized by precise, concrete images, free verse, and suggestion rather than complete statement

The correct answer is E.
The group known as the imagists was led by Ezra Pound at first, but he started the Vorticism movement and was replaced by Amy Lowell. Imagists rejected nineteenth-century poetry and were looking for clarity and exactness. Their poems were usually short and built around a single image. Other writers representative of the movement are Richard Addington, H.D. (Hilda Doolittle), F. S. Flint, D. H. Lawrence, Ford Madox Ford, and William Carlos Williams.

ENGLISH LITERATURE

19. Which choice below best defines naturalism?

   [A] A belief that the writer or artist should apply scientific objectivity in his or her observation and treatment of life without imposing values or judgments

   [B] The doctrine that teaches that the existing world is the best to be hoped for

   [C] The doctrine teaching that God is not a personality, but that all laws, forces, and manifestations of the universe are God-related

   [D] A philosophical doctrine professing that the truth of all knowledge must constantly be reexamined

   [E] A belief that enhancing a character's surroundings with the environment will improve the reader's understanding

The correct answer is A.
Naturalism is a movement that was started by French writers Jules and Edmond de Goncourt with their novel *Germinie Lacerteux* (1865), but its real leader is Emile Zola, who wanted to bring "a slice of life" to his readers. His saga *Les Rougon Macquart* consists of 22 novels (of which *La Bête Humaine* is particularly well-known) depicting various aspects of social life. Authors writing in English who are representative of this movement include George Moore and George Gissing in England, but the most important naturalist novel in English is Theodore Dreiser's *Sister Carrie*.

ENGLISH LITERATURE

20. The tendency to emphasize and value the qualities and peculiarities of life in a particular geographic area exemplifies:

[A] pragmatism

[B] regionalism

[C] pantheism

[D] abstract expressionism

[E] utilitarianism

The correct answer is B.
Regionalism emphasizes and values the defining details of life in a particular geographic area. Pragmatism (A) is a philosophical doctrine according to which there is no absolute truth. All truths change their trueness as their practical utility increases or decreases. The main representative of this movement is William James, who in 1907 published *Pragmatism: A New Way for Some Old Ways of Thinking*. Pantheism (C) is a philosophy according to which God is omnipresent in the world; everything is God and God is everything. The great representative of this sensibility is Spinoza. Also, the works of writers such as Wordsworth, Shelley, and Emerson illustrate this doctrine. Abstract expressionism (D) is one of the most important movements in American art. It began in the 1940s with artists such as Willem de Kooning, Mark Rothko, and Arshile Gorky. The paintings are usually large and nonrepresentational. Utilitarianism (E) is a form of ethics and philosophy that focuses on the well-being of the greater society and the consequence of actions.

21. The arrangement of words in sentences best describes:

[A] style

[B] discourse

[C] thesis

[D] syntax

[E] none of the above

The correct answer is D.
The analysis of sentence structure, and specifically the arrangement of words within sentences, is best captured by the term "syntax."

ENGLISH LITERATURE

22. The substitution of "went to his rest" for "died" is an example of:

[A] bowdlerism

[B] jargon

[C] euphemism

[D] malapropism

[E] simile

The correct answer is B.
A euphemism replaces an unpleasant or offensive word or expression with a more agreeable one. It also alludes to distasteful things in a pleasant manner, and it can even paraphrase offensive texts. Bowdlerism (A) removes potentially offensive text entirely. Jargon (B) is language specific to an industry or line of work. Malapropism (D) is the mistaken use of a word in place of a similar sounding one. Simile (E) is a figure of speech with the reference of one object/item to another, and also does not fit.

23. Explanatory or informative discourse is:

[A] exposition

[B] narration

[C] persuasion

[D] description

[E] discussion

The correct answer is A.
Exposition sets forth a systematic explanation of any subject. It can also introduce the characters of a literary work and their situations in the story.

ENGLISH LITERATURE

24. A conversation between two or more people is called a:

[A] parody

[B] dialogue

[C] monologue

[D] analogy

[E] diatribe

The correct answer is B.
Dialogues are indispensable to dramatic work, and they often appear in narratives and poetry. A parody (A) is a work that adopts the subject and structure of another work to ridicule it. A monologue (C) is a work or part of a work written in the first person. An analogy (D) illustrates an idea by means of a more familiar idea that is similar or parallel to it. A diatribe (E) is similar to a monologue but is negative and usually angry at a person or over a situation.

25. "Clean as a whistle" and "easy as falling off a log" are examples of:

[A] semantics

[B] parody

[C] clichés

[D] irony

[E] satire

The correct answer is C.
A cliché is a phrase or expression that has become dull due to overuse. Semantics (A) are small details on how something is accomplished. Parody (B) suggest making fun of a particular person. In irony (D), there is a reversal or opposition of meaning in which what is superficially true clashes with actuality. Satire (E) is the use of humor to reveal someone's stupidity.

ENGLISH LITERATURE

26. Addressing someone absent or something inhuman as though present and able to respond describes a figure of speech known as:

   [A] personification

   [B] synecdoche

   [C] metonymy

   [D] apostrophe

   [E] rhetorical strategy

The correct answer is D.
An apostrophe addresses an absent person or something inhuman as though that person or thing were present and able to respond. Personification (A) is about humanizing an object or animal. Synecdoche (B) is using a partial name to represent the whole, such as when a city's football team uses only the name of the city, but people understand the reference to the team. Metonymy (C) is substituting an item for the reference to someone or something (such as the case for a shipment of inventory). Rhetorical strategy (E) references a method used to organize evidence or sequences.

27. Slang or jargon expressions associated with a particular ethnic, age, socioeconomic, or professional group reflect:

   [A] aphorisms

   [B] allusions

   [C] idioms

   [D] Euphemisms

   [E] stereotypes

The correct answer is E.
Stereotypes, widely held but fixed and oversimplified ideas about a particular type of person or thing, can include (though they are not limited to) slang or jargon expressions. An aphorism (A) is a terse saying. An allusion (B) is a covert reference to an object from outside circumstances. Idioms (C) are a broad category of slang or informal expressions that are figurative in some way. Euphemisms (D) are a subtle way to reference a potentially indiscreet subject.

ENGLISH LITERATURE

The characters of the novel also show how deeply it has been meditated; for, though none of them may excite the personal interest which clings to Sam Weller or little Dombey, they are better fitted to each other and the story in which they appear than is usual with Dickens. They all combine to produce the unity of impression which the work leaves on the mind. Individually they will rank among the most original of the author's creations.
- from a review published in *The Atlantic Monthly*, 1861

28. In line 1, the critic refers to a particular novel by Charles Dickens. Which one?

    [A] *Great Expectations*

    [B] *The Old Curiosity Shop*

    [C] *David Copperfield*

    [D] *A Christmas Carol*

    [E] *Oliver Twist*

The correct answer is A.
The characters described only are visited in one of the novels by Dickens.

29. Which event triggered the beginning of Modern English?

    [A] Conquest of England by the Normans in 1066

    [B] Introduction of the printing press to the British Isles

    [C] Publication of Samuel Johnson's lexicon

    [D] The American Revolution

    [E] Creation of the British East India Company

The correct answer is B.
With the arrival of the written word, reading matter became mass produced, so the public tended to adopt the speech and writing habits printed in books, and the language became more stable. This laid the groundwork for the development of Modern English. The alternative answers A, D and E signify events of importance to the history of England as a country, but are not specifically linguistically important. Samuel Johnson's work (C) presupposed the existence of Modern English.

ENGLISH LITERATURE

30. Which of the following is not true about the English language?

[A] English is the easiest language to learn.

[B] English is the least inflected language.

[C] English has the most extensive vocabulary of any language.

[D] English originated as a Germanic tongue.

[E] A new word is added to the English Dictionary every two hours.

The correct answer is A.
Just like any other language, English has inherent difficulties that make it difficult to learn, even though English has no declensions such as those found in Latin, Greek, or contemporary Russian, or a tonal system such as Chinese.

31. Match each of the following poets to the poem that he or she wrote.

      I. Maya Angelou
     II. e. e. cummings
    III. Andrew Marvell
    IV. Sylvia Plath

"To His Coy Mistress" _____

"[in Just-]" _____

"Phenomenal Woman" _____

"Lady Lazarus" _____

The answers are: III., II., I., IV
Maya Angelou's "Phenomenal Woman," e.e. cumming's "[in Just-]", Andrew Marvell's "To His Coy Mistress," and Sylvia Plath's "Lady Lazarus."

ENGLISH LITERATURE

32. Children's literature became established as a distinct genre in the:

[A] sixteenth century

[B] seventeenth century

[C] eighteenth century

[D] nineteenth century

[E] twentieth century

The correct answer is B.
In the seventeenth century, works such as Jean de La Fontaine's *Fables*, Charles Perrault's *Tales of Mother Goose*, Madame d'Aulnoye's novels based on old folktales, and Madame de Beaumont's *Beauty and the Beast* began a new genre of children's literature. In England, Perrault was translated from French to English, and a work allegedly written by Oliver Smith, *The Renowned History of Little Goody Two-Shoes*, also helped establish children's literature in England.

33. What is the main form of discourse in this passage?

"It would have been hard to find a passer-by more wretched in appearance. He was a man of middle height, stout and hardy, in the strength of maturity; he might have been forty-six or seven. A slouched leather cap hid half his face, bronzed by the sun and wind, and dripping with sweat."

[A] Description

[B] Narration

[C] Exposition

[D] Persuasion

[E] Foreshadowing

The correct answer is A.
A description presents a thing or a person in detail and tells the reader about the appearance of whatever it is presenting. Narration (B) relates a sequence of events (the story) through a process of discourse, in which events are recounted in a certain order (the plot). Exposition (C) is an explanation or an argument within the narration. It can also be the introduction to a play or a story. Persuasion (D) strives to convince either a character in the story or the reader. Foreshadowing (E) gives context that precedes actual events in a story.

ENGLISH LITERATURE

34. Oral debate is most closely associated with which form of literary discourse?

[A] Description

[B] Exposition

[C] Narration

[D] Persuasion

[E] Poetic

The correct answer is D.
A participant in an oral debate may use multiple modes of discourse, but is primarily concerned with being persuasive.

35. Which of the following works is a satire?

[A] Boris Pasternak's Dr. Zhivago

[B] Albert Camus's The Stranger

[C] Henry David Thoreau's "On the Duty of Civil Disobedience"

[D] Benjamin Franklin's "Rules by Which a Great Empire May Be Reduced to a Small One"

[E] C. S. Lewis' Prince Caspian

The correct answer is D.
In this work, Benjamin Franklin adopts a scathingly ironic tone to warn the British about the probable outcome in their colonies if they persist with their policies. These are discussed one by one in the text, and the absurdity of each is condemned. So while not British, it was read by the British for the targeting of their policies (and foreshadowing of events to come). Answers A, B and E are twentieth century novels from Russia, France and England respectively. Thoreau's "Civil Disobedience" is an earnest political essay, not intended to be taken as satirical.

ENGLISH LITERATURE

36. Charles Dickens, Robert Browning, and Robert Louis Stevenson were:

[A] Classicists

[B] Medievalists

[C] Elizabethans

[D] Absurdists

[E] Victorians

The correct answer is E.
The Victorian Period is remarkable for the diversity and quality of its literature. Robert Browning wrote chilling monologues such as "My Last Duchess" and long poetic narratives such as *The Pied Piper of Hamlin*. Robert Louis Stevenson wrote his works partly for young adults, whose imaginations were quite taken by his *Treasure Island* and *The Case of Dr. Jekyll and Mr. Hyde*. Charles Dickens tells of the misery of the time and the complexities of Victorian society in novels such as *Oliver Twist* and *Great Expectations*. Answers A and B refer to literary scholars with particular areas of specialization, while absurdism (D) is a broad aesthetic movement that is more typical of the post-Victorian era. Elizabethans (C) is a collective term for people living in England under the reign of Queen Elizabeth I.

37. Which of the following is a characteristic of blank verse?

[A] Meter in iambic pentameter

[B] Clearly specified rhyme scheme

[C] Lack of figurative language

[D] Unspecified rhythm

[E] Presence of rhyming couplets

The correct answer is A.
An iamb is a metrical unit of verse having one unstressed syllable followed by one stressed syllable. This is the most commonly used metrical verse in English and American poetry. An iambic pentameter is a 10-syllable verse made of five of these metrical units, either rhymed as in sonnets or unrhymed as in free or blank verse.

ENGLISH LITERATURE

38. Which of the following is the correct chronological order of authors?

   [A] Defoe, Descartes, Dumas

   [B] Descartes, Dumas, Defoe

   [C] Dumas, Defoe, Descartes

   [D] Defoe, Descartes, Dumas

   [E] Descartes, Defoe, Dumas

The correct answer is E.
The correct order is Descartes (1596-1650), Defoe (1660-1731), and Dumas (1802-1870).

39. Her mother was jailed in Newgate Prison, given a reprieve and sent to America. Living with a foster mother, she grows up to be employed in a household where both brothers claim to love her, and she marries the younger brother. After the death of one of her children, she learns that her mother in law is really her biological mother - so her husband is her half-brother. What novel is described by this plot summary?

   [A] *Pride and Prejudice*

   [B] *Moll Flanders*

   [C] *Wuthering Heights*

   [D] *Novum Organum*

   [E] *Sons and Lovers*

The correct answer is B.
This is a plot summary from *Moll Flanders*. *Pride and Prejudice* (A) centers around five daughters in a proper high class household with the instruction of manners as well as their status-conscious friends. *Wuthering Heights* (C) depicts Yorkshire and the struggles of a wealthy yet uncouth land manager falling in love with the owner's daughter. *Novum Organum* (D) is Francis Bacon's major statement of his philosophy of science. *Sons and Lovers* (E) is a semi-autobiographical novel about an artist trying to get free from his old life, written by D. H. Lawrence.

ENGLISH LITERATURE

40. A passage about death and idyllic rural life is called a:

[A] ballad

[B] sonnet

[C] pastoral elegy

[D] metafiction

[E] lyric

The correct answer is C.
The definition provided is one of C, pastoral elegy. A ballad (A) is a narrative verse, usually to music (why the French call it a dancing song). A sonnet (B) is a poem and has specific line and meter quantities that need met. A metafiction (D) is a piece where the author alludes to the artificiality of an object to pose questions about reality versus fiction. A lyric (E) is similar to sonnet in that it has a brief recognized form, and yet is like a ballad in that it is typically sung.

41. The correct order of the following authors by birth is:

[A] Alexander Pope, Samuel Johnson, William Shakespeare, John Donne, William Thackeray

[B] William Shakespeare, John Donne, Samuel Johnson, Alexander Pope, William Thackeray

[C] John Donne, William Shakespeare, Alexander Pope, Samuel Johnson, William Thackeray

[D] William Shakespeare, John Donne, Alexander Pope, Samuel Johnson, William Thackeray

[E] John Donne, William Shakespeare, Samuel Johnson, Alexander Pope, William Thackeray

The correct answer is D.
In order of birth year: Shakespeare (1564), Donne (1572), Pope (1688), Johnson (1709) and Thackeray (1811).

ENGLISH LITERATURE

A mote it is to trouble the mind's eye.
In the most high and palmy state of Rome,
A little ere the mightiest Julius fell,
The graves stood tenantless and the sheeted dead
Did squeak and gibber in the Roman streets:
As stars with trains of fire and dews of blood,
Disasters in the sun; and the moist star
Upon whose influence Neptune's empire stands
Was sick almost to doomsday with eclipse:
And even the like precurse of fierce events,
As harbingers preceding still the fates
And prologue to the omen coming on,
Have heaven and earth together demonstrated
Unto our climatures and countrymen. o
But soft, behold! lo, where it comes again!

42. **Who speaks these lines?**

[A] Horatio

[B] Romeo

[C] Hamlet

[D] Othello

[E] Macbeth

The correct answer is A.
All of the characters listed are created by Shakespeare. However, only Horatio - in *Hamlet* - describes the vision of the ghost in this manner.

ENGLISH LITERATURE

43. A collection of twenty stories inspired by the Hundred Years War was written by:

[A] Walter Scott

[B] John Milton

[C] John Donne

[D] William Wordsworth

[E] Geoffrey Chaucer

The correct answer is E.
Chaucer wrote *Canterbury Tales* in 1483.

> These good folk, who have only just begun to think and act for themselves, are slow as yet to grasp the changed conditions which should attach them to these theories. They have only reached those ideas which conduce to economy and to physical welfare; in the future, if someone else carries on this work of mine, they will come to understand the principles that serve to uphold and preserve public order and justice. As a matter of fact, it is not sufficient to be an honest man, you must appear to be honest in the eyes of others. Society does not live by moral ideas alone; its existence depends upon actions in harmony with those ideas.

44. The passage describes:

[A] A judge's verdict

[B] A tax collector's dilemma

[C] The community view of a doctor

[D] A king's sovereign rights

[E] None of these are correct.

The correct answer is C.
This is an excerpt from *The Country Doctor* by Honoré de Balzac. It would not be a king, as the topic of equality is discussed. It would not be a tax collector as there is nothing in the passage regarding taxing in a community. Similarly, the first option, which it may appear could be legal in nature, is not the best choice as the doctor discusses the health of the community and inner-workings, so it is the better choice. E, or none of the above, is typically not a good or accurate choice in a college exam unless the other choices are so very divergent and disparate from the selection - and that is not the case here.

ENGLISH LITERATURE

Questions 45-47

Line 4

London was our present point of rest; we determined to remain several months in this wonderful and celebrated city. Clerval desired the intercourse of the men of genius and talent who flourished at this time; but this was with me a secondary object; I was principally occupied with the means of obtaining the information necessary for the completion of my promise, and quickly availed myself of the letters of introduction that I had brought with me, addressed to the most distinguished natural philosophers.

45. This is a passage written by:

[A] Mary Shelley

[B] Charles Dickens

[C] Jane Austen

[D] Percy Shelley

[E] Willa Cather

The correct answer is A.
Mary Shelley wrote *Frankenstein,* from which this is an excerpt.

46. What is the main theme of the selection?

[A] Travel discussions that compare where the characters have been

[B] Discussions about information gathering and solving an issue

[C] Meeting gentlemen for coffee

[D] Identifying the thought-leaders of the time

[E] How the traveler were going to select the next city they visit

The correct answer is B.
The two characters are discussing ways to find information while in London.

ENGLISH LITERATURE

47. In line 4 of the selection, intercourse means:

[A] crossroads

[B] relationship

[C] discussion

[D] meeting place

[E] sexual relations

The correct answer is C.
The most appropriate synonym is C, as the word can imply a variety of options, but discussion is the logical fit for this passage.

48. An example of a metaphysical poet would be:

[A] Christopher Marlowe

[B] George Peele

[C] William Shakespeare

[D] John Donne

[E] George Cascoigne

The correct answer is D.
John Donne's "The Sun Rising" or "The Good Morrow." All of the other options provided are Elizabethan poets.

ENGLISH LITERATURE

49. An example of a cavalier poet would be:

[A] Richard Lovelace

[B] Mary Sidney Hebert

[C] Lancelot Andrewes

[D] John Milton

[E] Hugh Latimer

The correct answer is A.
The correct answer is A, for Richard Lovelace, with an example such as "To Lucasta, Going to the Wars." The other examples are religious authors.

50. An example of a Jacobean poet would be:

[A] John Bale

[B] Margaret Cavendish

[C] John Skelton

[D] John Heywood

[E] Nicolas Udall

The correct answer is B.
Margaret Cavendish is one of the first poets taught in the Jacobean pattern. All of the other examples are Tudor.

ENGLISH LITERATURE

51. Charles Darwin did not write which of the following?

[A] *The Voyage of the Beagle*

[B] *The Origin of the Species*

[C] *The Descent of Man*

[D] *Bureaucracy*

[E] He only wrote two of these.

The correct answer is D.
Charles Darwin wrote the first three books (with the second selection having an update); he did not write *Bureaucracy*, a novel by Honoré de Balzac (D).

52. Which of the following was not actually written by Lewis Carroll?

[A] *Alice's Adventures in Wonderland*

[B] *Through the Looking Glass*

[C] *The Hunting of the Snark*

[D] *Sylvie and Bruno*

[E] *After Wonderland*

The correct answer is E.
Lewis Carroll wrote all of the books listed with the exception of *After Wonderland* (option E).

ENGLISH LITERATURE

53. Which of the following is not a mode of English literature?

[A] epistolary

[B] picaresque

[C] novella

[D] melodramatic

[E] chivalric

The correct answer is C.
The correct answer is C, as a novella is genre (or more precisely, a format) of fiction, not a mode. In the epistolary mode (A), the narrative is communicated by means of a series of published documents or letters. Stoker's *Dracula* is written in this mode. A picturesque novel (B) has a rogue as the main character, such as Henry Fielding's *Tom Jones* in the mid-1700s. Melodramas (D) have the main character making a decision between the timelessness of reality versus a constructed balancing act of an artificial nature. The chivalric mode (E) is a form of epic.

Questions 54-56

"Oh, Madam Mina," he said, "how can I say what I owe to you? This paper is as sunshine. It opens the gate to me. I am dazed, I am dazzled, with so much light, and yet clouds roll in behind the light every time. But that you do not, cannot comprehend. Oh, but I am grateful to you, you so clever woman. Madame,ds roll in behind the light every time. ed at this Helsing can do anything for your or yours, I trust you will let me know. It will be pleasure and delight if I may serve you as a friend, as a friend, but all I have ever learned, all I can ever do, shall be for you and those you love. There are darknesses in life, and there are lights. You are one of the lights. You are one of the lights. You will have a happy life and a good life, and your husband will be blessed in you."

ENGLISH LITERATURE

54. What type of novel is this?

[A] Gothic

[B] Renaissance

[C] Jacobean

[D] Medieval

[E] Restoration

The correct answer is A.
Bram (short for Abraham) Stoker wrote *Dracula*, which is a Gothic horror novel published in the late 1800s (1897). A is the correct answer; all other genres are from other literary eras.

55. Who is the author?

[A] Washington Irving

[B] Margaret Fuller

[C] Bram Stoker

[D] Horace Greeley

[E] Arthur Conan Doyle

The correct answer is C.
There are only two British authors on the list - C and E. Doyle wrote Sherlock Holmes; Stoker wrote *Dracula*.

ENGLISH LITERATURE

56. The phrase, "This paper is as sunshine. It opens the gate to me," means

[A] Madam Mina was holding a light in the next sentence that made it seem as bright as day.

[B] The character speaking has been given new glasses with which to see the sunshine.

[C] The character speaking has new information that is helpful to him.

[D] He is making a joke to Madam Mina.

[E] None of the above.

The correct answer is C.
This information is being compared to something the lead character very much needed to make sense of something, similar to opening a gate.

Questions 57-61

Strong man though he was, there is no doubt that he had behaved rather foolishly over the medicine. If he had a weakness, it was for thinking that all his life he had taken medicine boldly, and so now, when Michael dodged the spoon in Nana's mouth, he had said reprovingly, "Be a man, Michael."

57. The passage is excerpted from:

[A] Little Women

[B] The Adventures of Peter Pan

[C] Tess of the D'Urbervilles

[D] The Faerie Queene

[E] Oliver Twist

The correct answer is B.
The clue of Nana should give the novel away - Nana is the dog for the Darlings, and the story is Peter Pan.

ENGLISH LITERATURE

58. Is this the first time the main character was used by this author?

[A] Yes, there are no other references.

[B] No, the author used him as a cameo in *The Little White Bird*.

[C] No, the author used him in a magazine series.

[D] No, the author wrote several books before this one using him.

[E] No, the author used him in an advertisement first

The correct answer is B.
The character of Peter Pan was used previously by the author. The book written prior to this was *The Little White Bird,* so the correct answer is B.

59. Who is talking to Michael in the passage?

[A] Mrs. Darling

[B] Wendy

[C] Peter

[D] Mr. Darling

[E] John

The correct answer is D.
The female names are not appropriate as the masculine pronoun is used in the passage. Of the remaining characters, two are other children, and the tone is wrong for the context of action. Therefore, D is correct with Mr. Darling.

ENGLISH LITERATURE

60. In what chapter does the star of the story make his first appearance through reference and explanation?

[A] Chapter 1

[B] Chapter 2

[C] Chapter 3

[D] Chapter 4

[E] Chapter 5

The correct answer is A.
Peter Pan is mentioned only a few paragraphs into the first chapter.

61. The author of this novel is:

[A] J. M. Barrie

[B] Louisa May Alcott

[C] E. Nesbit

[D] Lucy Montgomery

[E] Mary Ann Evans

The correct answer is A.

62. Robert Louis Stevenson's most famous novel is:

[A] *Great Expectations*

[B] *Treasure Island*

[C] *Atonement*

[D] *Pilgrim's Progress*

[E] *Howard's End*

The correct answer is B.
He wrote B, *Treasure Island*. Charles Dickens wrote *Great Expectations*; Ian McEwan wrote *Atonement*, John Bunyan wrote *Pilgrim's Progress* and E.M. Forester wrote *Howard's End*.

ENGLISH LITERATURE

Question 63

> How sweet is the Shepherd's sweet lot!
> From the morn to the evening he strays;
> He shall follow his sheep all the day,
> And his tongue shall be filled with praise.
>
> For he hears the lamb's innocent call,
> And he hears the ewe's tender reply;
> He is watchful while they are in peace,
> For they know when their Shepherd is nigh.

63. The tone of the poem is:

   [A] peaceful.

   [B] argumentative.

   [C] mocking.

   [D] eclectic.

   [E] suspicious.

The correct answer is A.
The tone of this poem by William Blake is peaceful. It cannot be eclectic as that means wide-ranging. There is no evidence for argumentative, mocking or suspicious.

64. All of the following were written in the nineteenth century EXCEPT:

   [A] *Picture of Dorian Gray*

   [B] *Agnes Grey*

   [C] *Pickwick Papers*

   [D] *David Copperfield*

   [E] *Lord Jim*

The correct answer is E.
Lord Jim was written by Joseph Conrad in 1900, which is the twentieth century.

ENGLISH LITERATURE

65. The following authors all published in the 1800s EXCEPT:

   [A] Jonathan Swift

   [B] James Joyce

   [C] Virginia Woolf

   [D] Elizabeth Barrett Browning

   [E] Lewis Carroll

The correct answer is A.
All of the authors mentioned are English, and most were published in the Romantic Era. Jonathan Swift (A) published in the early 1700s. *Gulliver's Travels,* for instance, was published in 1726.

66. The following characteristics are true of post-colonial movement EXCEPT:

   [A] engagement with colonialism's power structures.

   [B] the destabilization of ideas of homeland.

   [C] a mother country's continued influence in the arts.

   [D] the presentation of concepts critical of non-western cultures.

   [E] the destabilization of ideas of the West

The correct answer is B.
All of the following are true except B, which states the exact opposite of what post-colonialism intends - challenging of previous ideas.

ENGLISH LITERATURE

67. Abstract imagery is:

[A] the reaction to the Symbolist movement.

[B] a type of catachresis known as a mixed metaphor.

[C] language that cannot be perceived with the five senses.

[D] updating older language to reflect the abstract movement.

[E] the creation of a sense of removed experience from an event.

The correct answer is C.
The definition is C; the other options mean, respectively: acmeism (A), abusio (B), a made up phrase (D), and aesthetic distance (E).

68. Alliteration is:

[A] addition of an extra unstressed syllable.

[B] transcription from a speaker.

[C] presentation of two alternatives in parallel structure.

[D] close proximity of repeated consonant sounds.

[E] insertion of an unnecessary vowel sound.

The correct answer is D.
The options are all literary terms, though only D is the correct answer. Respectively for the other options, they are the definitions of: anacrusis (A), amanuensis (B), juxtaposition (C) and anaptyxis (E).

ENGLISH LITERATURE

69. Who wrote *Paradise Lost*?

[A] John Ford

[B] John Milton

[C] John Webster

[D] John Fletcher

[E] John Donne

The correct answer is B.
All of the authors published in the same century (before 1660) but only John Milton wrote *Paradise Lost*.

70. Which famous author and friends dressed up in costumes in order to convince the Royal Navy they were Abyssinian Princes?

[A] Virginia Woolf

[B] Emily Bronte

[C] Charlotte Bronte

[D] Mary Shelley

[E] None of these authors did this.

The correct answer is A.
This is a funny anecdote that many people have heard, but you may not know the answer. Use deduction. As the Bronte sisters would likely have the same circle of friends, they can be eliminated from possibilities. None of the above is rarely a correct choice. Leaving the two last choices, Virginia Woolf was writing in the early 1900s while Mary Shelley was working in the early 1800s (Romantic period, when ladies were socially ostracized if they behaved as anything but staunch ladies). It is very unlikely a lady would have been able to do such antics, so pick Virginia Woolf.

ENGLISH LITERATURE

71. The earliest use of "wicked" to mean "cool" was included in a novel by which of the following authors?

[A] D. H. Lawrence

[B] Hugh Lofting

[C] F. Scott Fitzgerald

[D] Jonathan Swift

[E] T. S. Eliot

The correct answer is C.
F. Scott Fitzgerald created this nuance in *This Side of Paradise*. The other authors had recognizable achievements: D. H. Lawrence (*Lady Chatterley's Lover*), Hugh Lofting (*Doctor Dolittle*), Jonathan Swift (*Gulliver's Travels*); and while he was American-born, T. S. Eliot won the Nobel Prize in Literature in 1948, after becoming a British citizen in 1927.

72. Ben Jonson is known for:

[A] sonnets

[B] satirical plays

[C] medieval essays

[D] pastoral prose

[E] Elizabethan tragedy

The correct answer is B.
Ben Jonson is best known for satirical plays and is considered second only to Shakespeare during the time of James I. The other examples of genre do not apply to his works.

ENGLISH LITERATURE

73. Although he was a judge and legal administrator by avocation, he collected stories as a child in the Scottish highlands and began his writing career by translating German documents. This best describes:

    [A] G. Bernard Shaw

    [B] C. S. Lewis

    [C] John Banim

    [D] Robert Burns

    [E] Walter Scott

The correct answer is E.
They key in eliminating selections if you do not know The correct answer is "Scottish" - the first three authors are Irish. Of the last two, Robert Burns was from a literary family and was "just" a writer. Walter Scott was a barrister, who had great interest in writing and worked on it through his positions in legal administration, such as clerk of session.

74. Critics reviewed this novel and disliked "its dystopian satire of totalitarian regimes, nationalism, the class system, bureaucracy, and world leaders' power struggles," while others panned it as a "nihilistic prophesy on the downfall of humankind." Which novel does this describe?

    [A] *Animal House*

    [B] *1984*

    [C] *South of Broad*

    [D] *The Waste Land*

    [E] *Culture and Anarchy*

The correct answer is B.
Only the first two books are written by George Orwell, and the correct answer is 1984. It is one of the most discussed books about "big brother" replacing God and church, and this book is the foundation for "Orwellian" discourse and dissent against government.

ENGLISH LITERATURE

While the present century was in its teens and on one sunshiny morning in June, there drove up to the great iron gate of Miss Pinkertonreat iron g its teens and on oneChiswick Mall, a large family coach, with two fat horses in blazing harness, driven by a fat coachman in a three-cornered hat and wig, at the rate of four miles an hour.

75. This is the opening line of:

   [A] *Vanity Fair*

   [B] *The Great Gatsby*

   [C] *To Kill a Mockingbird*

   [D] *Hermann and Dorothea*

   [E] *Fair Maid of the West*

The correct answer is A.
That is the first line of *Vanity Fair*.

76. The author of the passage is:

   [A] John Fisher

   [B] Thomas Malory

   [C] Christopher Smart

   [D] William Makepeace Thackeray

   [E] Robert Greene

The correct answer is D.
The author of *Vanity Fair* is William Makepeace Thackeray.

ENGLISH LITERATURE

77. *Beowulf* **is set in what region of the world?**

[A] British Isles

[B] Scandinavia

[C] Prussia

[D] Russia

[E] Gaul

The correct answer is B.
Beowulf takes place in Scandinavia. Written perhaps as early as 1100 AD and more than 3,000 lines long, it is one of the staples of just about any British Literature course.

78. What is the primary focus of *Beowulf*?

[A] The Crusaders trying to return from the Middle East to Europe

[B] America's wealth, power, and influence over Russia

[C] Good over evil, with the king's funeral finishing the story

[D] The expansion of Russia towards the west and southward toward the Mediterranean Sea

[E] Examples of how the sun never sets over the British Isles

The correct answer is C.
Grendel attacks the kingdom and her loathsome mother takes revenge, and makes a brutal attack upon the king's hall. Beowulf seeks out the hag in her underwater lair, and slays her after an almighty struggle. Once more there is much rejoicing, and Beowulf is rewarded with many gifts. It closes with Beowulf's funeral.

ENGLISH LITERATURE

79. Which of the following is not one of the Canterbury Tales?

[A] "The Cook's Tale"

[B] "The Wife of Bath's Tale"

[C] "Sir Thopas' Tale"

[D] "The Manciple's Tale"

[E] "Sir Eduoard's Tale"

The correct answer is E.
E is a fictional story, and is not part of Canterbury Tales.

Question 80-82

> To be or not to be— that is the question
> Whether 'tis nobler in the mind to suffer
> The slings and arrows of outrageous fortune
> Or to take arms against a sea of troubles
> And by opposing end them. To die, to sleep —
> No more — and by a sleep to say we end
> The heartache, and the thousand natural shocks
> That flesh is heir to. 'Tis a consummation
> Devoutly to be wished. To die, to sleep—
> To sleep—perchance to dream…

80. This is an example of a:

[A] monologue

[B] soliloquy

[C] appeal

[D] benediction

[E] none of the above

The correct answer is B.
The only sensible options are A and B. Whereas a monologue is just a single person talking, a soliloquy is a character revealing inner thoughts.

ENGLISH LITERATURE

81. The character that speaks these lines is:

[A] Romeo

[B] Mercutio

[C] Ceasar

[D] Hamlet

[E] Macbeth

The correct answer is D.
Being one of the most famous pieces of all time, the answer should be recognized as D, *Hamlet*. If the student has not read *Hamlet*, it is advisable before the exam as it is probable examples may come from this play.

82. The tone of this selection is:

[A] despairing

[B] joyful

[C] longing

[D] remorseful

[E] self-promotion

The correct answer is A.
The soliloquy has Hamlet talking about his death and if it is better to die than continue in such agony.

ENGLISH LITERATURE

Nobody wanted your dance,
Nobody wanted your strange glitter, your floundering
Drowning life and your effort to save yourself,
Treading water, dancing the dark turmoil,
Looking for something to give.

83. This passage's tone is created by using one of the following means:

[A] allegories

[B] euphemisms

[C] alliteration

[D] irony

[E] metaphors

The correct answer is B.
From earlier definition review, The correct answer is euphemism as the depression and suicide of the person about whom the poem is written is too blunt for Ted Hughes' poetry.

84. Walter Scott wrote all of the following EXCEPT:

[A] *Rob Roy*

[B] *Ivanhoe*

[C] *Waverly*

[D] *The Talisman*

[E] *Kidnapped*

The correct answer is E.
Kidnapped was written by Robert Louis Stevenson.

ENGLISH LITERATURE

85. H. G. Wells wrote all of the following EXCEPT:

[A] *The Dream*

[B] *War of the Worlds*

[C] *Time Machine*

[D] *Vivian Grey*

[E] *Meanwhile*

The correct answer is D.
He wrote all of the following except Vivian Grey, which was penned by Benjamin Disraeli.

86. The correct order of Jane Austin's novels by publication is:

[A] Emma, Sense & Sensibility, Pride & Prejudice, Persuasion

[B] Emma, Persuasion, Sense & Sensibility, Pride & Prejudice

[C] Persuasion, Sense & Sensibility, Pride & Prejudice, Emma

[D] Sense & Sensibility, Pride & Prejudice, Emma, Persuasion

[E] Pride & Prejudice, Sense & Sensibility, Emma, Persuasion

The correct answer is D.
The correct order is Sense & Sensibility (1811), Pride & Prejudice (1813), Emma (1815) and Persuasion (1817).

ENGLISH LITERATURE

All the world's a stage
And all the men and women merely players;
They have their exits and their entrances,
And one man in his time plays many parts,
His acts being seven ages.

87. This is a passage from:

   [A] *The Tempest*

   [B] *As You Like It*

   [C] *Much Ado About Nothing*

   [D] *Twelfth Night*

   [E] *King Lear*

The correct answer is B.

88. The politician John Elwes, who had inherited a fortune but was reluctant to spend a penny - even living in empty apartments - is thought to have served as partial inspiration for which literary work?

   [A] A Christmas Carol

   [B] Tale of Two Cities

   [C] Pickwick Papers

   [D] Mystery of Edwin Drood

   [E] The Battle of Life

The correct answer is A.
All of these selections are written by Charles Dickens, but answer A provides the parallel for the life of Ebenezer Scrooge.

ENGLISH LITERATURE

89. Events taking place on a single day, following three major characters through Dublin, describes what 20th century novel?

   [A] *A Handful of Dust*

   [B] *The Third Man*

   [C] *Dubliners*

   [D] *Ulysses*

   [E] *The Heart of the Matter*

The correct answer is D.
Only C and D are written by James Joyce and set in Dublin. While *Dubliners* has the correct setting, the fact that *Ulysses* follows three main characters through a single day makes it the correct choice. *A Handful of Dust* (A) is written by Evelyn Waugh, where the English are wealthy but not necessarily substantial. *The Heart of the Matter* (E) is written by Graham Greene about an officer in a war-torn West African state. Also written by Greene, *The Third Man* (B) has the right number of men, but is set in Vienna when strange things occur as the protagonist goes to his friend's funeral.

90. In literature, evoking feelings of pity or compassion is creating:

   [A] colloquy

   [B] irony

   [C] pathos

   [D] paradox

   [E] emphatic response.

The correct answer is C.
A very well-known example of pathos is Desdemona's death in *Othello*, but there are many other examples of pathos.

XAMonline
The CLEP Specialist
Individual Sample Tests in eBook format with full explanations

eBooks

All 33 CLEP sample tests are available as eBook downloads from retail websites such as **Amazon.com** and **Barnesandnoble.com**

Title	ISBN
American Government	9781607875130
American Literature	9781607875079
Analyzing and Interpreting Literature	9781607875086
Biology	9781607875222
Calculus	9781607875376
Chemistry	9781607875239
College Algebra	9781607875215
College Composition	9781607875109
College Composition Modular	9781607875437
College Mathematics	9781607875246
English Literature	9781607875093
Financial Accounting	9781607875383
French	9781607875123
German	9781607875369
History of the United States I	9781607875178
History of the United States II	9781607875185
Human Growth and Development	9781607875444
Humanities	9781607875147
Information Systems	9781607875390
Introduction to Educational Psychology	9781607875451
Introductory Business Law	9781607875420
Introductory Psychology	9781607875154
Introductory Sociology	9781607875352
Natural Sciences	9781607875253
Precalculus	9781607875345
Principles of Macroeconomics	9781607875406
Principles of Microeconomics	9781607875468
Principles of Marketing	9781607875475
Principles of Management	9781607875468
Social Sciences and History	9781607875161
Spanish	9781607875116
Western Civilization I	9781607875192
Western Civilization II	9781607875208

TO ORDER Individual full length sample test are available from **amazon** or **BARNES & NOBLE** BOOKSELLERS

XAMonline
CLEP
Full Guides

TO ORDER — Complete study guides are available from amazon or BARNES&NOBLE BOOKSELLERS

CLEP College Algebra
ISBN: 9781607875307
Price: $34.99

CLEP Biology
ISBN: 9781607875314
Price: $34.99

CLEP Analyzing and Interpreting Literature
ISBN: 9781607875260
Price: $34.99

CLEP College Composition and Modular
ISBN: 9781607875277
Price: $16.99

CLEP College Mathematics
ISBN: 9781607875321
Price: $34.99

CLEP Psychology
ISBN: 9781607875291
Price: $34.99

CLEP Spanish
ISBN: 9781607875284
Price: $34.99

XAMonline
CLEP Subject Samplers

Collection by Topic
Sample Test Approach

CLEP Literature
ISBN: 9781607875833
Price: $24.99

CLEP Foreign Language
ISBN: 9781607875772
Price: $24.99

CLEP History
ISBN: 9781607875789
Price: $24.99

CLEP Sociology
ISBN: 9781607875796
Price: $24.99

CLEP Science
ISBN: 9781607875802
Price: $24.99

CLEP Mathematics
ISBN: 9781607875819
Price: $24.99

CLEP Business
ISBN: 9781607875826
Price: $24.99

TO ORDER Complete sample tests are available from **amazon** or **BARNES&NOBLE** BOOKSELLERS

XAMonline
CLEP Favorites
Collection by Topic
Sample Test Approach

CLEP 5
ISBN: 9781607875307
Price: $25.99

CLEP Military Favorites
ISBN: 9781607875314
Price: $25.99

TO ORDER Complete sample tests are available from **amazon** or **BARNES & NOBLE** BOOKSELLERS

www.ingramcontent.com/pod-product-compliance
Lightning Source LLC
Chambersburg PA
CBHW080724230426
43665CB00020B/2612